21世纪高等教育建筑环境与能源应用工程系列规划教材

建筑环境与能源应用工程概论
（中英文对照）

主　编　刘　立　范慧方
参　编（以拼音为序）
　　　　柳　靖　曲世琳　谢　慧　张　舸　吴延鹏
主　审　田贯三

机械工业出版社

本书是建筑环境与能源应用工程专业的中英文概述，内容包括室内空气品质、空气调节与制冷、供热工程、燃气工程、给水排水工程、建筑电气等。本书是对本专业的总体概述，为后续各门专业课的深入学习打下基础。本书各章都给出了本章要点、知识点和中英文双版，使学生掌握专业英文词汇，熟悉科技英文的阅读和写作，为将来英文论文写作打下坚实基础。

本书不仅可作为建筑环境与能源应用工程专业本科生的教材，而且对暖通空调工程师及从业人员也都有较高的参考价值。

本书配有电子课件，免费提供给选用本书的授课教师，需要者请根据书末的"信息反馈表"索取，或登录机械工业出版社教材服务网：www.cmpedu.com 下载。

图书在版编目（CIP）数据

建筑环境与能源应用工程概论：中英文对照/刘立，范慧方主编. —北京：机械工业出版社，2013.6（2025.2 重印）
21 世纪高等教育建筑环境与能源应用工程系列规划教材
ISBN 978-7-111-42177-1

Ⅰ.①建⋯ Ⅱ.①刘⋯②范⋯ Ⅲ.①建筑工程—环境管理—高等学校—教材—汉、英②房屋建筑设备—高等学校—教材—汉、英 Ⅳ.①TU – 023 ②TU8

中国版本图书馆 CIP 数据核字（2013）第 075577 号

机械工业出版社（北京市百万庄大街 22 号　邮政编码 100037）
策划编辑：刘　涛　责任编辑：刘　涛　臧程程　王晓艳　王雅新
版式设计：霍永明　责任校对：纪　敬
封面设计：路恩中　责任印制：张　博
北京雁林吉兆印刷有限公司印刷
2025 年 2 月第 1 版第 5 次印刷
184mm×260mm·15 印张·370 千字
标准书号：ISBN 978-7-111-42177-1
定价：32.00 元

电话服务　　　　　　　　　　网络服务
客服电话：010-88361066　　　机　工　官　网：www.cmpbook.com
　　　　　010-88379833　　　机　工　官　博：weibo.com/cmp1952
　　　　　010-68326294　　　金　书　网：www.golden-book.com
封底无防伪标均为盗版　　　　机工教育服务网：www.cmpedu.com

前　言

建筑环境与能源应用工程专业的学生在进入大学时，常常对本专业不是十分了解，学习过程中往往存在一定的盲目性，使得学习效果受到一定的影响。同时本专业的国际化程度越来越高，为了使学生能够了解国际动态，需要加强专业英语的培训。针对上述两个问题笔者编写了本书。本书围绕建筑环境与设备这一中心，系统地介绍了本专业所要学到的6门主要专业课的主要内容，包括室内空气品质（第2章）、供热工程（第3章）、空调工程（第4章）、燃气工程（第5章）、给水排水工程（第6章）、建筑电气系统（第7章和第8章）等系统的工作原理、系统构成、分类及其在建筑物中的重要作用和应用。通过本课程的学习对本专业形成良好总体认知。

本书针对这6门主要专业课的概述，给出了相应的英文。本书的英文覆盖了建筑环境与能源应用工程专业的所有专业英文描述，简洁并且实用。本书区别于传统的专业外语教材，涵盖了本专业不同领域的常用英文，也可以作为传统的专业外语课的教材。可以说，将来无论是进一步深造还是工作，本书都是不可多得的参考文献。

本书参考了多本美国及欧洲各国英文原版著作，并结合我国工程实践，作出了中英文对照版本。暖通空调（建筑环境与能源应用工程）工程师和从业人员可以从中文内容找到对应的标准英文表述，反之亦然。由于当前我国建筑环境与设备系统与国外有所不同，因而建筑环境与设备各个系统英文描述容易混淆，针对这一问题，本书清楚地给出了各个系统中英文描述，极大地方便了读者。

本书不仅可作为建筑环境与能源应用工程专业本科生的教材，而且对建筑环境与能源应用工程专业的工程师及从业人员也都有较高的参考价值。

本书第 1 章和第 8 章由北京科技大学刘立编写；第 2 章的 2.1 和 2.2 由吴延鹏编写，2.3 和 2.4 由柳靖编写；第 3 章和第 6 章由曲世琳编写；第 4 章由谢慧编写；第 5 章由范慧方编写；第 7 章由刘立和张舸编写。全书由田贯三主审。

在本书编写过程中，参阅了大量的中外文献资料，在此对各参考文献的作者表示衷心的感谢。

由于编者水平有限，书中难免存在疏漏与不足之处，恳请广大读者批评指正。

编　者

目 录

前言
第 1 章 建筑环境设备及其对建筑和环境的影响 ·············· 1
1.1 建筑环境设备工程的范围 ············· 1
1.2 建筑环境设备系统对空间规划的影响 ··· 2
1.3 建筑环境设备系统对建筑设计的影响 ··· 3
1.4 建筑环境设备工程系统对建筑造价的影响 ············· 4
1.5 建筑对环境的影响 ············· 4
1.6 不同系统的相互作用 ············· 5
习题 ············· 6

Chapter 1 The Scope & Impact of Building Environment and Equipment System ············· 7
1.1 The Scope of Building Environment and Equipment Engineering Systems ············· 8
1.2 The Impact on Space Planning ············· 8
1.3 The Impact on Architectural Design ············· 9
1.4 The Impact on Construction Cost ············· 11
1.5 The Impact of Buildings on Environment ············· 12
1.6 System Interfacing ············· 13
Questions ············· 13

第 2 章 室内环境 ············· 15
2.1 室内热环境和热舒适 ············· 15
2.2 室内空气品质 ············· 23
2.3 建筑声环境 ············· 29
2.4 建筑光环境 ············· 32
习题 ············· 34

Chapter 2 Indoor Environment ············· 36
2.1 Indoor Thermal Environment and Thermal Comfort ············· 36
2.2 Indoor Air Quality ············· 47
2.3 Architectural Acoustical Environment ············· 54
2.4 Architectural Luminous Environment ············· 58
Questions ············· 61

第 3 章 供热 ············· 63
3.1 热负荷 ············· 63
3.2 热水供热系统 ············· 65
3.3 集中供热系统的热源 ············· 69
习题 ············· 71

Chapter 3 Heating ············· 72
3.1 Heating Loss Calculation ············· 72
3.2 Hot-water Systems ············· 75
3.3 Heating Source of Central Heating Systems ············· 78
Questions ············· 81

第 4 章 空气调节与制冷 ············· 82
4.1 空气调节与空调系统 ············· 82
4.2 湿空气的物理性质 ············· 83
4.3 负荷计算 ············· 86
4.4 全空气系统 ············· 87
4.5 空气-水系统 ············· 94
4.6 冷剂式空调系统 ············· 95
4.7 制冷设备与系统 ············· 97
习题 ············· 99

Chapter 4 Air Conditioning & Refrigeration ············· 101
4.1 Air Conditioning and Air Conditioning Systems ············· 101
4.2 Thermodynamic Properties of Moist Air ············· 102

4.3　Load Calculations ……………… 106
4.4　All-air Systems ………………… 109
4.5　Air-water Systems ……………… 117
4.6　Refrigerant Air Conditioning Systems … 119
4.7　Refrigeration Equipment and Systems … 121
　　Questions ………………………… 125

第 5 章　燃气工程 ……………… 126
5.1　燃气气源 ………………………… 127
5.2　城市燃气输配系统 ……………… 130
5.3　燃气燃烧与应用简介 …………… 136
　　习题 ……………………………… 137

Chapter 5　Gas Engineering …………… 138
5.1　Gas Sources …………………… 140
5.2　City Gas Distribution Systems ……… 143
5.3　Gas Combustion and Its Appliances …… 151
　　Questions ………………………… 152

第 6 章　给水排水 ……………… 153
6.1　供水历史 ………………………… 153
6.2　给水工程 ………………………… 154
6.3　室内管道工程——背景与现状 …… 155
6.4　明渠流 …………………………… 156
6.5　泵和泵站 ………………………… 157
6.6　废水收集 ………………………… 157
6.7　废水的组成 ……………………… 158
6.8　水处理 …………………………… 160
　　习题 ……………………………… 161

Chapter 6　Water Supply ……………… 162
6.1　History of Water Supply ………… 162
6.2　Water-supply Engineering ……… 164
6.3　Plumbing—Background and Status … 165
6.4　Open Channel Flow …………… 166
6.5　Pumps and Pumping Stations …… 167
6.6　Collection of Wastewater ……… 168

6.7　Composition of Wastewater …… 170
6.8　Water Processing ……………… 172
　　Questions ………………………… 173

第 7 章　电力系统和设计 ……… 174
7.1　配电系统 ………………………… 174
7.2　电压差和电压分布 ……………… 175
7.3　接地 ……………………………… 175
7.4　短路和分断能力 ………………… 177
7.5　电力设备 ………………………… 177
7.6　电气系统设计及配线 …………… 178
　　习题 ……………………………… 182

Chapter 7　Power System and Electrical Design … 183
7.1　Power Distribution Systems …… 183
7.2　Voltage Spread and Profile …… 184
7.3　Grounding ……………………… 185
7.4　Short-circuit and Interruption Capacity … 187
7.5　Power Equipment ……………… 187
7.6　Electrical System Design ……… 189
　　Questions ………………………… 194

第 8 章　建筑照明 ……………… 196
8.1　光照与照明 ……………………… 196
8.2　照明设备及照明系统 …………… 201
8.3　建筑光环境设计 ………………… 206
　　习题 ……………………………… 211

Chapter 8　Building Lighting …………… 212
8.1　Light and Lighting ……………… 212
8.2　Lighting Equipment and Systems … 218
8.3　Building Lighting Design ……… 225
　　Questions ………………………… 231

参考文献 …………………………… 232

第1章
建筑环境设备及其对建筑和环境的影响

本章要点：介绍了建筑环境设备涵盖范围，论述了建筑环境设备对建筑空间、建筑风格、建筑造价及对大气环境的影响。

知识点：建筑环境设备，供热通风和空调，空间设计，建筑风格，建筑造价。

现代建筑的功能不再是简单的避风遮雨，而是为人们提供一个更加舒适的生活和工作的环境。建筑应设计为具有舒适的照明、温度、湿度和良好的空气品质，便利的供电和通信功能，高质量的卫生条件和可靠的保护生命财产安全的系统。所有这些功能都因为建筑环境与设备的技术进步而得以实现。

建筑环境设备的先进技术使得建筑设计在风格、形式和范围上的创新都成为可能。一些大商场采用无窗的方块形构筑，完全依赖于电气照明、通风和空调。

然而，这些优点的获得是有代价的。首先，建筑环境设备系统占用很大的地面和顶棚空间。在初始设计时必须预留足够的空间，否则必须重新设计，而且系统的功能往往也受制约。其次，建筑环境设备系统使房屋造价增高，对于复杂建筑（如医院和计算机中心等），有时超过工程总价的50%。

建筑环境设备系统的运行需要能源。建筑能耗（包括住宅、商业、公共机构、工业设备的能耗）占据一个工业国家总能耗的30%~50%。另外，建筑环境设备系统的运行费用占据整个建筑运行费用的大部分。建筑对能源大量和低效的使用是对环境造成破坏的主要因素。

设计正确的设备系统将会合理有效地利用空间和能源，从而降低建筑造价，减少对环境的影响。本章内容包含对建筑环境设备系统的总体描述，以及它们对空间规划、建筑设计、建造和运行费用及地球环境的影响。

1.1 建筑环境设备工程的范围

建筑环境设备工程系统随着社会生活标准、当地气候条件、住户性质和建筑质量而变化。例如，位于温和气候条件地区的建筑，无论建筑的质量如何都不需要供热也不需要供冷；储存大物件的仓库即便在寒冷地区也不一定需要供热；现代化医院必须备有医疗气体供应系统、备用电源和远距离通信系统以达到当前医学护理标准；小型办公楼可采用窗式空调而高层智能办公楼最可能选择的是中央空调系统并备有计算机自动管理控制系统。

建筑环境设备工程系统包括：①建筑环境系统；②供热通风空调系统；③给水排水系统；④燃气供应系统；⑤消防系统；⑥电气系统（包括供电系统、照明系统及附属设施）；⑦建筑运行系统（包括运输和自动化管理系统）。

1.2 建筑环境设备系统对空间规划的影响

建筑环境设备工程系统所需要的平面面积由于用户、气候条件、生活标准、建筑质量的不同而差别很大。两个坐落在不同地点但大小和结构一样的建筑，可能选择不同的建筑环境与设备工程系统。气候、经济和国家的文化背景都是影响建筑环境设备工程系统的选择因素。

建筑环境设备工程系统影响着总建筑面积、楼宇首层的面积和形状、层高、几何形状和建筑表达。在设计初始就应为建筑环境设备系统安排合理位置和空间。在建筑设计中，建筑环境设备工程系统的空间规划是最具挑战性的研究领域。

大型建筑的中央设备往往又高又大，使得层高为正常高度的 1.5～2 倍。一般，一个大型写字楼装有冷冻机组和泵房的楼层高度是 6～7m，几乎是正常楼层高的两倍。而一个大型商业楼，供热、空调、给水排水等复杂管道、照明、电缆等需要 0.6～0.9m 的屋顶空间。

对于一个写字楼，建筑环境设备系统将占整个建筑面积的 4%。换言之，对于一个 25 层建筑面积 50000m^2 的建筑，2000m^2 的建筑面积应预留给建筑环境与设备工程系统，相当于整整一层楼。同理，对于一个 50 层建筑，两层要预留给建筑环境与设备工程系统。显而易见，这么大的空间必须在建筑设计初始阶段进行规划，这就需要建筑设计师和建筑环境与设备工程工程师密切合作。

建筑环境与设备工程系统所需要的空间根据系统的选择而分为集中空间和分散空间。每个系统都需要在每层设置局部设备和输运空间。不同的是中央系统的主要设备集中放在一层或两层，其他每一层占有很小的局部空间，分散系统的设备空间与之相反。

如果一个建筑由单体窗式或墙式热泵加热和制冷，就不需要中央加热和制冷设备。然而，单体热泵有噪声、效率低、运行费用高并且不美观。所以，尽管设备需要空间，但高质量的建筑往往采用中央系统。

所有的高层建筑都有一或多层的地下层用于公共服务、物资的运送、燃料的储存等。同时，地下层为建筑提供坚实的结构基础。更重要的是地下停车场在许多城市越发成为不可缺少的需求。正常情况下，建筑环境设备系统应该设置在地下层。但是，这种安排有时无法实现，因为，设备系统需要靠近建筑中心，这样往往会妨碍停车场车辆的进出。加上其他原因，设备中心往往设在屋顶或中间层。影响设备中心位置的因素有：①装卸设备的容易度；②易于室外空气供给和废气排出；③足够的楼层高度；④不与停车场相干扰。同时还要考虑安全性，有些设备如锅炉、制冷机组和变压器内含巨大的能量或有毒液体，这些设备应该由防火墙围起来。以及设备系统的就近组合，如制冷机组与冷却塔要便于设备系统的管理，减小设备的振动和噪声的影响，兼顾整体美观。

1.3 建筑环境设备系统对建筑设计的影响

在有可靠和可行的建筑环境设备系统之前，建筑设计往往遵循一个简单的规则：每个房间必须设置外窗以供给自然光和通风。这样，大多数建筑是 L 形、U 形或 H 形，通道一侧或两侧住人；大型方形建筑往往在中间设天井来供给阳光和空气；楼的高度受到人们能够徒步上下的高度所限制。现代建筑，由于具有了建筑环境设备，建筑形状可以有更多形式，高度也可以更高。为高层建筑设计的现代电梯速度可以达到 150~750m/min。这样，除去等待和上下电梯时间，30s 内就能到达 30 层楼。近年来随着城市土地短缺，在城市环境中高层建筑，甚至是超高层建筑越来越受欢迎。

然而，任何事物都具有两面性。低层建筑（6 层及更低）比高层建筑造价低、效率高。理论上，对建筑的最有效利用是内部空间的百分之百都用来居住。这种最高效只能在空调设备等设置在屋顶或屋外的小单层房屋实现。随着建筑高度的增加更多的建筑空间用于楼梯、电梯、建筑环境设备系统等，使得使用空间缩小。

建筑环境设备系统对建筑的影响不仅仅在高度上，还在风格、外观和形式上。建筑与结构的结合在建筑史上早已得到了很好的研究。建筑与建筑环境设备系统的结合在巴黎的蓬皮杜中心艺术博物馆得到了良好的体现。蓬皮杜中心艺术博物馆将所有的机械设备的管道都暴露在博物馆外。建于 20 世纪 80 年代的汇丰银行创立了另一种风格，把结构和建筑设备的机械元素的暴露作为主要的建筑风格。事实上，许多现代建筑受到建筑设备的影响，如：

（1）在顶层辅助空间的设计 在屋顶建一个更小面积的一层或防护结构来容纳电梯设备、电梯加长导轨（使最高一层的电梯导轨加长来使电梯减速，以防电梯停不下来）、冷却塔、废气扇和其他设备。这是在屋顶隐藏建筑设备的最基本的设计理念，是很多城市和国家要求的设计原则。

（2）平屋顶建筑设计 高层建筑的顶层或次顶层统筹设计成为容纳中央建筑设备和隐藏建筑设备上方部分，如冷却塔、空气处理系统和电梯设备。

（3）中间设备层设计 超过 30 层的高楼往往设计成由一个或多个中间楼层来放置中央建筑环境与设备工程系统。因为安装设备的楼层需要比较高的楼层高度，对该层的楼表面设计往往与其相邻的楼层的表面设计有所不同。高层建筑中这些楼层很容易与其他楼层区分开来。中国台北的远东大楼在低层、中间和顶层设置了设备楼层。

（4）设计风格 20 世纪 90 年代的后设计脱离了平屋顶设计风格，偏向于显示个性和雕塑风格的屋顶设计。具有雕塑风格的设计往往以不同的方法来隐藏冷却塔。冷却塔可能放在地面（或附近）或楼中间。

图 1-1 所示是现代高层和超高层建筑和摩天大楼的几种流行设计风格。

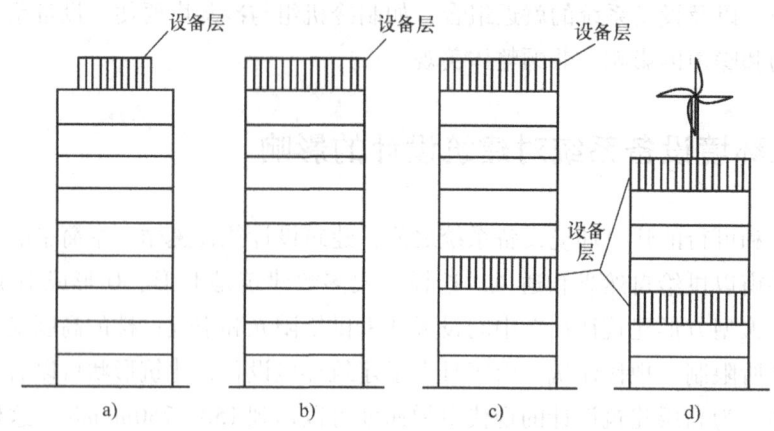

图 1-1 现代高层和超高层建筑的风格
a) 在屋顶设有房屋的设计 b) 平屋顶建筑设计 c) 中间设备层设计 d) 风格设计

1.4 建筑环境设备工程系统对建筑造价的影响

随着建筑物高度的增加，需要更多的时间和提升设备以及严格的工作流程把建筑材料运送到更高的楼层。而很多建筑工人整天都在高空中作业，使得工作效率降低。建筑结构和建筑环境设备系统更加复杂，建造方法也不相同。对高于 10 层的建筑物，第二个五层的单位面积造价将会增加 5%～15%，随后，每五层单位面积造价将以 10%～15% 递增。

随着楼层的增高，投资增加的幅度变化很大，因为它受到建筑地址，建材运输便利程度，建筑细节，工人的技术和承包者高层建筑的经验多少等因素影响。但是建筑高度对建筑投资的影响存在一个大致估算。

建筑环境设备系统对建筑造价产生很大的影响。随着建筑类型、生活质量标准、建筑设计、建筑设备系统的选择，高层建筑的建筑设备系统造价占总造价的 15%～25%，而计算机中心的建筑环境与设备工程系统占总造价的 30%～60%。

建筑运行费用包含正常维护费、修理费、置换费和水电煤气费。大多数建筑和结构元素（除了屋顶）寿命很长，都不需要经常更换。对于建筑设备系统则不然，不仅需要耗能，而且需要不停地维修和更换。事实上，在整个寿命周期，运行维护建筑环境与设备工程系统的费用有时可能超过整个建筑初期总投资。由此可知，建筑环境设备系统的合理选择和管理是非常重要的。

1.5 建筑对环境的影响

1.5.1 技术对环境的影响

从全球来看，工业、交通业、电力行业、建筑供热和供冷对石油、煤、天然气的使用在不断增加。这就增加了大气层中的二氧化碳含量及其吸收太阳能的比例，这种现象被称为温室效应。温室效应是引起全球气温升高的主要原因。

直到 20 世纪 90 年代，氟利昂一直是制冷和空调系统的主要制冷剂，还用来清洁。大量氟利昂的使用使得高于地球 24~32km 的臭氧层被破坏。臭氧层可以降低太阳辐射到地球表面的紫外线能量。随着臭氧层的破坏，更多的有害的可引起癌症的紫外线到达地面。国际上达成共识，禁止使用氟利昂而使用其他不伤害臭氧层的制冷剂。但是其他化学试剂也不是无害的。只有通过更有效的设计和控制减少能源消耗，才能最大限度地降低人类对环境的破坏。

1.5.2 建筑能耗带来的空气污染

根据统计，发达国家每年消耗的能源 1/3 是用在建筑上。随着人民生活水平的大幅提高，我国建筑能耗也快速增长。目前，我国建筑能耗占总能耗的 27.5%。建筑每消耗 1kW·h 的电能，就需要燃煤发电厂中燃烧，放出 1.1kg 的二氧化碳、0.01kg 的二氧化硫和 0.005kg 的氮氧化物。如果通过更好的设计和管理使用于建筑的能源年消耗量降低 20%，二氧化碳排放量就可以减少 150×10^6 t，相当于减少 3 千万辆车的二氧化碳排放。从而可知建筑节能对环境的重要性。

1.6 不同系统的相互作用

前面讲述了建筑环境设备与空间规划、建筑理念与全球环境间的相互关联。在某个领域的决定可能会影响所有其他领域。图 1-2 指出，建筑和工程决策需要不同领域的相互协作。

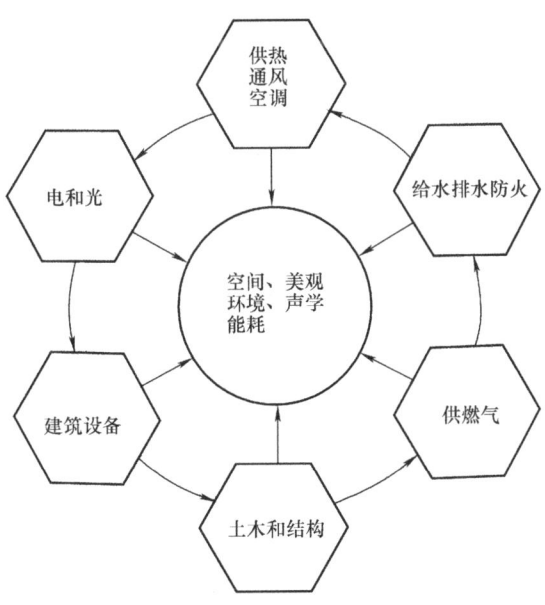

图 1-2 不同系统的相互作用

设计现代建筑需要团队协作。没有一个专业人士是全知全能的。在建筑设计和建造中，建筑设计师是项目的主要负责人，需要其他专家的支持和意见，比如，土木、结构、机械、电子、照明和声学专家。只有所有职业人士通力合作，才能构筑最优化、功能平衡、低造价、高品质的建筑。

习　　题

1. 现代建筑的哪些特点依赖于建筑环境设备系统？
2. 在现代的建筑环境设备兴起之前，办公建筑，比如写字楼，往往局限于几种简单的建筑格局，为什么？
3. 现代建筑设计程序需要不同专业的专家共同合作，通常是由建筑设计师统筹安排，对否？
4. 建筑外表面对建筑环境设备系统有何影响？
5. 为什么建筑表面风格设计关系到建筑环境设备系统？
6. 为什么关心能源消耗？为什么建筑应该是绿色建筑？

Chapter 1

The Scope & Impact of Building Environment and Equipment System

Abstract: This chapter introduces the scope of building environment and equipment system. It also discusses impacts of building environment and equipment system on building planning, architectural style, construction cost and atmospheric environments.

Key points: building environment and equipment system, HVAC, space planning, architectural style, construction cost.

Modern buildings are no longer just shelters from wind and snow. Rather, they are built to create better environments in which to live and to work. Building must be designed with features to provide comfortable lighting, temperature, humidity, air quality; convenient power and communication capability; high-quality sanitation and reliable systems for the protection of life and property. All these desirable features have become a reality with recent advances in the technology of building environment and equipment system (BE/E).

These advances make possible of architectural design innovations in style, form and scope. Block-type buildings without windows, such as department stores, are totally dependent on electrical lighting, ventilation and air conditioning. High-rise buildings must rely on high-speed vertical transportation and high-pressure water for drinking, cleaning purposes and for protection against fire.

However, all these benefits are achieved with penalties. BE/E systems demand considerable floor and ceiling space. During the preliminary planning phase of a project, proper space must be allocated. Otherwise, the process may have to be started over again and often the system performances are compromised. Furthermore, BE/E systems add to the cost of construction of a building, in some instances approaching or exceeding 50 percent of the total cost. Sophisticated buildings, such as hospitals and computer centers, are just a few examples.

BE/E systems require energy to operate them. Energy consumed by occupied buildings, including residential, commercial, institutional, and industrial facilities, accounts for over 30 to 50 percent of all energy usage by an industrialized country. In addition, it accounts for a large portion of the operating cost of such buildings. The high and inefficient use of energy by building is the major contributing factor to the deterioration of our environment.

Properly designed BE/E systems utilize space and energy efficiently, thereby reducing building costs and minimizing impacts on environment. This chapter provides an overview of BE/E systems and their impact on space planning, architectural design, construction and operating costs and the greater environment.

1.1 The Scope of Building Environment and Equipment Engineering Systems

The complexity of BE/E systems varies with the living standards of the society, climatic conditions of the region, and occupancy and quality of the building. For example, a house located in a mild climate may not require either heating or cooling, regardless of the quality of the house; a warehouse for bulk storage may not require any heating even in a freezing climate; a modern hospital must have a supply of medical gas, standby electrical power, and telecommunications systems to meet present health care standards; and a small office building may appropriately have window-type air conditioner, whereas an intelligent high-rise office building would most likely be designed with a central HVAC systems complete with computer-based building automatic management controls.

BE/E systems may be classified into the following major categories: ①Building Environmental Systems. ②HVAC Systems. ③Water Supply and Drainage Systems. ④Gas Supply Systems. ⑤Fire Prevention Systems. ⑥Electrical Systems, including Electrical Power Supply System, Illuminating Systems and Ancillary Facilities. ⑦Building Operation Systems, including transportation and automation Management Systems.

1.2 The Impact on Space Planning

The floor area necessary for BE/E systems in a building varies widely, depending on the occupancy, climatic conditions, living standards, and quality and general architectural design of the building. Two buildings of similar size and configuration located on different sites may favor different BE/E systems and central plant locations. Climate and the economic and cultural background of a country are other factors that affect the selection of a BE/E system.

The BE/E system affects the gross floor area, footprint the size and shape of the building's ground floor, floor-to-floor height, geometry, and architectural expression. Reasonable allocations made during the space programming phase allow BE/E space to be appropriately sized and strategically located. Space planning for BE/E system is one of the most challenging and least developed procedures in the architecture design process.

Central equipment used for large buildings is usually bulky and tall, requiring floor-to-floor height of 1.5 to 2 times the normal height. For example, floor-to-floor height of a chiller and pump room of a large office computer building is 6 to 7 meters, about twice the normal height. Pipes, lighting and wiring of a commercial building require 0.6 to 0.9 meter of ceiling cavity.

For example, the average BE/E floor space in an office building is about 4 percent of the total building gross floor area. In other words, for a 25-story building with a gross floor area of 50000 sq meters, 2000 sq meters should be initially allocated as BE/E equipment space. This is equivalent to one full floor of the building. Similarly, two floors are needed for BE/E equipment in a 50-story building. Needless to say, these are not incidental spaces that can be added at will, except during the initial programming phase of the project. Optimum solutions are a result of close coordination between the architect and the BE/E engineers.

Space for BE/E system may be centralized or decentralized, depending on the system selected. With either plan, there is always a need for on-floor (local) equipment and distribution (shaft) space on every floor. The major difference is that centralized planning concentrates major equipment on one or two floors with smaller on-floor BE/E spaces, whereas the decentralized plan is just the opposite.

If a building is to be heated and cooled by the unitary window or through-the-wall heat pumps, then the need for central heating and cooling equipment will be eliminated. On the other hand, unitary heat pumps are noisy and less energy-efficient, require high maintenance, and are unaesthetic. Thus most high-quality buildings have central systems in spite of the increased requirements for equipment space.

Without exception, all high-rise buildings have one or more underground levels for utility service, delivery of supplies, fuel storage, etc.. Furthermore, underground levels provide better structural stability for the foundation of the building. More important, underground parking for automobiles is an unavoidable demand in most city codes. Normally, a BE/E central plant should be located in an underground level. However, this is not always feasible, since BE/E system risers must be close to the core of the building, which frequently hinders access to and from the parking garage. For this and other reasons, the BE/E central plant may be located on the rooftop or on other, intermediate levels. Factors affecting the location of a central plant include the following: Accessibility for loading/unloading equipment. Proximity to the outside air supply and exhaust air discharge. Adequacy of floor height. Interference with a convenient parking plan. Safety. Some equipment, such as boilers, chillers, and liquid-filled transformers, contains considerable stored energy or toxic material. This equipment should be confined within fireproof walls. Proximity of system components, such as between the chiller and the condenser with cooling towers. Ease of maintenance. Vibration and noise from equipment. Aesthetics.

1.3 The Impact on Architectural Design

Prior to the development of reliable and affordable BE/E systems, buildings designed for human occupancy followed a simple rule: every room must have exterior operable windows for the introduction of daylight and for natural ventilation. Accordingly, most buildings are L-, U-, or H-shaped, having either single or double-loaded corridors. Deep block-type buildings usually have an open interior court for access to daylight and outside air. Height of a building is pretty much limited by a human's ability to walk up and down stairs. With technique of BE/E, architecture of modern buildings has more varieties and height is not limited. Modern elevators for high-rise buildings are designed to travel between 150 ~ 750m per minute. At that speed, it would take less than 30 seconds to reach the top of a 30-story building, excluding the waiting and loading time at each stop. High-rise buildings and even skyscrapers have become increasingly popular in urban settings in recent years as urban land is in short supply.

However, the side effect is that high-rise buildings are more expensive to build and less efficient to use than low-rise buildings (six stories or lower). Theoretically, a building is most efficient if 100 percent of the interior space can be utilized for occupancy. This is possible for a small, single-story building with all major BE/E equipment located on the roof or at the exteriors. Multistory buildings gradually lose space utilization efficiency, owing to their need for stairways, elevators, and BE/E equipment space.

The major influence on BE/E systems on modern architecture has been not only in building height, but in architectural style, facade, form, and expression. Architectural and structural system interfacing has long been established in the history of architecture. Architectural and BE/E system interfacing became a reality only when the Pompidou Center Art Museum in Paris daringly exposed all BE/E system ducts, pipes, and conduits on the exterior of the museum. Since then, the Hong Kong-Shanghai Bank in Hong Kong, built in the 1980s, created another sensation, with exposed structural and BE/E elements as the main feature of its architectural design. In fact, most modern buildings are influenced by the presence of BE/E systems, as evidenced by the following architectural design styles:

(1) Penthouse design At the top of the roof is a smaller floor or screened structure to enclose the elevator equipment and elevator overtravel (the extension of the elevator shaft above the last floor to slow down the elevator, should it fail to stop as intended), cooling towers, exhaust fans, and other equipment. This is a fundamental design concept to conceal equipment on the roof and is a building code requirement in many cities and countries.

(2) Flattop design The top one or two floors of a high-rise building are usually designed to house central BE/E equipment and to conceal upper-level BE/E equipment, such as cooling towers, air-handling units, and elevator equipment.

(3) Intermediate floor bands design High-rise buildings of over 30 stories are usually designed with one or more intermediate floors to house central BE/E equipment. Because extra floor-to-floor height is required for this equipment, the facade of these intermediate floors is usually treated differently from the adjacent occupied floors. Such floors are easily detected in most high-rise buildings. The BE/E floors of Far Eastern Plaza building in Taipei on the lower, middle, and top levels

are readily distinguished from the rest of occupied floors.

(4) Signature design Postmodern design in the 1990s has deviated from the flattop style in favor of individuality and sculpture-type rooftops. With the sculptured roof design, cooling towers must be concealed in a different manner. They may be located at or near the ground level or may be concealed within the building.

Illustrated in Fig. 1-1 are the popular architectural design styles of the modern high-rise buildings and skyscrapers.

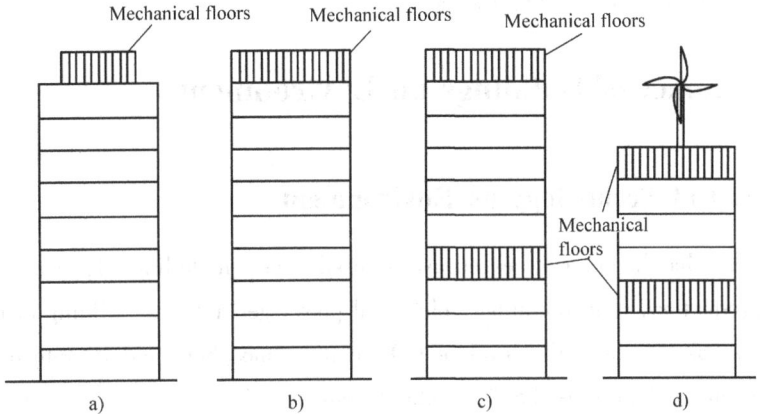

Fig. 1-1 Styles of modern high-rise buildings and skyscrapers
a) Penthouse design b) Flattop design c) Intermediate floor bands design d) Signature design

1.4　The Impact on Construction Cost

When the building is taller, it will require more time and hoisting equipment and complicated scheduling to raise the material onto the upper floors. In fact, most construction workers may have to stay on the upper levels during the entire workdays, losing productivity. The structural and BE/E systems will be more complex, and the method of construction will be different. For a building taller than 10 stories, the unit cost per floor area will increase about 5 to 15 percent for the next 5 stories and another 10 to 15 percent for each additional 5 floors.

The wide spread of the incremental cost for the increased building height is to be expected, because the increase is very much affected by the site conditions, ease of material handling, architectural details, labor skills, and contractor's experience with constructing high-rise buildings. Nevertheless, the general rule can serve as a base for determining the impact of building height on the overall construction cost.

The impact of BE/E systems on construction cost varies greatly, depending on the type of building, standard of living of the country, architectural design, and BE/E systems selected. BE/E systems cost of high-rise buildings accounts for 15% ~25% of total cost of buildings, while BE/

E systems cost of computer center is 30% ~60% of the total cost.

The operating cost of a building includes the cost of routine maintenance, repairs, replacements, and utilities. Most architectural and structural components of a building (except the roof) are normally long-lasting, without the need for frequent replacement. This is not the case, however, for most BE/E systems, which not only consume energy but also require ongoing maintenance and repair. Indeed, over a life cycle, the cost of owning and operating BE/E systems may outweigh the initial capital investment of the entire building. Naturally, the importance of efficient BE/E systems and management can not be overemphasized.

1.5 The Impact of Buildings on Environment

1.5.1 Impact of Technology on Environment

Globally there has been an increased use of fossil fuels, including oil, coal, and natural gas, for industrial production, transportation, electrical power generation, building heating, and building cooling. This has increased the level of CO_2 in the atmosphere and its rate of absorbing energy. This phenomenon, known as the "greenhouse effect", is suspected to be the primary cause of global warming.

Up to the 1990s, carbon fluorocarbons (CFCs) were the primary refrigerant for refrigeration and air-conditioning systems. CFCs are also used as cleaning agent. Their increased use has caused the destruction of the ozone (O_3) layer in the lower part of stratosphere, 24 to 32 kilometers above the earth. The ozone layer decreases the ultraviolet energy that penetrates down to the earth's surface. With the destruction of the ozone layer, more harmful cancer-causing ultraviolet energy reaches the earth. International agreement has banned the future use of CFCs and promotes the use of alternative chemicals which do not deplete the ozone layer so much. However, these chemicals themselves are by no means harmless. The most effective way to reduce environmental damage from pollutants is to minimize the use of energy through more efficient design and controls.

1.5.2 Air Pollutants Due to Building Energy Consumption

According to statistics, an industrialized country consumes more than 2 trillion kilowatt-hours of electrical energy annually, about one-third in buildings. With rapid increase of living standard in China, energy consumed in buildings jumped to a record high level. 27.5% of China's annual energy consumption is used in buildings. For every kilowatt-hour of electrical energy consumed in a building, a coal-fired power generation plant will release 1.09kg of CO_2, 9g of SO_2, and 4.4g of NO. For the case of above mentioned country, if its annual energy consumption in building is reduced by a mere 20 percent through better design and management, total CO_2 emissions may be reduced by about 150 million tons, the equivalent of taking 30 million cars off the road. The impact of building energy conservation on the environment could not be more dramatically demonstrated.

1.6 System Interfacing

The various topics covered in this chapter—from space planning and other architectural concepts to the global environment—are all interrelated. A decision in one area will affect all the others. Fig. 1-2 illustrates the need for close coordination and interfacing between the various design disciplines, revolving around architectural and engineeing decisions.

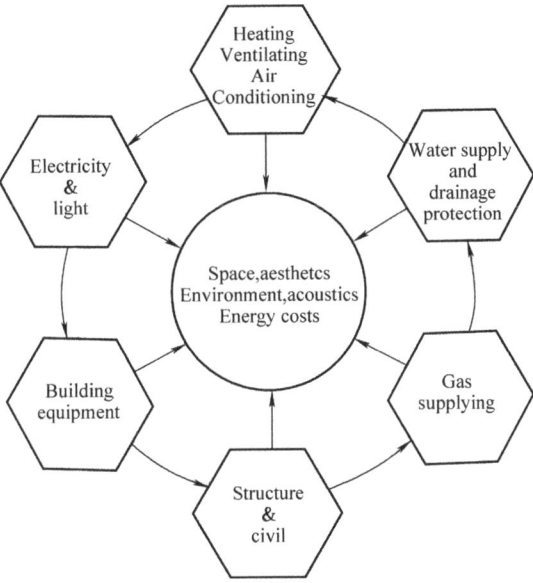

Fig. 1-2 The interaction of different systems

The design of modern buildings requires a team effort. No single designer or professional knows all of the solutions. In building design and construction, the architect is the prime professional on a project, with the support and consultation of specialists such as civil, structural, mechanical, electrical, lighting, and acoustical engineers as well as contractors and construction managers. Only through a close interface among all professionals can a building achieve its optimum vale, balancing function, cost, and quality.

Questions

1. Name some features in modern buildings which are dependent on building environment and equipment systems.

2. Prior to the installation of modern building environment and equipment system, buildings designed for workplaces, such as offices, are usually limited to a few simple building configurations. Why?

3. What are the differences between mechanical engineering system in western country and building environment

and equipment system in China?

4. Modern building design process requires close interfacing of design professionals. Normally, the architect coordinates the team effort. True or false?

5. What influence does a building's external facade have on building environment and equipment system?

6. Why should architectural/techninal facade solutions concern building environment and equipment system?

7. Why should we be concerned about energy consumption and whether our buildings should be "green"?

第 2 章
室内环境

本章要点：本章介绍了人体热感觉的生理基础、室内热舒适的基本概念及其预测方法。本章还简要描述了室内主要空气污染物及室内空气品质改善策略。本章也介绍了建筑光环境的基本概念、天然采光与人工照明以及常用灯具的种类，并阐述了光污染问题，强调了建筑光环境节能的重要性，并给出建筑声环境的基本概念、噪声的来源以及控制噪声的方法。

知识点：人体热感觉的生理基础，人体热平衡，PMV-PPD 指标，病态建筑综合征，室内主要空气污染物，改善室内空气品质的基本策略，光环境，表观颜色，遮光板，视亮度，彩度，色度，明度，显色指数，色温，天然采光，直接眩光，失能眩光，光通量，照度，发光强度，亮度，照度均匀度，视觉功效，工作面，白炽灯，荧光灯，卤钨灯，高压汞灯，高压钠灯，半导体发光二极管，声学，环境噪声，分贝，噪声控制，吸声材料，吸声系数，声压级，声功率级，隔振。

2.1 室内热环境和热舒适

供热通风空调系统的基本作用就是为人类热舒适提供条件。国际公认的热舒适的定义是"对热环境表示满意的意识状态"（ISO7330，ASHRAE 标准 55）。因此，热舒适会受人的不同情绪、文化背景和其他个人因素、群体因素以及社会因素的影响。基于以上定义，舒适度不是外部条件的状态，而是一种心理状态。热舒适的定义为具体什么是满意的意识状态留有很大的空间，但是其确实强调了判断舒适性是一个感知的过程，其中包括许多因素的影响，如身体条件、生理状况、心理状态等。本章介绍人体温度调节和舒适性的基本原理。

2.1.1 热感觉和温度调节的生理基础

人体的体温调节系统能够在一定的不利环境条件下使体温保持一个相对恒定的温度。众所周知，人体温度调节主要通过中枢神经系统控制。该系统的三个要素包括：用来感受温度的感受器、能够比较感知温度与"正常"温度进而激发适当响应的中枢整合机构、被激发后能够改变温度的效应器。

系统的第一个要素（感受器）位于皮肤内部。除了皮肤的温度感受器外，位于大脑底部的下丘脑也能够对局部温度变化直接作出反应。也有人认为，感受器可能存在于人体中心的其他部位，但是支持这种理论的证据还不够充分。

皮肤的温度感受器分为两种类型，冷感受器和热感受器。在对皮肤的试验研究中描绘出了只对冷感觉有反应的非常小的区域以及另外的只对热感觉有反应的区域。两者之间的空间似乎对冷热都不敏感。前臂上每平方厘米大约发现了13~15个冷点，相对而言，每平方厘米只有一两个热点。研究发现冷点和热点都有很快的适应性，尤其对温度的变化很敏感。这说明热感觉会随温度的渐变或突变而不同。

系统的第二个要素（中枢整合机构）能够处理感受器输入的信息，然后作出适当的响应。尽管大脑皮层和脊髓有辅助功能，但下丘脑是主要的中枢神经系统。下丘脑作为主要的整合部位，是一个位于大脑底部的很小的器官。它有两个热控制区域，每一个区域都有一些功能。后部主要抵御寒冷，它的活动导致血管收缩，以此来保持热量守恒。前部控制热消散。下丘脑的一部分可以引起血管舒张以使人体出汗以及动物大口喘气。其功能是在中心系统的控制下，使一种行为抑制另一种行为，从而保持一种平衡。当环境恶劣到使上述反应失去体温调节作用的时候，将会产生严重的后果。零下27℃以下时，颤抖反应失灵，呼吸作用被抑制，生命受到严重的威胁。42℃是保持存活的大脑温度的上限值，当然人体是不能长时间忍受这个温度的。

效应器是对中枢整合机构发出的信号作出响应的身体结构，并且在被激活时能够帮助系统回到平衡状态。效应机制首先是改变组织的隔热性能。当改变组织的隔热性能不足以维持体温的热中性时，那么其他的生理反应，如颤抖或者出汗就会发生。

人体对热应力的反应主要包括皮肤血管扩张和汗腺活动。

在受到刺激的几分钟内，皮肤血管扩张会增加通过皮肤的血液流量。通常情况下这使得皮肤温度升高，使之接近空气温度，因此，减少从环境中吸热。在炎热的环境中，循环系统为保持人体热平衡起到关键作用，其作为一种媒介将内部组织产生的热量传导到皮肤和呼吸系统，然后散出体外。

汗液蒸发是人体消散多余热量的主要途径。这种防卫机制是冷却皮肤和增加内部散热的有效方法。有两种汗腺：大泌腺和小汗腺。运动、情绪紧张以及热刺激都会引起出汗。对热刺激产生反应所分泌的汗液主要由分布于整个皮肤表面的小汗腺产生。当热应力增加或工作中新陈代谢增加时，排汗速率也会增加。环境适应性、疲劳与否、盐的吸收以及个体差异等也会影响排汗速率。

2.1.2　人体与环境的热作用

人体对于热舒适和热不舒适的意识结论来自直接的皮肤温湿度感觉、身体内部温度和体温调节所需要的努力。总之，当体表温度控制在一个小的范围内，皮肤湿度较低，生理调节最小时人体感觉最舒适。

人体代谢活动几乎全部以热量的形式体现，这些热量必须不断被消散和调节，从而使身体保持正常的温度。散热不足会导致过热（体温过高），而散热过多又会导致身体冷却（体温过低）。所以说人体与环境的热交换是影响热舒适的最重要的因素之一。

1. 人体热平衡

图2-1为人体与其周围环境的热交换示意图。体内的总代谢率M是人体活动代谢率M_{act}

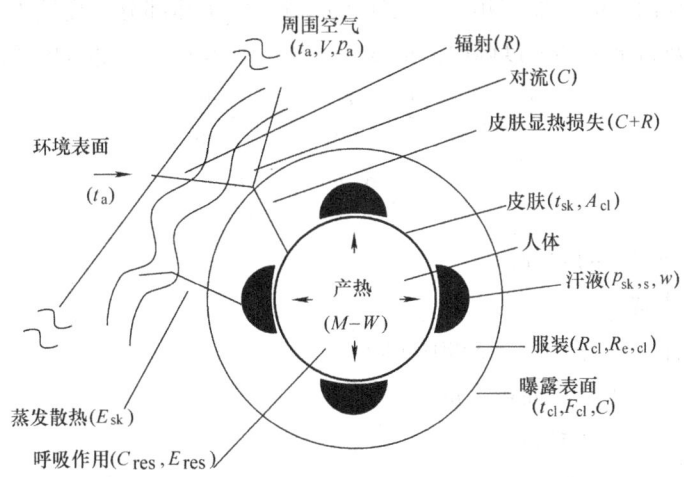

图 2-1 人体与其周围环境的热交换

与有颤抖发生时的代谢率 M_{shiv}（当颤抖发生时）之和。人体产生的部分能量做机械功 W；产生的净热量 $M-W$ 通过皮肤表面（q_{sk}）和呼吸道（q_{res}）散发到环境中，如有剩余或者不足则为蓄热（S），蓄热引起人体温度的上升或下降。

$$M - W = q_{sk} + q_{res} + S = (C + R + E_{sk}) + (C_{res} + E_{res}) + (S_{sk} + S_{cr}) \tag{2-1}$$

式中 M——人体产热代谢率（W/m²）；

W——人体所做的机械功率（W/m²）；

q_{sk}——皮肤总散热率（W/m²）；

q_{res}——呼吸作用总散热率（W/m²）；

$C+R$——皮肤显热散热率（W/m²）；

E_{sk}——皮肤通过蒸发作用的总散热率（W/m²）；

C_{res}——呼吸作用通过对流作用的散热率（W/m²）；

E_{res}——呼吸作用通过蒸发作用的散热率（W/m²）；

S_{sk}——皮肤蓄热率（W/m²）；

S_{cr}——体内蓄热率（W/m²）。

人体通过以下几种热交换方式向周围环境散热：皮肤显热流 $C+R$；汗液蒸发潜热流 E_{rsw} 和皮肤表面散湿蒸发潜热流 E_{dif}，呼吸作用显热流 C_{res}；以及呼吸作用过程中湿气蒸发潜热流 E_{res}。通过皮肤散发的显热可能是个复杂的混合作用，包括导热、对流以及服装的辐射；然而其与外衣表面（或裸露的皮肤表面）的总对流传热量 C 以及辐射传热量 R 是相等的。

来自皮肤的显热与潜热损失一般采用环境因素、皮肤温度 t_{sk} 以及皮肤表面湿度 w 来计算。服装的保温性与透湿性同样也是影响皮肤热损失的重要因素。关于环境的独立变量可以概括为空气温度 t_a，平均辐射温度 $\bar{t}_r$，相对风速 V 以及环境的蒸汽压力 p_a。影响热舒适的与人有关的独立变量有活动量和衣着情况。

体内蓄热率与内能的增加率相等。人体可以看做两个热部分：皮肤表面与身体内部。可以根据热容量以及每部分的温度随时间的变化率来分别计算每一部分的蓄热率。

$$S_{cr} = \frac{(1-\alpha_{sk})mc_{p,b}}{A_D} \cdot \frac{dt_{cr}}{d\theta} \tag{2-2}$$

$$S_{sk} = \frac{\alpha_{sk}mc_{p,b}}{A_D} \cdot \frac{dt_{sk}}{d\theta} \tag{2-3}$$

式中　α_{sk}——皮肤部分的质量；

m——人体质量（kg）；

$c_{p,b}$——人体比热容，$c_{p,b}=3490\text{J}/(\text{kg}\cdot\text{K})$；

A_D——DuBois 皮肤表面积（m^2）；

t_{cr}——核心温度（℃）；

t_{sk}——皮肤表面温度（℃）；

θ——时间（s）。

皮肤部分的质量 α_{sk} 取决于血液流向皮肤表面的速率。

对于人体能量平衡需结合理论与试验方法精确描述人体与环境的热交换。基本传热理论用来表述各种显热交换与潜热交换的机理，经验公式用来确定这些热交换率的数值。经验公式还用来作为人体皮肤温度与核心温度的函数来描述热生理学控制机理。

2. 皮肤散失的显热

皮肤必须通过服装来与周围环境进行显热交换。这一系列路径可描述为从皮肤表面热交换开始，通过服装，再由服装外表面进入周围环境中。

从人体衣服外表面向环境的对流散热量 C 和辐射散热量 R 都可以用传热系数以及服装外表面的平均温度 t_{cl} 与周围环境温度的差值来表示。

$$C = F_{cl}h_c(t_{cl}-t_a) \tag{2-4}$$

$$R = F_{cl}h_r(t_{cl}-\bar{t_r}) \tag{2-5}$$

式中　h_c——表面传热系数 [W/($\text{m}^2\cdot$K)]；

h_r——线性辐射传热系数 [W/($\text{m}^2\cdot$K)]；

F_{cl}——服装的表面系数 A_{cl}/A_D，其中 A_D 表示人体裸身表面积，A_{cl} 表示人体着装后的实际表面积。

h_c 和 h_r 均由服装表面积求得。式（2-4）和式（2-5）通常结合使用，再结合操作温度 t_o 和传热系数 h 来描述显热交换。

$$C + R = F_{cl}h(t_{cl}-t_o) \tag{2-6}$$

$$t_o = \frac{h_r\bar{t_r}+h_ct_a}{h_r+h_c} \tag{2-7}$$

$$h = h_r + h_c \tag{2-8}$$

根据式（2-7），操作温度 t_o 可以定义为辐射温度与周围空气温度的平均值，分别由其传热系数计算得出。

通过服装的实际显热传递过程包含对流、传导和辐射。为了方便起见，通常将这些因素

归纳成一个热阻值 R_{cl}，定义为

$$C + R = (t_{sk} - t_{cl})/R_{cl} \tag{2-9}$$

式中　R_{cl}——服装热阻值（$m^2 \cdot K/W$）。

由于在计算中常常不方便得知服装表面温度，故可以联立式（2-6）和式（2-9）来消除参数 t_{cl}。

$$C + R = \frac{t_{sk} - t_o}{R_{cl} + 1/(F_{cl}h)} \tag{2-10}$$

其中，t_o 参见式（2-7）中的定义。

3. 皮肤蒸发散热

皮肤蒸发散热 E_{sk} 取决于皮肤的湿度以及皮肤与周围环境的水蒸气分压力之差。

$$E_{sk} = \frac{w(p_{sk,s} - p_a)}{R_{e,cl} + 1/(F_{cl}h_e)} \tag{2-11}$$

式中　w——皮肤的无量纲湿度；

　　　$p_{sk,s}$——皮肤的水蒸气分压力，通常认为等于饱和蒸汽压（kPa）；

　　　p_a——周围空气的水蒸气分压力（kPa）；

　　　$R_{e,cl}$——服装层的蒸发传热热阻（类似于 R_{cl}）（$m^2 \cdot K/W$）；

　　　h_e——蒸发传热系数（类似于 h_c）[$W/(m^2 \cdot K)$]。

皮肤湿度是实际蒸发散热量与相同条件下完全浸湿的皮肤（$w=1$）的最大蒸发散热量 E_{max} 的比值。

皮肤的蒸发散热量是体温调节控制机制下的排汗蒸发量 E_{rsw} 与皮肤表面自然散湿量 E_{dif} 的和。

$$E_{sk} = E_{rsw} + E_{dif} \tag{2-12}$$

调节排汗的蒸发散热与调节出汗的蒸发散热成正比。

$$E_{rsw} = \dot{m}_{rsw} h_{fg} \tag{2-13}$$

式中　h_{fg}——水的汽化热，$h_{fg} = 2.43 \times 10^6 J/kg$（在30℃的时候）；

　　　$\dot{m}_{rsw}$——调节出汗的速率 [$kg/(s \cdot m^2)$]。

人体皮肤湿度 w_{rsw} 是汗液蒸发量与完全浸湿蒸发量之比。

$$w_{rsw} = E_{rsw}/E_{max} \tag{2-14}$$

皮肤湿度在确定蒸发散热时有重要作用。当 $w=1$ 时取最大蒸发量 E_{max}。皮肤湿度与热不舒适有很强的关联性，能够很好地衡量热应力。理论上说，当人体仍然保持在可控制的体温调节范围内时，皮肤湿度可以接近1.0。在大多数情况下，其值很难超过0.8。推荐0.5为一个健康的、适应环境的、可持续活动的人体的实际上限值。

4. 呼吸散热

在呼吸作用过程中，通过呼吸道与吸入空气的热对流和水分蒸发作用，人体既散失显热又散失潜热。一大部分热量与呼吸作用有关是因为空气在环境温度时被吸入，而呼出时接近饱和，温度只比 t_{cr} 低一点。

由呼吸作用造成的总散热量和散湿量分别为

$$q_{\text{res}} = C_{\text{res}} + E_{\text{res}} = \frac{\dot{m}_{\text{res}}(h_{\text{ex}} - h_{\text{a}})}{A_{\text{D}}} \tag{2-15}$$

$$\dot{m}_{\text{w,res}} = \frac{\dot{m}_{\text{res}}(w_{\text{ex}} - w_{\text{a}})}{A_{\text{D}}} \tag{2-16}$$

式中 $\dot{m}_{\text{res}}$——肺部通气率（kg/s）；

h_{ex}——呼出空气的焓值［J/kg（干空气）］；

h_{a}——吸入（环境）空气的焓值［J/kg（干空气）］；

$\dot{m}_{\text{w,res}}$——肺部失水率（kg/s）；

w_{ex}——呼出空气的湿度比率［kg（水气）/kg（干空气）］；

w_{a}——吸入（环境）空气的湿度比率［kg（水气）/kg（干空气）］。

通常情况下，肺部通气率主要是新陈代谢率的函数。

$$\dot{m}_{\text{res}} = K_{\text{res}} M A_{\text{D}} \tag{2-17}$$

式中 M——人体代谢率（W/m²）；

K_{res}——比例常数（1.43×10^{-6} kg/J）。

对于典型的室内环境，呼气温度与湿度由环境条件确定。

$$t_{\text{ex}} = 32.6 + 0.066 t_{\text{a}} + 32 w_{\text{a}} \tag{2-18}$$

$$w_{\text{ex}} = 0.0277 + 0.000065 t_{\text{a}} + 0.2 w_{\text{a}} \tag{2-19}$$

其中，环境温度 t_{a} 和呼气温度 t_{ex} 的单位是℃。在极端条件下，例如对于冬天的室外环境，可能就有不同的关系了。

周围空气的含湿量可根据大气压力 p_{t} 和环境水蒸气分压力 p_{a} 表达为

$$w_{\text{a}} = \frac{0.622 p_{\text{a}}}{p_{\text{t}} - p_{\text{a}}} \tag{2-20}$$

呼吸散热常由显热散热 C_{res} 和潜热散热 E_{res} 来表示。两个近似值通常用于简化式（2-18）和式（2-19）。首先，在热平衡中，与其他散热相比，干空气中的呼吸散热的值相对较小，t_{ex} 的平均值在标准条件（即空气温度20℃，相对湿度50%，海平面）下通过式（2-18）计算得出。其次，注意到式（2-19）中，t_{a} 的影响很微弱，式（2-19）的第二项以及式（2-20）的分母相当于标准状况。在标准条件下，C_{res} 和 E_{res} 可表示为

$$C_{\text{res}} = 0.0014 M (34 - t_{\text{a}}) \tag{2-21}$$

$$E_{\text{res}} = 0.0173 M (5.87 - p_{\text{a}}) \tag{2-22}$$

式中，p_{a} 的单位是 kPa；t_{a} 的单位是℃。

2.1.3 热舒适及其预测

根据 Fanger 教授的理论，六个基本因素的相互作用定义了人类热环境和热舒适的感觉。这些参数又被划分为环境因素与人为因素。环境温度、平均辐射温度、湿度、风速为四个基

本的环境变量；人体代谢率和服装（热阻与透湿性）为影响人类对热环境反应的人为变量。因此，任何与热应力有关的问题都应该研究这六个因素。

在这六个因素间建立其对人体舒适性的影响关系，可以推断出另外五个因素对环境温度 t_a 的影响。

1) 代谢率：每增加 17.5W（静止水平以上）相当于 t_a 增加了 1℃。
2) 服装热阻（clo）：每变化 1clo 相当于休息时变化 5℃，运动时变化 10℃。
3) 平均辐射温度（MRT）：MRT 每变化 1℃ 相当于 t_a 变化 1℃。
4) 风速：风速每变化 0.1m/s 相当于温度变化 0.5℃（直到 1.5℃ 止）。
5) 湿度：相对湿度每变化 10% 相当于 t_a 变化 0.3℃。

Fanger 定义了 3 个限制因素来描述人体热舒适：①人体处于热平衡状态；②排汗率在舒适的范围内；③皮肤平均温度在舒适的范围内。这些定义热舒适的概念可描述为可测量的术语，如人体核心温度的变化范围是 36.5~37.5℃，在皮肤温度的最低值为 30℃，躯干和头部温度为 34~35℃，在以上情况下人体可免于出汗。任何温度值与以上的值有偏差都会引起热不舒适。关于式（2-1），当通过辐射与对流的方式使人体散热率与产生的净代谢率（$M-W$）相等时，人体感到热舒适，因此，蓄热率 S 为零。换言之，热应力是由于人体承受的工作环境的需求量与人体所能消除的热负荷（以服装修正）不平衡导致的。由此得出结论，热舒适与汗液蒸发作用有直接联系。热舒适可以表达为 E_{sk}/E_{max}。当这个比率超过 0.2 时，人体感觉从"舒适"变为"不舒适"；增加到 0.4~0.6 时，人体机能递减；超过 0.6 时，人体将不能工作或者只能在有限的时间范围内行动；超过 0.8 时，人就会有中暑的危险。

热感觉和热舒适都有两极，"太冷"和"太热"，舒适或温度适中处于中间。这种感觉可分几个级别描述。不舒适的主观等级与相应的生理关系总结于表 2-1 中。

表 2-1 热感觉标度和热舒适标度

投票值①	投票值②	热感觉	热舒适	热效应区域
—	9	很热	很不舒适	不可忍受的热
+3	8	热	不舒适	
+2	7	暖	稍不舒适	可忍受的出汗
+1	6	稍暖		
0	5	正常	舒适	—
-1	4	稍凉		可忍受的血管收缩
-2	3	凉	稍不舒适	可忍受的颤抖
-3	2	冷	—	
—	1	很冷	不舒适	不可忍受的冷

① 热标度依据为 ASHRAE 标准 55（美国采暖、制冷与空调工程师学会标准）。
② 热标度依据为 Rohles 的研究成果。

热舒适和热感觉可以有几种预测方法。一种方法是利用图 2-2 和表 2-2 通过调整不同的衣着与活动水平来获得。更数字化与严格的预测需利用模型来进行，如 PMV-PPD 模型、双节点模型以及自适应模型。这一部分只介绍 PMV-PPD 模型。

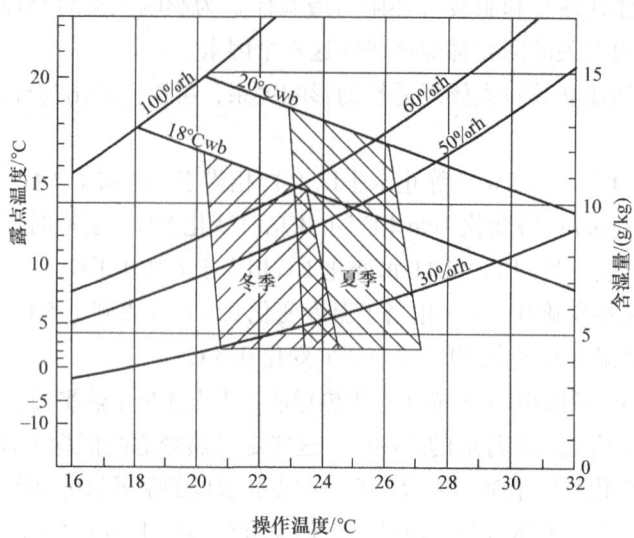

图 2-2 ASHRAE 夏季和冬季舒适区

表 2-2 男性、女性两者以及共同的预测热感觉等式

曝露时间/h	试验对象	回归方程[①,②] t（干球温度）/℃ p（蒸汽压）/kPa
1.0	男性	$Y = 0.220t + 0.233p - 5.673$
	女性	$Y = 0.272t + 0.248p - 7.245$
	男性和女性	$Y = 0.245t + 0.248p - 6.475$
2.0	男性	$Y = 0.221t + 0.270p - 6.024$
	女性	$Y = 0.283t + 0.210p - 7.694$
	男性和女性	$Y = 0.252t + 2.40p - 6.859$
3.0	男性	$Y = 0.212t + 0.293p - 5.949$
	女性	$Y = 0.275t + 0.255p - 8.622$
	男性和女性	$Y = 0.243t + 0.278p - 6.802$

① Y 值指 ASHRAE 热感觉等级。

② 对于年轻的久坐的成年人，穿着热阻大约为 0.5clo 的衣服，$\bar{t}_r \approx \bar{t}_a$，风速小于 0.2m/s。

Fanger 提出的预测平均评价（PMV）指标用来预测人群的平均反应，其依据是 ASHRAE 的热感觉标度。房间中的人们根据 ASHRAE 的热感觉七点标度来描述他们的感受。通过所有处于同一设定条件中的试验对象提供的感觉平均值，得出一个平均评价（MV）。Fanger 将特定环境中人体实际热流与最佳舒适条件所需热流间的不平衡与 PMV 联系起来，得到式 (2-23)。

$$PMV = [0.303\exp(-0.036M) + 0.028]L \qquad (2-23)$$

式中 L——人体热负荷，定义为假设一个处于舒适状态的人其内部产热与散失到环境中的热量之差。

预测不满意百分比（PPD）用来预测感觉劣于稍暖和稍凉的人的百分比（也就是说倾向于抱怨环境的人的比例）。Fanger利用热感觉七点标度（-3～+3）提出：反应值为±2和±3的均确定为不舒适。那些反应值为±1和0的人们被认为是舒适的。受访者反应±2和±3所占的比例确定为每一级别的PMV值；变量为PPD值。PMV和PPD的关系为

$$PPD = 100 - 95\exp[-(0.03353PMV^4 + 0.2179PMV^2)] \quad (2\text{-}24)$$

这个关系的价值在于它揭示了关于热中性的完美对称（$PMV=0$）。可以从图2-3看出，即使PMV指标为0时，仍然有一些对温度水平不满意的个体，尽管他们的着装和活动与其他人类似。这是由于不同的人对热舒适的评价不一样造成的。这意味着$PMV=0$时，允许最多有5%的人不满意。

Fanger的PMV-PPD热舒适模型对于热舒适理论以及评价建筑室内热环境作出了突破性的贡献。其被广泛应用于热舒适的设计和评估领域，并获得认可。但是，应该注意的是，PMV-PPD模型仅对静止状态的舒适反应有效果，不能应用于预测生理反应或者瞬时情形的反应。

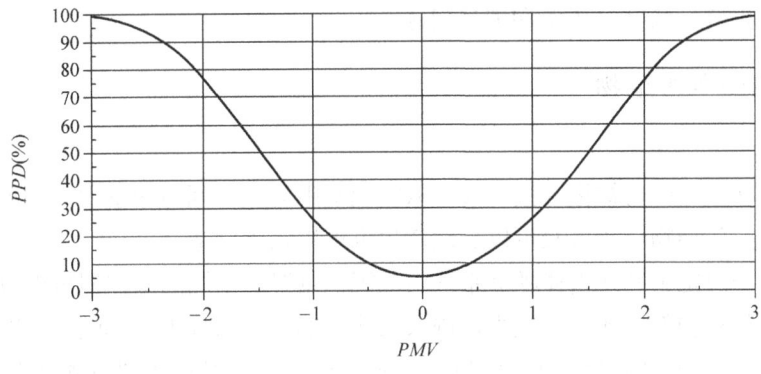

图2-3　PMV和PPD的关系

2.2　室内空气品质

人们一天中大部分时间是在家里、办公室、学校、商店或其他私人或公共建筑室内环境中度过的。建筑物内部空气的品质已经成为人们健康与幸福的重要决定因素。但不幸的是，室内空气中含有各种自然的或者人为的污染物，如细菌、病毒、真菌、氡气、燃烧副产物等。近年来，室内空气中又被检测出石棉、甲醛等有机化学污染物。研究表明，这些污染物在家中以及其他建筑内部的含量可能高于室外空气。这一情况即使在大城市也不例外。

本章描述了建筑物内常见的空气污染物的来源、暴露于污染物中对健康的潜在影响以及改善室内空气品质的方法。

2.2.1　病态建筑综合征和建筑相关疾病

美国环境保护署（EPA）将建筑环境引起的急性健康问题大致分为两类：病态建筑综合

征和与建筑相关的疾病。

病态建筑综合征（SBS）是室内人员表现出的一种急性健康和舒适反应。室内人员的这种反应一般出现于清晨，在下午达到高峰，离开工作场所不久后消失。由于没有被正式命名，所以有多种名称（如环境疾病、二十世纪病等）。病态建筑综合征（SBS）是使用最广泛的一种表述，并被世界卫生组织所采用。

具体地说，病态建筑综合征是非确定性症状，其不符合任何特定的疾病模式，不能关联到一个可识别的病源。而且病态建筑综合征的性质使其诊断非常困难，常见的症状包括头痛、头晕、恶心、流鼻涕、眼睛灼热、喉咙沙哑、持续的干咳。还有一些其他比较常见的症状，如疲劳、烦躁、紧张、注意力不集中等。

相比而言，建筑相关疾病（BRI）比较容易诊断，但是其表现得更为严重。建筑相关疾病属于非传染性疾病，其有诊断的可能，可与特定的建筑物内污染物相关联。建筑相关疾病的原因通常可以追溯到病毒、细菌、真菌或其他微生物，它们在加湿系统和空气调节系统等潮湿环境下会大量繁殖。其受害者出现如军团病、湿热症、过敏性肺炎、气喘等临床确定的疾病。建筑相关疾病，还有一个特征是会表现出类似流感的症状，包括眼睛流泪、打喷嚏和咳嗽、气短、发烧、嗜睡、头晕和消化问题。

2.2.2 室内空气污染物

1. 颗粒物

颗粒分散在空气中也被称为气溶胶。从沙尘暴中的沙粒到洁净室中的不可见微粒都属于空气传播的颗粒污染物。气溶胶可以自然产生也可以人为制造。

粒子的大小决定了其在人体呼吸系统内的沉积位置。不同的采样器可以收集不同粒径的颗粒物。这些颗粒物都会或多、或少地进入人体肺部。大部分被人体吸入的颗粒在鼻腔通道内被捕获。可入胸颗粒物（国内常称为可吸入颗粒物）是其中可进入肺支气管的部分，用中位切割直径 $10\mu m$（PM10）的样本表示。可入胸颗粒物是可进入肺部气体交换区域的部分。美国环保署（EPA）将其定义为可用中位切割点 $2.5\mu m$ 收集的颗粒（PM2.5）。而美国政府工业卫生专家会议（ACGIH）将其定义为中位切割点为 $4\mu m$ 的颗粒。

环境烟草烟气（ETS）是颗粒物的重要来源，其由吸烟者呼出的主流烟气和香烟燃烧排放出的侧流烟气组成。大约有 70%~90% 的烟是侧流烟气，它的化学成分与主流烟气有所不同。实验室研究已确定的环境烟草烟气中的化学物质已达 4700 多种，包括已知的致癌有毒化学物，如一氧化碳、氨、甲醛、尼古丁以及烟草含有的亚硝胺、苯、镉、镍、芳香胺化合物。这些成分在侧流烟气中的含量比主流烟气要集中得多。对有吸烟许可的住宅和办公楼的研究表明，烟草烟气是多种气体多环芳香烃化合物的重要来源。

接触燃烧产物对健康的影响取决于许多因素，包括含量、毒性和个体易感性或对特殊物质的敏感性。燃烧产生的多环芳香烃化合物含有许多已被证明是对动物有致癌作用的芳香碳氢化合物。环境烟草烟气已被证明与成年人肺癌，以及呼吸道感染、哮喘发作、中耳积液、儿童低出生率有关。美国环境保护署已把 ETS 列为已知的人类致癌物。ETS 对健康的影响也包括心脏病、头痛和刺激等。

2. 生物气溶胶

生物气溶胶是指任何由空气传播的细菌颗粒物。虽然通常被认为源自微生物（真菌、细菌、病毒、原生动物、藻类），生物气溶胶也可能源自植物（花粉、植物碎片）、动物（狗和猫的毛、皮屑和唾液，尘螨）。除了完整的生物（如细菌），其部分（真菌孢子和片段）、成分（内毒素、过敏原）及产物（尘螨含抗原类粒和真菌毒素）也包含在生物气溶胶的定义内。对于抗原或毒素，很少的量也可能引起机体的反应；很多过敏或毒性反应都是由微量的抗原或毒素引起的。公共利益的重点是由空气传播的可引起疾病和感染的微生物，主要是细菌和病毒。

在室内环境中，地板和地板覆盖物可以变成微生物的聚集场所，这些微生物随后会悬浮到空气中。日常活动，包括步行、吸尘、地毯清洗都可能促进微生物的再悬浮。有些病毒可能会存活于无孔表面长达八个星期。

人群是室内空气中的细菌和病毒的重要来源。当病原微生物感染宿主，进而感染另一个宿主时，传染性疾病就已开始蔓延。在室内，受感染的人群就变为传染疾病的主要来源和传播者。病毒支原体可以由皮肤的损伤部释放出来，或在咳嗽、打喷嚏、说话时分散于空气中。唾液的飞沫、牙科和呼吸道疾病治疗程序中的呼吸道分泌物也是人群受感染的途径。

一定剂量的微生物才能使室内易感人群感染疾病。当大小、密度、电荷相同时，空气中传播的致病颗粒物的物理特性和任何其他颗粒物相同。两者的主要区别是，生物气溶胶可通过多种方式（如感染、过敏性反应、中毒）引发疾病，这取这决于生物体种类、剂量，以及接触人群的易感性。虽然室内环境中一般都存在微生物，但是有丰富的水分和养分的室内空间会促进真菌、细菌、原生动物、藻类，甚至线虫的生长。因此，加湿器、水喷雾系统、湿润的多孔表面就成为它们生长的载体。空气湿度过大也会加快这些微生物在室内的繁殖。空气处理机组的起动引起的湍流也会提高空间中的细菌和真菌的含量。

接触空气中的真菌孢子、菌丝片段或其代谢产物可引起过敏性疾病，包括过敏性鼻炎、哮喘和过敏性肺炎，以及传染性疾病，如组织胞浆菌病、芽生菌病、曲霉菌病。此外，急性中毒和癌症都被归因于呼吸道接触到的真菌毒素。

3. 无机气体

多种无机气体由于对人类健康和舒适以及材料的影响而受到人们的关注。这些无机气体包括二氧化碳、一氧化碳、氮氧化物、二氧化硫、臭氧和氨。它们大多数同时源于室外污染源和室内污染源。

二氧化碳（CO_2）是由人类呼吸产生的。它通常不被认为是一种有毒的空气污染物，但它可以在诸如潜艇密闭空间内造成单纯的缺氧窒息。二氧化碳在城市周边环境中的含量是$330\sim370\times10^{-4}\%$。在城市环境中$CO_2$的含量较高，这可能是由于汽油发动机或柴油发动机的汽车尾气排放量较大造成的。室内空间CO_2含量已被广泛用于评价供应给室内空间的室外空气质量。

一氧化碳（CO）是一种无色、无味的气体，由碳氢化合物的不完全燃烧产生。它是一种常见的空气污染物，具有很强的毒性。CO与氧相比，与血红蛋白具有更强的结合能力（约为氧气的240倍），而且其对氧解离曲线的不利偏移使得吸入一氧化碳会导致搏动性头痛。一氧化碳通过形成碳氧血红蛋白抑制氧在血液中的运输，同时也抑制细胞中的细胞色素氧化酶含量。普通室内的一氧化碳来源包括燃气灶、煤油灯和加热器、主流和侧流烟气、火炉、无排气或不适当地排气的燃烧源。当大厦的进气口位于路边或临近停车场等产生CO的场所时，也会将室外的CO带入室内环境。

氮氧化物（NO_x）是一种有刺激性气味的腐蚀性气体。二氧化氮具有较低的水溶性，因此可进入肺部深处，在那里它会导致延迟性炎症反应。二氧化氮可产生自由基，因此被认为是一种潜在致癌物。在含量高时，二氧化氮由于其氧化性能直接导致肺部损伤，并通过增加机体对呼吸道感染易感性间接引起健康问题。氮氧化物主要来自室内灶具、守夜灯和无排气管的加热器。产生一氧化碳（CO）的污染源往往也会产生一氧化氮（NO）以及二氧化氮（NO_2）。地下或临近的停车库都会提高室内的氮氧化物的含量。在烹调时，可能会出现$0.2 \sim 0.4 \times 10^{-4}$%的峰值。城市地区汽车尾气排放的氮氧化物会进入室内。氮氧化物也会产生于主流和侧流烟气。目前，一氧化氮和二氧化氮是人们最关心的氮氧化物。

二氧化硫（SO_2）是一种有刺鼻气味的无色气体。在含量约0.5×10^{-4}%时会被察觉。采用煤油的空间加热器会产生二氧化硫，同时燃烧化石燃料、民用燃料油和汽油或燃烧含硫的任何材料都会产生二氧化硫。因此，二氧化硫在许多城市地区是一种常见的空气污染物。由于二氧化硫极易溶于水，它极易与呼吸道的水气反应，刺激上呼吸道黏膜。

臭氧（O_3）是对肺有刺激性的气体，在约0.12×10^{-4}%的含量时就会改变肺功能。暴露在$60 \sim 80 \times 10^{-6}$%的含量下会引起炎症、支气管狭窄，增加气管的反应。在地表附近，当碳氢化合物及氮氧化物在紫外线照射下反应产生光化学烟雾时会产生臭氧。臭氧也可由电气或办公室设备（包括激光打印机和复印机）的冠状放电产生。当室内使用臭氧发生设备时（通常为市场上的便携式空气净化器和负离子空气净化器）也会产生臭氧。

氨（NH_3）是一种具有强烈的刺激性气味的无色气体。它比空气轻，易溶于水。氨本身就是一种制冷剂、肥料，也是一种高容量工业化学品，可用于制造多种产品（如氮肥、硝酸、合成纤维、炸药等）。在自然界，氨是动物代谢的副产品，由尿酸分解产生。作为室内空气污染物，氨的来源一般是合成清洁剂和新陈代谢的副产品。

4. 挥发性有机气体

所有的室内有机污染物按照其挥发性被分为了三个级别，见表2-3。依据有机污染物沸点所划分的三个级别之间并没有明显的区分界限。而挥发性有机物（VOCs）在非工业环境中的影响引起了人们相当多的注意。这类有机物的沸点范围大致为$50 \sim 250$℃，饱和压力大致为$10^{-3} \sim 10^{-4}$mmHg（1mmHg = 133.322Pa）。这些有机物的来源包括两方面，其一是工业环境中的各种溶剂、试剂和去污脱脂剂，另外是非工业环境中的诸如家具、陈设、墙壁和地板饰面，清洁和维护产品等物品，甚至室内的办公和娱乐活动都可以产生这类有机物。

表2-3 室内有机化合物的挥发性分类

说 明	缩 写	沸点范围/℃
高挥发性有机化合物	VVOCs	<0 ~ (50 ~ 100)
一般挥发性有机化合物	VOCs	(50 ~ 100) ~ (240 ~ 260)
半挥发性有机化合物（农药、多环芳烃化合物、增塑剂）	SVOCs	(240 ~ 260) ~ (380 ~ 400)

Berglund 发现，由于潜在来源的多变特性，使得非工业室内环境中 VOCs 的来源变得不可确定。室内挥发性有机物的排放可以按其排放的持续性和排放速率是否固定来分类。例如建筑材料和家具的挥发性有机物排放是持续的而且其速率也是固定的（例如地毯和复合木家具），而其他类型的排放有的是持续的但速率是不固定的（例如装修工程中的油漆），有的是间断的但速率是固定的（例如燃气灶的燃烧产物或者清洁产物中的 VOCs），有的是间断的而且其挥发速率并不固定（例如地毯清洗剂）。

很多"湿"散发源（油漆和粘合剂）在刚刚使用的时候有着很高的挥发速率，但是随着时间的推移其速率会急剧下降直至物品被粘和或者变干。而新的"干"式材料（例如地毯、糊墙纸、家具）在变旧之前也以很高的速率挥发着化学物质。这些高含量污染源衰减到正常散发水平通常需要几周到几个月，时间的长短取决于挥发速度、材料表面积以及通风情况。一些改造措施可以用来提高挥发性有机物衰减的速度。在刚刚入住的新办公建筑中 VOCs 的总含量可以达到室外空气中含量的 50~100 倍。在同样的新办公建筑里，经过四至五个月的充分通风后，这个比率就下降到了不到 5 倍。

在室内发现了众多 VOCs 以及分别识别它们的困难性导致了总有机挥发性气体（TVOCs）概念的产生。一些研究人员已经使用 TVOCs 来代表所有检测到的有机挥发性气体的总和。TVOCs 的含量通常是指通过光电探测器或者火焰离子探测器等检测方法所检测到的空气中的所有物质的含量。由于不同类别的 VOCs 会导致探测器的不同变化，所以从本质上说所有 TVOCs 含量检测方法的精度介于低精度到中等精度之间。虽然有这些不足，但是 TVOCs 的概念还是很有用的，并且已经广泛应用于大气中混合污染物的研究。

目前，对非工业环境室内 VOCs 对健康的潜在负面影响的了解并不充分，但是这些影响可能包括以下几方面：刺激性效果，包括吸入难闻气体，刺激黏膜和恶化哮喘；全身效应，如疲劳，注意力难以集中；毒性以及慢性效果，如致癌。

由于一些经常在室内空气中发现的 VOCs 可能导致人类（苯）以及动物（氯仿、三氯乙烯、四氯化碳、二氯苯）致癌，所以 VOCs 挥发量对人体健康的慢性不利影响被人们所重视。理论风险研究表明挥发性有机化合物暴露在住宅的室内空气中的慢性危害比在室外空气以及饮水中的危害要大。

5. 放射性污染物

放射性污染物可以是颗粒状的或是气态的，而且和普通的工业污染物非常相似。很多放射性物质在高含量的情况下会有化学毒性，然而在很多情况下放射性本身会限制它们在空气中的含量。大部分的放射性空气污染物在被人体吸收并且残留在人体内部时会对人体产生影响。这种影响就是内部辐射伤害。

放射性颗粒可能会落到地面上，从而污染植物最终进入食物链和人体。地面沉积物可以增加外部辐射。然而，这样的外部辐射是不会有太大危害的，除非有来自核武器或者是严重的核反应堆事故的放射性沉降物。

放射性物质表现出多种不同问题。高含量的放射性物质可以产生足够的热量，损坏过滤设备或使材料自燃。对大多数的放射性物质而言，只需要比普通材料小得多的含量就会变成有害的物质。这样，就应该用特殊的电子仪器来检测放射性物质的危险水平。

空气中的大部分气体放射性来自于氡。氡（Rn）是一种天然的、无色、无味的惰性放射性气体。它产生于镭的放射性衰变，而镭是通过铀和钍的衰变过程产生的。

氡广泛存在于自然界中。在氡衰变之前，它可以在非常小的空间内（如土壤颗粒与岩石之间）移动有限的距离，从而进入室内。室内氡的其他来源是地下水（氡具有很好的水溶性）和含镭的一些建筑材料。

氡气主要是通过地基的缝隙，在压力驱动流的作用下进入建筑。氡气侵入建筑的路径包括混凝土地基中的裂缝、接头和一些其他孔洞；直接通过多孔混凝土砌砖；通过低矮走廊天花板上的接头盒开口；还可以通过嵌在楼层板或者位于走廊的暖通空调管道系统的泄露点进入。在氡含量高的情况下，压力驱动流是氡侵入建筑物的主要方式。

2.2.3 改善室内空气品质的基本策略

1. 源控制

一般来说，最有效的改善室内空气质量的方法是消除污染物的来源，或减少其排放。一些含有石棉的污染源，可以密封。而其他的，如燃气灶，可以进行调整，以减少排放量。在许多情况下，与增加通风换气次数相比，源控制也是一个更具经济性的保持室内空气品质的方法，因为增加通风会增加能源消耗。

2. 改进通风系统

另一种用于降低建筑物室内空气污染物含量的方法是增加室内的通风量。大多数家庭取暖和供冷系统都不是通过机械方式将新鲜空气引入屋内的。打开窗户和门，当天气允许的时候打开窗口或阁楼的风扇，或者打开具有通风控制的窗式空调器以增加通风效率。室内卫生间或厨房的排气风扇，可以直接去除排气风扇所在房间内的污染物，同时也可以增加室外空气的通风率。

特别重要的是，人们在短期活动中应尽可能多地运用这些方法。因为在短期活动中，可能产生高含量的污染物。例如绘画、脱漆、煤油炉取暖、烹饪或从事维修工作，如焊接、锡焊或砂纸打磨。

3. 空气净化器

市场上有很多类型与型号的空气净化器，范围从相对便宜的台式净化器到复杂、昂贵的全房间系统。一些空气净化器在除尘方面是非常有效的，然而，有些类型，包括大多数台式机型都不是很有效。空气净化器通常并不是为了去除气体污染物而设计的。

一个空气净化器的有效性取决于它如何很好地收集室内空气污染物和它能够驱动多少空气通过清洗或过滤元件。具有低空气流通率的高效率收集器是不会有效的，或者高空气流通率的低效率收集器也是同样不会有效的。任何空气净化器的长期性能取决于根据制造商的指示进行维护。

另一个决定空气净化器性能的重要因素是污染源强度。特别是台式空气净化器，有可能无法有效去除由附近的强污染源产生的污染物。对特定污染源非常关注的人们会发现，努力消除污染源，才能发挥空气净化器的作用。

在过去的几年里，出现了一些宣传声称盆栽植物已被实验证明可以减少某些化学物质的含量。但是目前还没有证据来证明消除家庭和办公室大量污染物所需的合理的盆栽植物数量。室内盆栽植物，不应过分浇水，因为过分潮湿的土壤可促进微生物生长，从而影响过敏体质的人群。

2.3 建筑声环境

2.3.1 噪声概述

1. 声音和噪声

随着近代工业的发展，环境污染也随之产生。噪声污染是环境污染的一种，已经成为人类健康的一大危害。噪声污染、水污染、大气污染是世界范围内的三个主要环境问题。现代城市中人们约90%以上的时间是在人工环境中度过的。建筑声环境与热环境、光环境构成了建筑物理环境，它们既相互区别又相互联系。如果一个建筑的室内声环境不能令人满意，就可以说该室内环境不能令人满意。随着城镇化程度的加重，建筑隔声和噪声控制问题成为各类建筑的一个普遍性问题。

声音在主观上是人们听到的物体在空气中振动的传播。局部的空气压缩和扩展使得声音在空气中传播。可以用声级计测量这些振动产生的波动压力，图2-4所示为声级计。

声音由物体振动引起，以波的形式在一定的介质（如固体、液体、气体）中传播。通常听到的声音为空气声。一般情况下，人耳可听到的声波频率为20～20000Hz，称为可听声；低于20Hz，称为次声波；高于20000Hz，称为超声波。人们所听到声音的音调的高低取决于声波的频率，高频声听起来尖锐，而低频声给人的感觉较为沉闷。声音的大小是由声音的强弱决定的。图2-5所示是一些不同频率和波长的具有单一频率特性的声音。

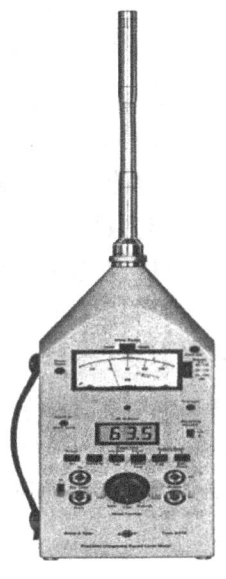

图2-4 声级计

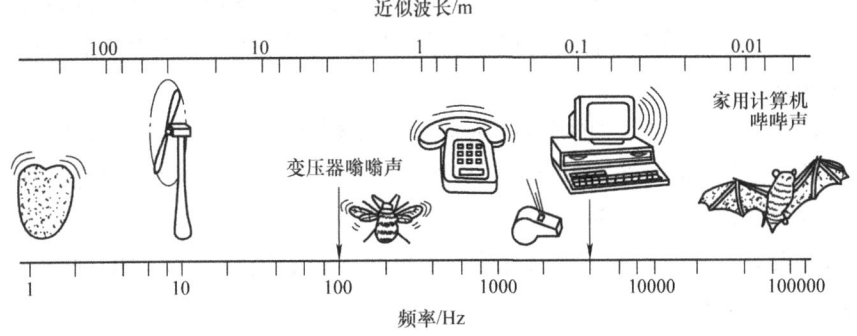

图2-5 日常可以听到的不同频率和波长的声音

噪声是由各种不同频率、不同强度的声音杂乱、无规律地组合而成的。

建筑设备工程设计主要关注的是锅炉、送风机和排风机、制冷压缩机、水泵等产生的噪声。

2. 噪声的分类与特征

按声源的机械特点可分为：气体扰动产生的噪声、固体和液体振动产生的噪声、撞击产生的噪声以及电磁作用产生的电磁噪声。

按声音的频率，噪声可分为三类：小于400Hz的低频噪声、400~1000Hz的中频噪声及大于1000Hz的高频噪声。

按时间变化的属性可分为：稳态噪声、非稳态噪声、起伏噪声、间歇噪声以及脉冲噪声等。

3. 噪声的主要来源

（1）交通噪声　包括机动车辆、船舶、地铁、火车、飞机等的噪声。由于机动车辆数目的迅速增加，使得交通噪声成为城市的主要噪声。

（2）工业噪声　工厂的各种设备产生的噪声。工业噪声的声级一般较高，对工人及周围居民有较大的影响。

（3）建筑噪声　主要是建筑机械发出的噪声。建筑噪声的特点是强度较大，且多发生在人口密集地区，因此严重影响居民的休息与生活。

（4）空调系统噪声　空调系统噪声按产生形式可分为空气动力性噪声和机械性噪声，按噪声发生部位也可分为两大类：设备噪声、风管及部件噪声。空调设备包括冷水机组、水泵、风机（包括空调机组、风机盘管机组、通风机）、冷却塔等，在运行中均可能因为压缩机、电动机、风叶运转，设备振动而产生机械性噪声，属于噪声源。风管和风管部件（主要是送风口）的噪声为涡流噪声（空气涡流产生的气流噪声）和振动噪声（风管及部件振动产生的噪声）。

（5）社会噪声　包括人们的社会活动和家用电器、音响设备发出的噪声。

4. 噪声污染的危害

噪声给人带来生理上和心理上的危害，主要有以下几方面：

（1）损害听力　有关资料表明，当人连续听摩托车声，8h以后听力就会受损；若是在摇滚音乐厅，0.5h后人的听力就会受损；若在80dB以上的噪声环境中生活，造成耳聋的可能性可高达50%。

（2）损害视力　噪声会严重影响听觉器官，甚至使人丧失听力，尽人皆知。然而，耳朵与眼睛之间有着微妙的内在"联系"，当噪声作用于听觉器官时，也会通过神经系统的作用"波及"视觉器官，使人的视力减弱。

（3）损害人的心血管系统　我国对城市噪声与居民健康的调查表明，噪声每上升1dB，高血压发病率就增加3%。

（4）刺激人的神经系统　长期在噪声环境下工作，还会引起人的神经衰弱症候群（如头痛、头晕、耳鸣、记忆力衰退、视力降低等）。

（5）影响睡眠　突然的噪声在40dB时，可使10%的人惊醒；达到60dB时，可使70%

的人惊醒。

2.3.2 噪声的控制方法

1. 噪声控制的基本原理

(1) 噪声源的控制　降低噪声源的噪声，一般有两种方法：一是控制噪声源，如改进设备结构，提高部件加工精度和装配质量，采用合理的操作方法等，从而降低噪声的发生功率；二是根据吸收、反射、干涉等原理，采用吸声、隔声、减振和隔振等技术及消声措施，控制声源的辐射功率。

(2) 传播途径的控制　合理规划防噪布局，切断噪声的传播途径。把噪声源与居民区、文教区等隔开。利用土坡、山冈等屏障或树木来建立隔声屏障。

(3) 个人防护　当不能从噪声源和传播途径控制噪声时，可采用个人防护的办法，一般采用耳塞、防声棉、耳罩和头盔等，也可以采用轮班作业，缩短个人在强噪声环境中的暴露时间。

2. 控制方法

在设计阶段就考虑到噪声控制是最有效的。在建筑的设计和施工方法中使用替代装置可以排除设备和技术中潜在的噪声。

(1) 吸声降噪　吸声降噪是一种在传播途径上控制噪声强度的方法。物体的吸声作用是普遍存在的，吸声的效果不仅与吸声材料有关，还与所选的吸声结构有关。这种技术主要用于室内空间。

(2) 消声降噪　消声器是一种既能使气流通过，又能有效地降低噪声的设备。通常可用消声器降低各种空气动力设备的进出口的噪声或沿管道传递的噪声。

(3) 隔声降噪　把产生噪声的机器设备封闭在一个小的空间内，使它与周围环境隔开，以减少噪声对环境的影响，这种做法叫做隔声。隔声屏障和隔声罩是主要的两种设计，其他隔声结构还有：隔声室、隔声墙、隔声幕、隔声门等。

3. 空调系统噪声控制措施

在设计和安装过程中采取有效措施来降低空调系统的噪声。

(1) 风管及部件减噪

1) 设计风速不宜过高，以减小空气涡流产生的噪声。一般干管内风速控制在8m/s以内，支管风速不高于3m/s，送风口风速控制在2m/s以内。

2) 在管路布置时人为地增加风管走向变化，以便合理利用噪声的自然衰减。

3) 各支路风管的设计风量尽量达到自然平衡。

4) 送风量与回风量应尽量接近平衡，避免室内外形成明显的压力差。

5) 风管变径要采用渐扩或渐缩管，不能发生截面巨变。

6) 风管弯头与弯头的间距不宜过小，避免涡流严重而产生噪声。

7) 风管与墙体、楼板之间不能刚性接触，要做隔振处理，如图2-6和图2-7所示。

(2) 冷却塔减噪

1) 优选低噪声型冷却塔。

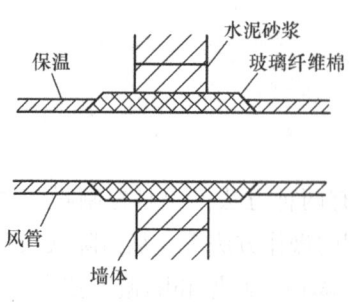
图 2-6　风管穿墙的隔振设计

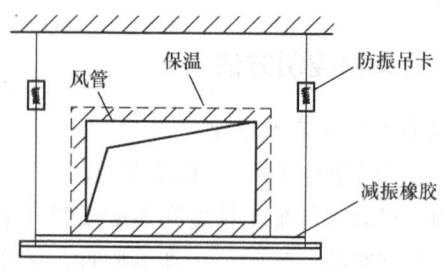
图 2-7　风管与楼板的隔振设计

2）冷却塔应设置在对周边建筑影响最小处，并避开建筑物的主立面和主出入口。

3）在塔基和混凝土基础间应设减振垫或减振器。

4）冷却塔可以加装消声器。

5）如果需要，可以在冷却塔和周边建筑物间建造隔声墙。

2.4　建筑光环境

视觉是人类最重要的一种感观。人们用眼睛去感知环境，行动于四处并且完成各项工作。光以及光的效果刺激着人们的视觉，所以从自然光和人工光方面实现对光的控制成为人工环境的重要特征。

光是一种电磁辐射形式的能源。它是一种特殊的电磁辐射，能够被人的视觉所感知。能够被人眼所感知的电磁辐射的范围在整个电磁辐射光谱中只是非常狭窄的一部分，如图 2-8 所示。对于肉眼来说，可见电磁辐射的波长范围大约在 380~760nm 之间。

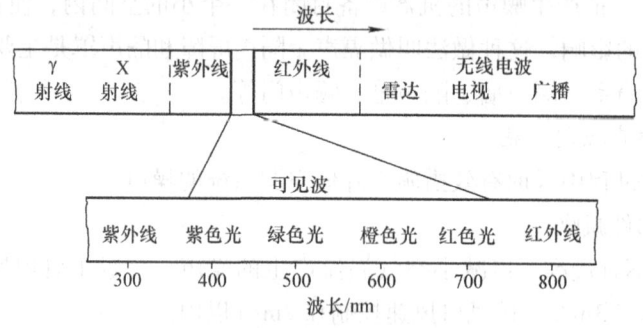
图 2-8　电磁光谱

光是自然的一个最基本的要素。视觉是光的一种探测。光探测刺激视觉，使人们看见并认知周围的环境。人类对光有着本能的生理需求和心理依赖，在物质极大丰富、产品日新月异的今天，人们有条件追求更高质量的光，不仅要求照明，更希望针对不同的场合对光线进行精确的控制。与此同时，人们对于光还有着越来越高的装饰和艺术感的需求。

2.4.1　自然光和人工光

现阶段人工环境中的自然光源主要有三种——散射光（通过云层或局部多云的天空漫

反射的光)、直射光（晴朗或局部多云的天空下直射的太阳光束）和反射光（通过自然或人工表面发射的光）。根据不同的光源种类采用相应的措施对建筑物进行合理的天然采光就显得尤为重要，对应不同的建筑类型选择适宜的自然采光形式（侧面采光、顶部采光、中庭采光）是建筑天然采光设计阶段的重要环节。办公室、卧室等小型民用、公用房间宜采用侧面采光形式。侧面采光不仅能使室内人员透过采光玻璃直接看到外部自然界和人，而且不受高度限制，但是可能会使室内人员在局部位置产生眩晕感，对于这种产生眩光的可能性，可以采用局部隔挡加以控制调节。对人员流动较少的仓库、车间等建筑，可以采用眩光率较低（尤其在低太阳高度角时）的顶部采光即顶棚天窗采光。对于商场、办公楼等大型建筑宜采用中庭采光，它不仅能满足人对外界的视觉欣赏要求而且产生眩光的概率又极低，对高度没有任何的限制，可以获得极佳的光线穿透深度。但是并不是所有建筑都能满足设计中庭的需要，如设置中庭则其全晴天日光照射下顶层与底层有较大的温度差，这就使得空调设计可能需要进行负荷计算改进，因此，中庭采光仅局限于部分建筑群体。

虽然自然光具有很多优点，但它的应用却受到时间、地点、外部气候条件等的限制，因此，太阳能导光管作为一种新型的自然光采光设施被设计开发出来。太阳能导光管照明是一种新型照明装置，该装置无需常规能源就能提供白天室内照明，减小由常规能源带来的环境污染，是一种绿色健康、节能环保的系统。图2-9和图2-10所示为北京科技大学体育馆太阳能导光管系统。

图2-9　北京科技大学体育馆
太阳能导光管系统（室外部分）

图2-10　北京科技大学体育馆
太阳能导光管系统（室内部分）

天然光在任意时刻不能满足建筑照明的需要时，人工照明就可以弥补。建筑内不仅在自然光较弱的夜间需要利用人工照明。根据人工光的用途可以把其分为工作照明（功能性照明）和装饰照明（艺术性照明）。在进行人工照明设计时，需要综合考虑光源、灯具、照明功率密度、照明质量及相应的供电线路和设备。由于光源的革新及装饰材料的发展，人工照明已不只是满足室内一般照明和工作照明的需要，而且进一步向环境照明和艺术照明发展。它在商业、居住以及大型公共建筑的室内环境中，已成为不可或缺的室内环境设计要素。

2.4.2 光环境的设计

建筑光环境设计中要综合考虑自然光与人工光的搭配运用。在设计人工照明时又要考虑光源与灯具等的配合方式，同时也要照顾到建筑室内人员的情绪波动等。在进行光环境设计时，应充分考虑到光环境给人带来的心理上的效果。明亮的环境能够使人心境开阔。一个均匀的高照度的白光会给人以透明的感觉。当一个高照度区域位于大空间之中，照明亮度不均匀变化，包括极端的闪烁、移动或闪光照明，以及用刺激色所形成的周边环境，这些都会给人以兴奋感，并使人乐于交谈。人处于黑暗的环境时，会产生不安全感和恐怖感。

2.4.3 光环境的节能措施

（1）合理布置房间 通常把经常使用的房间布置在建筑的南向或东向，而把不经常使用的房间如会议室、卫生间、楼梯间布置在建筑的北向，提高天然光利用效率，减少人工照明的时间。

（2）合理选择光源 应根据场所特点及使用条件，用高效光源。此外，还应重视发展和应用高效灯具及与光源配套的电气附件，特别是节能的镇流器等。在办公室内用显色性好的光源，达到与显色性差的光源同样令人满意的照明效果，照度可降低25%，节能效果显著。

（3）正确选择照度标准值 照明系统设计中首先要考虑一个表面光的数量多少。这个数量是通过光通量密度，即照度来确定的，用勒克斯（lx）来度量。某一特定作业所需要的照度取决于该作业的视觉难度，人的视力水平以及所期望达到的结果。光照度水平影响工作的速度和精确度。如 GB 50034—2004《建筑照明设计标准》规定普通办公室及会议室照度标准值为300lx（工作面0.75m高），高档办公室照度标准值为300lx。

（4）照明控制与节能 为了方便使用和节能，应重视照明控制开关的设计。以下是对控制开关的设置要求：

1）有利于利用天然光。
2）有利于无人时自动关灯。
3）便于管理，集中或自动定时开关灯。
4）大房间应便于部分人或区段工作时分组开关灯。

习　题

1. 人体的舒适性主要受哪些因素影响？
2. 写出人体热舒适方程并简要说明每一项的物理意义。
3. 什么是 *PMV-PPD* 指标？
4. 室内空气污染物主要有哪些？
5. 减少室内空气污染物主要有哪几种方法？
6. 写出描述光环境的基本术语。

7. 在现代建筑中天然采光和人工照明如何合理配置？特别是眩光和发射光如何控制？
8. 如何解决现代都市中的光污染问题？
9. 计算长宽为 15m×10m，高为 3m 的教室的室形系数，工作面距离地面 0.75m。
10. 对比不同灯具的能耗和显色性，并指出每种灯具的适用场合。
11. 提出三种适合大型商场的天然采光和人工照明的组合方案，找出最佳方案。
12. 说明建筑构造是如何传递声音的。
13. 空调建筑的噪声源主要有哪些？
14. 说明不同吸声材料的性能及作用。
15. 某建筑内装有 5 台风机，1 台风机开启时室内平均噪声为 50dB，当 2 台或 5 台同时开启时室内平均噪声各为多少？
16. 根据自己的生活经验，举例说明噪声的干扰，现实生活中如何减少噪声的干扰。

Chapter 2
Indoor Environment

Abstract: This chapter introduces physiological basis of thermal sensation, basic concepts of indoor thermal comfort and its prediction. This chapter briefly describes typical indoor air pollutants and basic strategies to improve indoor air quality. This chapter also describes the basic concepts of building light environment, daylighting and artificial lighting and types of lamps. The problems of light pollution are mentioned. The energy efficiency of light environment is emphasized. This chapter gives the basic concepts of building acoustics, the sources of noise and methods of noise control.

Key points: physiological basis of thermal sensation, energy balance of the human body, PMV-PPD index, sick building syndrome, typical indoor air pollutants, basic strategies to improve indoor air quality, luminous environment, apparent color, baffle, brightness, chroma, chromaticity, lightness, color rendering index, color temperature, daylighting, direct glare, disability glare, luminous flux, illuminance, luminous intensity, luminance, uniformity of illuminance, visual performance, work plan, incandescent lamp, fluorescent lamp, tungsten-halogen lamp, high-pressure mercury lamp, high-pressure sodium lamp, light-emitting diode (LED), acoustics, ambient noise, decibel, noise control, sound absorption material, sound absorption coefficient, sound pressure level, sound power level, vibration isolation.

2.1 Indoor Thermal Environment and Thermal Comfort

A principal purpose of HVAC is to provide conditions for human thermal comfort. An internationally-accepted definition of thermal comfort is the condition of mind which expresses satisfaction with the thermal environment (ISO7330, ASHRAE STANDARD55). As such, it will be influenced by personal differences in mood, culture and other individual, organizational and social factors. Based on the above definitions, comfort is not a state of condition, but rather a state of mind. The definition of thermal comfort leaves open as to what is meant by condition of mind or satisfaction, but it correctly emphasizes that the judgment of comfort is a cognitive process involving many inputs influenced by physical, physiological, psychological, and other factors. This chapter summarizes the fundamentals of human thermoregulation and comfort.

2.1.1 Physiological Basis of Thermal Sensation and Thermoregulation

The human thermoregulatory system is capable of maintaining a fairly constant deep body temperature under a range of adverse environmental conditions. It is agreed that human temperature regulation is mediated primarily through the activity of the central nervous system. The three essential elements of the system include: the receptors of sensors, which sense the temperature; the integrative structure, which has the ability to compare the sensed temperature to the "normal" temperature and then to activate appropriate responses; and the effectors, which, when activated, would be capable of altering the temperature.

The first element of the system (the receptors) is located within the skin. Besides the cutaneous thermoreceptors, the hypothalamus, which is situated at the base of the brain, has been shown to be capable of responding directly to local changes in temperature. It has also been suggested that receptors may exist in other places within the body's core; however, support for this theory is not universal.

The cutaneous thermoreceptors appear to be of two distinct types, cold receptors and warm receptors. Exploration of the skin, conducted in research experiments, has delineated very small areas that respond only to a sensation of cold and other areas which respond only to warmth. The spaces between seem to be sensitive to neither. About thirteen to fifteen cold spots per square centimeter were found on the forearm, as compared with only one or two warm spots per square centimeter. It was found that both warm and cold spots show rapid adaptation and are particularly sensitive to rate of change of temperature. This implies that thermal sensation differ depending on whether the temperature change is effected gradually or rapidly.

The second element of the system (the integrative structures) is capable of processing inputs from the receptors and then designating appropriate responses. The hypothalamus appears to be the major central nervous system integrative site, although the cortex and the spinal cord have subsidiary functions. The major integrative site, the hypothalamus, is a small organ situated at the base of the brain. The hypothalamus appears to have two regions concerned with heat control, each having separated functions to some degree. The posterior section is the main center for protection against cold. Its activity induces vasoconstriction and shivering to promote and control heat conservation. The anterior portion promotes and controls heat dissipation. This portion of hypothalamus induces vasodilation and sweating in man and panting in animals. It appears that the centers operate in a manner such that the activity of one inhibits the activity of the other, thereby maintaining a balance. When environmental conditions are such that these mechanisms of control can no longer bring about the necessary adjustments, the situation becomes very serious. Below $-27℃$, shivering reactions may fail, respiration may be depressed, and cardiac output may become abnormal, presenting a serious threat. $42℃$ is the upper limit of temperature for the brain to survival, thus this temperature cannot be tolerated by human for long periods of time.

The effectors are mechanisms of the body that respond to signals from central integrative structures. When activated, the effectors have the capacity of helping the system return to a balanced state. The effector mechanisms include first of all changes in tissue insulation. If a change in tissue insulation is insufficient to maintain thermal neutrality, other mechanisms as shivering or sweating are necessitated.

The human body's responses to heat stress mainly involve cutaneous vascular dilation and sweat gland activity.

Cutaneous vascular dilation results in an increased blood flow through the skin within a few minutes of sensory stimulation. Ordinarily this raises the skin temperature, making it closer to air temperature, and thus reduces the body's heat gain from the environment. The circulation system plays a critical role in maintaining heat balance in the body in hot environments by being a vehicle for the conductance of heat from the tissues producing it to the skin and the respiratory system for dissipation.

Sweat evaporation is the principal avenue for dissipation of excess body heat. This defense mechanism is a powerful way to cool the skin and increase heat loss from the core. There are two types of sweat glands: the apocrine glands and the eccrine glands. The secretion of sweat may be caused by muscular exercise, emotional or mental stress, and thermal stimuli. Sweat, secreted in response to heat stimuli, is produced chiefly by the eccrine glands which are distributed over the entire skin. The rate of sweating increases as the heat stress becomes more severe and as the metabolic rate in work increases. Acclimatization, fatigue, salt intake, and individual variation also affect rate of sweating.

2.1.2 Thermal Interaction of the Human Body with Its Environment

The conscious mind appears to reach conclusions about thermal comfort and discomfort from direct temperature and moisture sensations from the skin, deep body temperatures, and efforts necessary to regulate body temperatures. In general, comfort occurs when body temperatures are held within narrow ranges, skin moisture is low, and the physiological effort of regulation is minimized.

Metabolic activities of the body result almost completely in heat that must be continuously dissipated and regulated to maintain normal body temperatures. Insufficient heat loss leads to overheating (hyperthermia), and excessive heat loss results in body cooling (hypothermia). So heat exchange between people and the environment is one of the most important factors which affect thermal comfort.

1. Energy Balance of the Human Body

Fig. 2-1 shows the thermal interaction between a human body and its environment. The total metabolic rate M within the body is the metabolic rate required for the person's activity M_{act} plus the metabolic level required for shivering M_{shiv} (should shivering occur). A portion of the body's energy production may be expended as external work W; the net heat production $M - W$ is transferred to the environment through the skin surface (q_{sk}) and respiratory tract (q_{res}) with any surplus or deficit stored (S), causing the body's temperature to rise or fall.

$$M - W = q_{sk} + q_{res} + S = (C + R + E_{sk}) + (C_{res} + E_{res}) + (S_{sk} + S_{cr}) \qquad (2-1)$$

Where M—rate of metabolic heat production (W/m^2);

W—rate of mechanical work accomplished (W/m^2);

q_{sk}—total rate of heat loss from skin (W/m^2);

q_{res}—total rate of heat loss through respiration (W/m^2);

$C + R$—sensible heat loss from skin (W/m^2);

E_{sk}—total rate of evaporative heat loss from skin (W/m^2);

C_{res}—rate of convective heat loss from respiration (W/m^2);

E_{res}—rate of evaporative heat loss from respiration (W/m^2);

S_{sk}—rate of heat storage in skin compartment (W/m^2);

S_{cr}—rate of heat storage in core compartment (W/m^2).

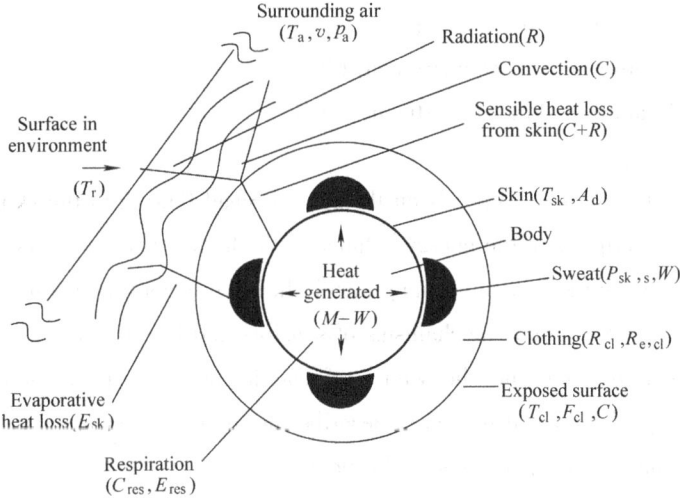

Fig. 2-1 The thermal interaction between a human body and its environment

Heat dissipates from the body to the immediate surroundings by several modes of heat exchange: sensible heat flow $C + R$ from the skin; latent heat flow from sweat evaporation E_{rsw} and from evaporation of moisture diffused through the skin E_{dif}; sensible heat flow during respiration C_{res}; and latent heat flow from evaporation of moisture during respiration E_{res}. Sensible heat flow from the skin may be a complex mixture of conduction, convection, and radiation for a clothed person; however, it is equal to the sum of the convection C and radiation R heat transfer at the outer clothing surface (or exposed skin).

Sensible and latent heat losses from the skin are typically expressed in terms of environmental factors, skin temperature t_{sk}, and skin wettedness w. Factors also account for the thermal insulation and moisture permeability of clothing. The independent environmental variables can be summarized as air temperature t_a, mean radiant temperature $\bar{t}_r$, relative air velocity V, and ambient water vapor pressure p_a. The independent personal variables that influence thermal comfort are activity and clothing.

The rate of heat storage in the body equals the rate of increase in internal energy. The body can be considered as two thermal compartments: the skin and the core. The storage rate can be written separately for each compartment in terms of thermal capacity and time rate of change of temperature in each compartment.

$$S_{cr} = \frac{(1 - \alpha_{sk})mc_{p,b}}{A_D} \cdot \frac{dt_{cr}}{d\theta} \tag{2-2}$$

$$S_{sk} = \frac{\alpha_{sk}mc_{p,b}}{A_D} \cdot \frac{dt_{sk}}{d\theta} \tag{2-3}$$

Where α_{sk}—fraction of body mass concentrated in skin compartment;

m—body mass (kg);

$c_{p,b}$—specific heat capacity of body, $c_{p,b}$ = 3490J/ (kg · K);

A_D—DuBois surface area (m^2);

t_{cr}—temperature of core compartment (℃);

t_{sk}—temperature of skin compartment (℃);

θ—time (s).

The fractional skin mass α_{sk} depends on the rate of blood flowing to the skin surface.

Mathematical description of the energy balance of the human body combines rational and empirical approaches to describing thermal exchanges with the environment. Fundamental heat transfer theory is used to describe the various mechanisms of sensible and latent heat exchange, and empirical expressions are used to determine the values of coefficients describing these rates of heat exchange. Empirical equations are also used to describe the thermophysiological control mechanisms as a function of skin and core temperatures in the body.

2. Sensible Heat Loss from Skin

Sensible heat exchange from the skin must pass through clothing to the surrounding environment. These paths are treated in series and can be described in terms of heat transfer from the skin surface, through the clothing insulation, to the outer clothing surface, and from the outer clothing surface to the environment.

Both convective C and radiative R heat losses from the outer surface of a clothed body can be expressed in terms of a heat transfer coefficient and the difference between the mean temperature t_{cl} of the outer surface of the clothed body and the appropriate environmental temperature.

$$C = F_{cl}h_c(t_{cl} - t_a) \tag{2-4}$$

$$R = F_{cl}h_r(t_{cl} - \bar{t}_r) \tag{2-5}$$

Where h_c—convective heat transfer coefficient [W/ (m^2 · K)];

h_r—linear radiative heat transfer coefficient [W/ (m^2 · K)];

F_{cl}—clothing area factor, $F_{cl} = A_{cl}/A_D$, A_D is nude body surface area, and A_{cl} is actual surface area of the clothed body.

The coefficients h_c and h_r are both evaluated at the clothing surface. Equations (2-4) and (2-5) are commonly combined to describe the total sensible heat exchange by these two mechanisms in terms of an operative temperature t_o and a combined heat transfer coefficient h.

$$C + R = F_{cl} h (t_{cl} - t_o) \quad (2\text{-}6)$$

$$t_o = \frac{h_r \bar{t}_r + h_c t_a}{h_r + h_c} \quad (2\text{-}7)$$

$$h = h_r + h_c \quad (2\text{-}8)$$

Based on Equation (2-7), operative temperature t_o can be defined as the average of the mean radiant and ambient air temperatures, weighted by their respective heat transfer coefficients.

The actual transport of sensible heat through clothing involves conduction, convection, and radiation. It is usually most convenient to combine these into a single thermal resistance value R_{cl}, defined by

$$C + R = (t_{sk} - t_{cl})/R_{cl} \quad (2\text{-}9)$$

Where R_{cl}—the thermal resistance of clothing ($m^2 \cdot K/W$).

Because it is often inconvenient to include the clothing surface temperature in calculations, Equations (2-6) and (2-9) can be combined to eliminate t_{cl}.

$$C + R = \frac{t_{sk} - t_o}{R_{cl} + 1/(F_{cl} h)} \quad (2\text{-}10)$$

Where t_o is defined in Equation (2-7).

3. Evaporative Heat Loss from Skin

Evaporative heat loss E_{sk} from skin depends on the amount of moisture on the skin and the difference between the water vapor pressure at the skin and in the ambient environment.

$$E_{sk} = \frac{w(p_{sk,s} - p_a)}{R_{e,cl} + 1/(F_{cl} h_e)} \quad (2\text{-}11)$$

Where w—skin wettedness dimensionless;

$p_{sk,s}$—water vapor pressure at skin, normally assumed to be that of saturated water vapor (kPa);

p_a—water vapor pressure in ambient air (kPa);

$R_{e,cl}$—evaporative heat transfer resistance of clothing layer (analogous to R_{cl}) ($m^2 \cdot K/W$);

h_e—evaporative heat transfer coefficient (analogous to h_c) [$W/(m^2 \cdot K)$].

Skin moisture is the ratio of the actual evaporative heat loss to the maximum possible evaporative heat loss E_{max} with the same conditions and a completely wet skin ($w = 1$).

Evaporative heat loss from the skin is a combination of the evaporation of sweat secreted because of thermoregulatory control mechanisms E_{rsw} and the natural diffusion of water through the skin E_{dif}.

$$E_{sk} = E_{rsw} + E_{dif} \quad (2\text{-}12)$$

Evaporative heat loss by regulatory sweating is directly proportional to the rate of regulatory sweat generation.

$$E_{rsw} = \dot{m}_{rsw} h_{fg} \tag{2-13}$$

Where h_{fg}—heat of vaporization of water, $h_{fg} = 2.43 \times 10^6 \text{J/kg}$ (at 30℃);

$\dot{m}_{rsw}$—rate at which regulatory sweat is generated [kg/(s·m²)].

The portion w_{rsw} of a body that must be wetted to evaporate the regulatory sweat is

$$w_{rsw} = E_{rsw}/E_{max} \tag{2-14}$$

Skin wettedness is important in determining evaporative heat loss. Maximum evaporative potential E_{max} occurs when $w = 1$. Skin wettedness is strongly correlated with warm discomfort and is also a good measure of thermal stress. Theoretically, skin wettedness can approach 1.0 while the body still maintains thermoregulatory control. In most situations, it is difficult to exceed 0.8. 0.5 is recommended as a practical upper limit for sustained activity for a healthy, acclimatized person.

4. Respiratory Losses

During respiration, the body loses both sensible and latent heat by convection and evaporation of heat and water vapor from the respiratory tract to the inhaled air. A significant amount of heat can be associated with respiration because air is inspired at ambient conditions and expired nearly saturated at a temperature only slightly cooler than t_{cr}.

The total heat and moisture losses due to respiration are

$$q_{res} = C_{res} + E_{res} = \frac{\dot{m}_{res}(h_{ex} - h_a)}{A_D} \tag{2-15}$$

$$\dot{m}_{w,res} = \frac{\dot{m}_{res}(w_{ex} - w_a)}{A_D} \tag{2-16}$$

Where $\dot{m}_{res}$—pulmonary ventilation rate (kg/s);

h_{ex}—enthalpy of exhaled air [J/kg (dry air)];

h_a—enthalpy of inspired (ambient) air [J/kg (dry air)];

$\dot{m}_{w,res}$—pulmonary water loss rate (kg/s);

w_{ex}—humidity ratio of exhaled air [kg (water vapor)/kg (dry air)];

w_a—humidity ratio of inspired (ambient) air [kg (water vapor)/kg (dry air)].

Under normal circumstances, pulmonary ventilation rate is primarily a function of metabolic rate

$$\dot{m}_{res} = K_{res} M A_D \tag{2-17}$$

Where M—metabolic rate (W/m²);

K_{res}—proportionality constant (1.43×10^{-6} kg/J).

For typical indoor environments, the exhaled temperature and humidity ratio are given in terms of ambient conditions.

$$t_{ex} = 32.6 + 0.066 t_a + 32 w_a \qquad (2\text{-}18)$$

$$w_{ex} = 0.0277 + 0.000065 t_a + 0.2 w_a \qquad (2\text{-}19)$$

Where ambient t_a and exhaled t_{ex} air temperatures are in centigrade (℃). For extreme conditions, such as outdoor winter environments, different relationships may be required.

The humidity ratio of ambient air can be expressed in terms of total or barometric pressure p_t and ambient water vapor pressure p_a.

$$w_a = \frac{0.622 p_a}{p_t - p_a} \qquad (2\text{-}20)$$

Respiratory heat loss is often expressed in terms of sensible C_{res} and latent E_{res} heat losses. Two approximations are commonly used to simplify Equations (2-18) and (2-19) for that purpose. First, because dry respiratory heat loss is relatively small compared to the other terms in the heat balance, an average value for t_{ex} is determined by evaluating Equation (2-18) at standard conditions of 20℃, 50% rh, sea level. Second, noting in Equation (2-19) that there is only a weak dependence on t_a, the second term in Equation (2-19) and the denominator in Equation (2-20) are evaluated at standard conditions. At standard conditions, C_{res} and E_{res} can be determined by

$$C_{res} = 0.0014 M (34 - t_a) \qquad (2\text{-}21)$$

$$E_{res} = 0.0173 M (5.87 - p_a) \qquad (2\text{-}22)$$

Where p_a is expressed in kPa and t_a is in ℃.

2.1.3 Thermal Comfort and Its Prediction

According to Professor Fanger, the interactions of six fundamental factors define the human thermal environment and its sensation of thermal comfort. These parameters are subcategorized into environmental factors and behavioral factors. Ambient temperature, mean radiant temperature, humidity, and air movement are the four basic environmental variables; the metabolic rate and clothing (insulation and moisture permeability characteristics) provide the behavioral variables that affect human response to thermal environment. Thus, any consideration of thermal stress should explore these six factors.

Tradeoffs have been established between these six factors with respect to their effects on human comfort. We can infer five effects on ambient temperature t_a.

1) Metabolic rate: an increase of 17.5W (above resting level) is equivalent to a 1℃ increase in t_a.

2) Clothing insulation (clo): a change of 1 clo is equivalent to a change in 5℃ at rest and 10℃ while exercising.

3) Mean radiant temperature (MRT): a change of 1℃ in MRT can be offset by a 1℃ in t_a.

4) Wind speed: a change in 0.1 m/sec in wind speed is equivalent to a change in 0.5℃ in t_a (up to 1.5℃).

5) Humidity: a 10% change in relative humidity can be offset by a 0.3℃ in t_a.

Fanger defined 3 parameters for a person to be in thermal comfort: ①the body is in heat balance; ②sweat rate is within comfort limits; ③mean skin temperature is within comfort limits. These conceptual requisites for determining thermal comfort can be expressed by measurable terms as: body-core temperature within a very narrow range of 36.5 ~ 37.5℃, a skin temperature of 30℃ at the extremity and 34 ~ 35℃ at body stem and head, and the body will be free of sweating. Any deviation from these assertions results in sensation of discomfort. In reference to equation (2-1), thermal comfort will be attained when the rate of heat dissipation from the body by means of radiation and convection will equal the rate of net metabolic heat production ($M - W$) and, consequently, heat storage S will be nil. In other words heat stress results from imbalance between the demands imposed on the worker by the task and the environment, and the worker's capacity to eliminate the heat load as modified by clothing. It follows that thermal comfort is directly related to sweat evaporation. This can be expressed by the ratio of demand to capacity (E_{sk}/E_{max}). As this ratio exceeds 0.2 (20%), the worker is moved from a "comfort" condition to "discomfort". As the ratio increases to 0.4 ~ 0.6, the worker is subject to performance decrements. Above 0.6, work will be usually discontinued or will be performed for only a limited period and above 0.8 there is substantial risk of heat illness.

Thermal sensation and thermal comfort are bipolar phenomena ranging from "too cold" to "too hot" with comfort or neutral sensation in the middle. This continuum of sensations has been described by several scales. The subjective ratings of discomfort and the corresponding physiological correlates are summarized in Table 2-1.

Table 2-1　Thermal sensation scale and comfort sensation scale

Vote value①	Vote value②	Thermal sensation	Comfort sensation	Zone of thermal effect
—	9	Very hot	Very uncomfortable	Incompensable heat
+3	8	Hot	Uncomfortable	Sweat evaporation compensable
+2	7	Warm	Slightly uncomfortable	
+1	6	Slightly warm		
0	5	Neutral	comfortable	—
-1	4	Slightly cool		Vasomotor compensable
-2	3	Cool	Slightly uncomfortable	Shivering compensable
-3	2	Cold		
—	1	Very cold	Uncomfortable	Incompensable cold

① Thermal scale according to ASHRAE 55.
② Thermal scale according to research findings of Rohles.

Thermal comfort and thermal sensation can be predicted in several ways. One way is to use Fig. 2-2 and Table 2-2 and adjust for clothing and activity levels that differ from those of the figure. More numerical and rigorous predictions are possible by using models such as the PMV-PPD model, two-node model and adaptive models. Only the PMV-PPD is described in this section.

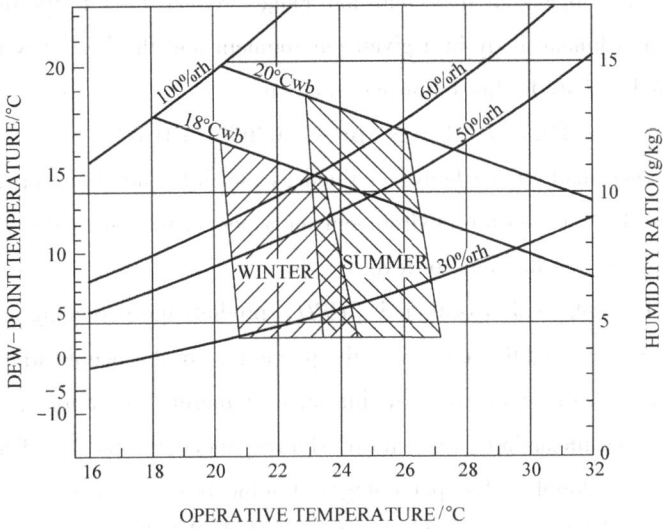

Fig. 2-2 ASHRAE summer and winter comfort zones

Table 2-2 Equations for predicting thermal sensation (Y) of men, women, and men and women combined

Exposure Period/h	Subjects	Regression Equations[1],[2] t (dry-bulb temperature) /℃ p (vapor pressure) /kPa
1.0	Men	$Y = 0.220t + 0.233p - 5.673$
	Women	$Y = 0.272t + 0.248p - 7.245$
	Both	$Y = 0.245t + 0.248p - 6.475$
2.0	Men	$Y = 0.221t + 0.270p - 6.024$
	Women	$Y = 0.283t + 0.210p - 7.694$
	Both	$Y = 0.252t + 2.40p - 6.859$
3.0	Men	$Y = 0.212t + 0.293p - 5.949$
	Women	$Y = 0.275t + 0.255p - 8.622$
	Both	$Y = 0.243t + 0.278p - 6.802$

[1] Y values refer to the ASHRAE thermal sensation scale.

[2] For young adult subjects with sedentary activity and wearing clothing with a thermal resistance of approximately 0.5 clo, $\bar{t}_r \approx \bar{t}_a$ and air velocities < 0.2 m/s.

The Predicted Mean Vote (PMV) index suggested by Fanger predicts the mean response of a large group of people according to the ASHRAE thermal sensation scale. Subjects exposed to the climate chambers are asked to give their opinions according to the ASHRAE seven-point scale of thermal sensation. A mean vote (*MV*) is obtained for a given condition by finding the mean value of the feeling given by all the subjects for that condition. Fanger related *PMV* to the imbalance between the actual heat flow from a human body in a given environment and the heat flow required for optimum comfort at a specified activity by the following equation.

$$PMV = [0.303\exp(-0.036M) + 0.028]L \tag{2-23}$$

Where *L*—the thermal load on the body, defined as the difference between internal heat production and heat loss to the environment for a person hypothetically kept at comfort values of t_{sk} and E_{rsw} at the activity level.

The Predicted Percentage of Dissatisfied (*PPD*) predicts the percentage of the people who felt more than slightly warm or slightly cold (i.e. the percentage of the people who inclined to complain about the environment). Using the seven-point scale of thermal sensation (-3 ~ +3), Fanger postulated: are declared uncomfortable all those who responded ±2 and ±3. Those who responded ±1 and 0 are declared comfortable. The percentages of subjects who responded ±2 and ±3 are determined for each class of *PMV*; that variable has been called *PPD*. The relationship between *PPD* and *PMV* is given by

$$PPD = 100 - 95\exp[-(0.03353PMV^4 + 0.2179PMV^2)] \tag{2-24}$$

The merit of this relation is that, it reveals a perfect symmetry with respect to thermal neutrality (*PMV* = 0). Fig. 2-3 shows that even when the *PMV* index is 0, there are some individual cases of dissatisfaction with the level of temperature, although all are dressed in a similar way and that the level of activity is the same. This is due to some differences of approach in the evaluation of thermal comfort from one person to another. It is shown that at *PMV* = 0, a minimum rate of dissatisfied of 5% exists.

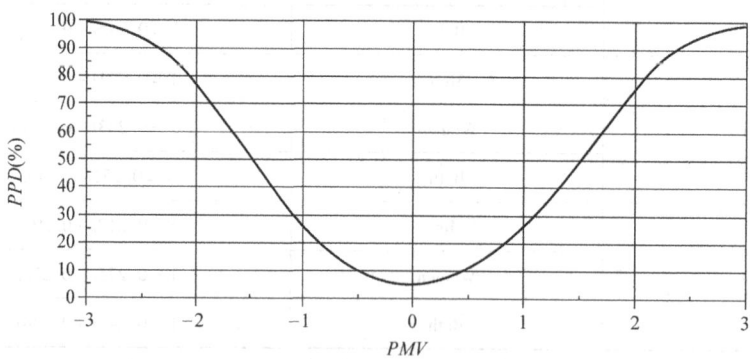

Fig. 2-3 Relationship *PMV* versus *PPD*

Fanger's *PMV-PPD* model on thermal comfort has been a path breaking contribution to the theory of thermal comfort and to the evaluation of indoor thermal environments in buildings. It is widely used and accepted for design and field assessment of thermal comfort. However, it should be noted that the *PMV-PPD* model is useful only for predicting steady-state comfort responses and can not be used to predict physiological responses or responses to transient situations.

2.2 Indoor Air Quality

People spend a large part of their time each day indoors: in homes, offices, schools, shops or other private or public buildings. The quality of the air they breathe in those buildings is an important determinant of their health and well-being. Unfortunately, indoor air has always contained natural and man-made impurities such as bacteria, viruses, fungi, radon gas, and combustion byproducts from burning. In recent years, additional contaminants such as asbestos, formaldehyde, and other organic chemicals have been identified in indoor air. Research indicates that the air within homes and other buildings can have higher levels of these contaminants than the outdoor air, even in large cities.

This chapter describes the sources of common air pollutants inbuildings, the potential health effects from exposure to these pollutants, and methods to improve indoor air quality.

2.2.1 Sick Buildings Syndrome and Building Related Illness

There are two general cases classified by the US Environmental Protection Agency (EPA) for acute health complaints attributed to the occupancy of modern non-industrial buildings: sick building syndrome and building related illness.

The term sick building syndrome (SBS) refers to situations in which building occupants experience acute health and comfort effects that appear early in the morning, peak in the afternoon and disappear shortly after leaving the work premises. Due to its anonymous nature, this environmental condition is often identified by a plethora of terminology (e.g., environmental illness, twentieth century disease). However, SBS is the most widely used term preferred by the World Health Organization.

Specifically, SBS is characterized by non-specific symptoms that do not fit the pattern of any particular illness and cannot be linked to an identifiable source. While the nature of SBS makes diagnosis of symptoms very difficult, common maladies include headache, dizziness, nausea, a runny nose, burning eyes, a scratchy throat, and a dry, persistent cough. Some complains are even more general such as fatigue, irritability, nervousness, or lack of concentration.

Building Related Illness (BRI), though easier to diagnose, is a more serious manifestation of the same architectural phenomenon. They are classified as non-communicable illnesses that may be diagnosable and can be linked to specific pollutants or contaminants inside buildings. The cause of BRI is often be traced back to viruses, bacteria, fungi or other microorganisms that tend to flourish in the moist environments of humidifying and air conditioning systems. Its victims suffer from clinically definable illnesses such as Legionnaire's Disease, humidifier fever, hypersensitivity pneumonitis, or asthma. BRI is also characterized by flu-like symptoms, including watery-eyes, sneezing and coughing, shortness of breath, fever, lethargy, dizziness and digestive problems.

2.2.2 Indoor Air Pollutants

1. Particulate Matter

Particles dispersed in air are also known as aerosols. Airborne particulate contamination ranges from dense clouds of desert dust storms to completely invisible and dilute cleanroom particles. It may be man-made or completely natural.

The size of a particle determines where in the human respiratory system particles are deposited, and various samplers collect particles that penetrate more or less deeply into the lungs. Most of the inhalable mass is captured in the nasal passages. The thoracic particle mass is the fraction that can penetrate to the lung airways and is represented by a sample with a median cut point of $10\mu m$ (PM10). The respirable particle mass is the fraction that can penetrate to the gas-exchange region of the lungs, which EPA defines as particles collected by a sampler having a median cut-point of $2.5\mu m$ (PM2.5), while American Conference of Governmental Industrial Hygienists (ACGIH) defines respirable particles as having a median cut point of $4\mu m$.

An important source of particulates, environmental tobacco smoke (ETS) consists of exhaled mainstream smoke from the smoker and sidestream smoke emitted from the smoldering tobacco. Approximately 70% to 90% of ETS results from sidestream smoke, which has a chemical composition somewhat different from mainstream smoke. More than 4,700 compounds have been identified in laboratory-based studies, including known human toxic and carcinogenic compounds such as carbon monoxide, ammonia, formaldehyde, nicotine, tobacco-specific nitrosamines, benzene, cadmium, nickel, and aromatic amines. Many of these constituents are more concentrated in sidestream smoke than in mainstream smoke. In studies conducted in residences and office buildings with tobacco smoking permitted, ETS was a substantial source of many gaseous and particulate polycyclic aromatic compounds.

The health effects of exposure to combustion nuclei depend on many factors, including concentration, toxicity, and individual susceptibility or sensitivity to the particular substance. Combustion-generated polycyclic aromatic compounds include many polycyclic aromatic hydrocarbons that have been shown to be carcinogenic in animals. ETS has been shown to be causally associated with lung cancer in adults and respiratory infections, asthma exacerbations, middle ear effusion, and low birth mass in children. The US Environmental Protection Agency classifies ETS as a known human carcinogen. Health effects can also include heart disease, headache, and irritation.

2. Bioaerosol

Bioaerosol refers to any airborne biological particulate matter. Though often thought of as originating as microorganisms (fungi, bacteria, viruses, protozoa, algae), bioaerosols may also be derived from plants (pollen and plant fragments), and animals (hair, dander, and saliva from dogs and cats; dust mites). In addition to the intact organisms (e.g., bacteria), their parts (fungal spores and fragments), components (endotoxins, allergens), and products (dust mite antigen-containing fecal pellets and fungal mycotoxins) may be included in the definition. The antigen or toxin to which the body reacts may be quite small; trace amounts are all that are required for many allergic or toxic reactions. Public interest has focused on airborne microorganisms responsible for diseases and infections, primarily bacteria and viruses.

In the indoor environment, floors and floor coverings can be reservoirs for organisms that are subsequently resuspended into the air. Routine activities, including walking and vacuuming and carpet cleaning, may even promote resuspension. Some viruses may persist up to 8 weeks on nonporous surfaces.

People are an important source of bacteria and viruses in indoor air. Contagious diseases spread when pathogenic organisms infect a host that, in turn, infects another individual. Indoors, infected humans are the primary sources and disseminators of contagious disease. Virulent agents can be released from skin lesions or dispersed during coughing, sneezing, or talking. Other means for direct release from infected humans include sprays of saliva and respiratory secretions during dental and respiratory therapy procedures.

For a microorganism to cause illness in building occupants, it must be transported in sufficient dose to a susceptible occupant. Airborne infectious particles behave physically in the same way as any other aerosol-containing particles with similar size, density, and electrostatic charge. The major difference is that bioaerosols may cause disease by several mechanisms (infection, allergic reaction, toxicosis), depending on the organism, the dose, and the susceptibility of the exposed population. Although microorganisms are normally present in indoor environments, the presence of abundant moisture and nutrients in interior spaces results in the growth of fungi, bacteria, protozoa, algae, or even nematodes. Thus, humidifiers, water spray systems, and wet porous surfaces can be reservoirs and sites for growth. Excessive air moisture can also result in proliferation of these microorganisms indoors. Turbulence associated with the start-up of air-handling unit plenums may also elevate concentrations of bacteria and fungi in occupied spaces.

Exposure to airborne fungal spores, hyphal fragments, or metabolites can cause respiratory problems ranging from allergic diseases, including allergic rhinitis, asthma, and hypersensitivity pneumonitis, to infectious diseases, such as histoplasmosis, blastomycosis, and aspergillosis. In addition, acute toxicosis and cancer have been ascribed to respiratory exposure to mycotoxins.

3. Inorganic Gases

Several inorganic gases are of concern because of their effects on human health and comfort and on materials. These include carbon dioxide, carbon monoxide, oxides of nitrogen, sulfur dioxide, ozone, and ammonia. Most have both outdoor and indoor sources.

Carbon dioxide (CO_2) is produced by human respiration. It is not normally considered to be a toxic air contaminant, but it can be a simple asphyxiant in confined spaces such as submarines. CO_2 is found in the ambient environment at 330 to 370 ppm. Levels in the urban environment may be higher because of emissions from gasoline and, more often, diesel engines. Measurement of CO_2 in occupied spaces has been widely used to evaluate the amount of outdoor air supplied to indoor spaces.

Carbon monoxide (CO) is an odorless, colorless gas produced by the incomplete combustion of hydrocarbons. It is a common ambient air pollutant and is very toxic. Inhalation of CO causes a throbbing headache because hemoglobin has a greater affinity for CO than for oxygen (about 240 times greater), and because of a detrimental shift in the oxygen dissociation curve. Carbon monoxide inhibits oxygen transport in the blood by forming of carboxyhemoglobin and inhibiting cytochrome oxidase at the cellular level. Common indoor sources of CO include gas stoves, kerosene lanterns and heaters, main stream and side stream tobacco smoke, wood stoves, and unvented or improperly vented combustion sources. Building makeup air intakes located at street level or near parking garages can entrain CO from automobiles and carry it to the indoor environment.

Oxides of nitrogen (NO_x) is a corrosive gas with a pungent odor. NO_2 has low water solubility, and is therefore inhaled into the deep lung, where it causes a delayed inflammatory response. NO_2 is reported to be a potential carcinogen through free radical production. At high mass concentration, NO_2 causes lung damage directly by its oxidant properties, and may cause health effects indirectly by increasing host susceptibility to respiratory infections. NO_x indoors result mainly from cooking appliances, pilot lights, and unvented heaters. Sources generating CO often produce nitric oxide (NO) and nitrogen dioxide (NO_2), as well. Underground or attached parking garages can also contribute to indoor concentrations of NO_x. During cooking, 0.2 to 0.4 ppm peak levels may be reached. Ambient air pollution from vehicle exhausts in urban locations can contribute NO_x to the indoor environment in makeup air. Oxides of nitrogen also are present in mainstream and sidestream tobacco smoke; NO and NO_2 are of most concern.

Sulfur dioxide (SO_2) is a colorless gas with a pungent odor detected at about 0.5 ppm. SO_2 can result from emissions of kerosene space heaters; combustion of fossil fuels such as coal, heating oil, and gasoline; or burning any material containing sulfur. Thus, sulfur dioxide is a common ambient air pollutant in many urban areas. Because SO_2 is quite soluble in water, it readily reacts with moisture in the respiratory tract to irritate the upper respiratory mucosa.

Ozone (O_3) is a pulmonary irritant and alters human pulmonary function at mass concentration of approximately 0.12 ppm. Exposure to ozone at 60 to 80 ppb causes inflammation, bronchoconstriction, and increased airway responsiveness. O_3 forms at ground level when hydrocarbons and oxides of nitrogen react with ultraviolet radiation in sunlight to produce photochemical smog. Ozone can be emitted by electrical or coronal discharges from office equipment, including laser printers and photocopiers. It can also form when ozone-generating devices (often marketed as portable air cleaners and ionizers) are used in the indoor environment.

Ammonia (NH_3) is a colorless gas with a sharp and intensely irritating odor. It is lighter than air and readily soluble in water. Ammonia is itself a refrigerant and fertilizer and is also a high-volume industrial chemical used in the manufacture of a wide variety of products (e. g., nitrogen fertilizers, nitric acid, synthetic fibers, explosives, and many others). In nature, ammonia is an animal metabolism byproduct formed by decomposition of uric acid. As an indoor air contaminant, ammonia generally originates in synthetic cleaners and as a metabolic byproduct.

4. Volatile Organic Compounds

The entire range of organic indoor pollutants has been categorized by volatility as indicated in Table 2-3 (WHO). No sharp limits exist between the categories, which are defined by boiling point ranges. Volatile organic compounds (VOCs) have attracted considerable attention in nonindustrial environments. They have boiling points in the range of approximately 50 ~ 250℃ and vapor pressures greater than about 10^{-3} ~ 10^{-4} mm Hg (1mm Hg = 133.322Pa). Sources of VOCs include solvents, reagents, and degreasers in industrial environments; and furniture, furnishings, wall and floor finishes, cleaning and maintenance products, and office and hobby activities in nonindustrial environments.

Table 2-3 Classification of indoor organic contaminants by volatility

Description	Abbreviation	Boiling Point Range/℃
Very volatile organic compounds	VVOCs	<0 to 50 ~ 100
Volatile organic compounds	VOCs	50 ~ 100 to 240 ~ 260
Semivolatile organics (pesticides, polynuclear aromatic compounds, plasticizers)	SVOCs	240 ~ 260 to 380 ~ 400

Berglund et al. found that the sources of VOCs in nonindustrial indoor environments are confounded by the variable nature of emissions from potential sources. Emissions of VOCs from indoor sources can be classified by their presence and rate patterns. For example, emissions are continuous and regular from building materials and furnishings (e. g., carpet and composite-wood furniture), whereas emissions from other sources can be continuous but irregular (e. g., paints used in renovation work), intermittent and regular (e. g., VOCs in combustion products from gas stoves or cleaning products), or intermittent and irregular (e. g., VOCs from carpet shampoos).

Many "wet" emission sources (paints and adhesives) have very high emission rates immediately after application, but rates drop steeply with time until the product has cured or dried. New "dry" materials (carpets, wall coverings, and furnishings) also emit chemicals at higher rates until aged. Decay of these elevated VOC concentrations to normal constant-source levels can take weeks to months, depending on emission rates, surface areas of materials, and ventilation protocols. Renovation can cause similar increases of somewhat lower magnitude. The total VOC concentration in new office buildings at the time of initial occupancy can be 50 to 100 times that present in outdoor air. In new office buildings with adequate outdoor air ventilation, these ratios often fall to less than 5:1 after 4 or 5 months of aging.

The large number of VOCs, usually found indoors, and the impossibility of identifying all of them in samples, led to the concept of total VOCs (TVOCs). Some researchers have used TVOCs to represent the sum of all detected VOCs. TVOCs concentrations are often reported as everything detected in the air by analysis methods such as photoionization detectors (PID) or flame ionization detectors (FID). Therefore, all methods for TVOCs determination are intrinsically of low to moderate accuracy because of variations in detector response to different classes of VOCs. Despite the limitations, TVOCs can be useful, and is widely used for mixed contaminant atmospheres.

Potential adverse health effects of VOCs in nonindustrial indoor environments are not well understood, but may include irritant effects, including perception of unpleasant odors, mucous membrane irritation, and exacerbation of asthma; systemic effects, such as fatigue and difficulty concentrating; and toxic, chronic effects, such as carcinogenicity.

Chronic adverse health effects from VOCs exposure are of concern because some VOCs commonly found in indoor air are human (benzene) or animal (chloroform, trichloroethylene, carbon tetrachloride, p-dichlorobenzene) carcinogens. Theoretical risk assessment studies suggest that the risk from chronic VOCs exposures in residential indoor air is greater than that associated with exposure to VOCs in the outdoor air or in drinking water.

5. Radioactive contaminants

Radioactive contaminants can be particulate or gaseous and are similar to ordinary industrial contaminants. Many radioactive materials would be chemically toxic if present in high concentrations; however, in most cases, the radioactivity necessitates limiting their concentration in air. Most radioactive air contaminants affect the body when they are absorbed and retained. This is known as the internal radiation hazard.

Radioactive particulates may settle to the ground, where they contaminate plants and eventually enter the food chain and the human body. Deposited material on the ground increases external radiation exposure. However, except for fallout from nuclear weapons or a serious reactor accident, such exposure is insignificant.

Radioactive materials present distinctive problems. High concentrations of radioactivity can generate enough heat to damage filtration equipment or ignite the material spontaneously. The concentrations at which most radioactive materials are hazardous are much lower than those of ordinary materials; as a result, special electronic instruments that respond to radioactivity must be used to detect these hazardous levels.

A major source of airborne radioactive exposure to the population comes from radon. Radon (Rn) is a naturally occurring, chemically inert, colorless, tasteless radioactive gas. It is produced from the radioactive decay of radium, which is formed through several intermediate steps of decay of uranium and thorium.

Radon is widely found in the natural environment. Before it decays, radon can move limited distances through very small spaces, such as those between particles of soil and rock, and enter indoor environments. Additional but secondary sources of indoor radon include groundwater (radon is quite soluble in water) and radium-containing building materials.

Radon gas enters a house or building primarily through leakage paths in the foundation and is transported by pressure-driven flow. Entry occurs through cracks, joints, and other holes in concrete foundations; directly through porous concrete blocks; through the joints and openings in crawlspace ceilings; and through leakage points in HVAC ductwork embedded in slab floors or located in crawlspaces. Pressure-driven flow is the dominant radon entry mechanism in houses with elevated radon concentrations.

2.2.3 Basic Strategies to Improve Indoor Air Quality

1. Source Control

Usually the most effective way to improve indoor air quality is to eliminate individual sources of pollution or to reduce their emissions. Some sources, like those that contain asbestos, can be sealed or enclosed; others, like gas stoves, can be adjusted to decrease the amount of emissions. In many cases, source control is also a more cost-efficient approach to protecting indoor air quality than increasing ventilation because increasing ventilation can increase energy costs.

2. Ventilation Improvements

Another approach to lowering the concentrations of indoor air pollutants in buildings is to increase the amount of outdoor air coming indoors. Most home heating and cooling systems do not mechanically bring fresh air into the house. Opening windows and doors, operating window or attic fans, when the weather permits, or running a window air conditioner with the vent control open increases the outdoor ventilation rate. Local bathroom or kitchen fans that exhaust outdoors remove contaminants directly from the room where the fan is located and also increase the outdoor air ventilation rate.

It is particularly important to take as many of these steps as possible while people are involved in short-term activities that can generate high levels of pollutants, for example, painting, paint stripping, heating with kerosene heaters, cooking, or engaging in maintenance activities such as welding, soldering, or sanding.

3. Air Cleaners

There are many types and sizes of air cleaners on the market, ranging from relatively inexpensive table-top models to sophisticated and expensive whole-house systems. Some air cleaners are highly effective at particle removal, while others, including most table-top models, are much less so. Air cleaners are generally not designed to remove gaseous pollutants.

The effectiveness of an air cleaner depends on how well it collects pollutants from indoor air and how much air it draws through the cleaning or filtering element. A very efficient collector with a low air-circulation rate will not be effective, nor will a cleaner with a high air-circulation rate but a less efficient collector. The long-term performance of any air cleaner depends on maintaining it according to the manufacturer's directions.

Another important factor in determining the effectiveness of an air cleaner is the intensity of the pollutant source. Table-top air cleaners, in particular, may not remove satisfactory amounts of pollutants from strong nearby sources. People with sensitivity to particular sources may find that air cleaners are helpful only in conjunction with concerted efforts to remove the source.

Over the past few years, there has been some publicity suggesting that houseplants have been shown to reduce levels of some chemicals in laboratory experiments. There is currently no evidence, however, that a reasonable number of houseplants remove significant quantities of pollutants in homes and offices. Indoor houseplants should not be over-watered because overly damp soil may promote the growth of microorganisms which can affect allergic individuals.

2.3 Architectural Acoustical Environment

2.3.1 Noise

1. Sound and Noise

With the development of modern industry, environmental pollution increases as side product. As one of the pollution, noise pollution has become a major hazard to human health. Noise pollution, water pollution and air pollution are considered as the three major worldwide environmental problems. Modern urban people spend 90% of time in the built environment. Architectural physics environment contain sound, heat and light environment. They are both mutually distinguishes and mutually contact. For example, if the indoor acoustical environment of one building does not satisfy certain requirements, the indoor environment of this building is unsatisfying. With the urbanization increasing, the problems of building noise are common in modern buildings.

Subjectively, sound is something that human hears as a result of vibration in the air. As sound travels through air, air is locally compressed and expanded. The sound pressure created by vibration can be measured on a sound level meter. Fig. 2-4 shows a sound level meter.

Sound is caused by the object vibrating and spread by the form of waves in certain medium (such as solid, liquid, gas). Human usually hear the air sound. Under normal circumstances, humans have a hearing range from 20 Hz up to 20,000 Hz, known as the audible sound, less than 20Hz, known as the sub-sonic and higher than 20,000 Hz, known as ultrasound. Depending on the level of the frequency of sound waves, high-frequency acoustics sounds sharp and the low-frequency sound gives the feeling of boredom. The volume of sound is determined by the strength of the sound. Fig. 2-5 illustrates the frequencies and wavelength of some sounds with single frequency characteristics.

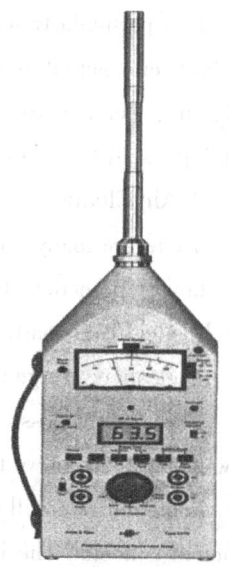

Fig. 2-4　Sound level meter

Noise is formed by a variety of different or irregular degrees of voice

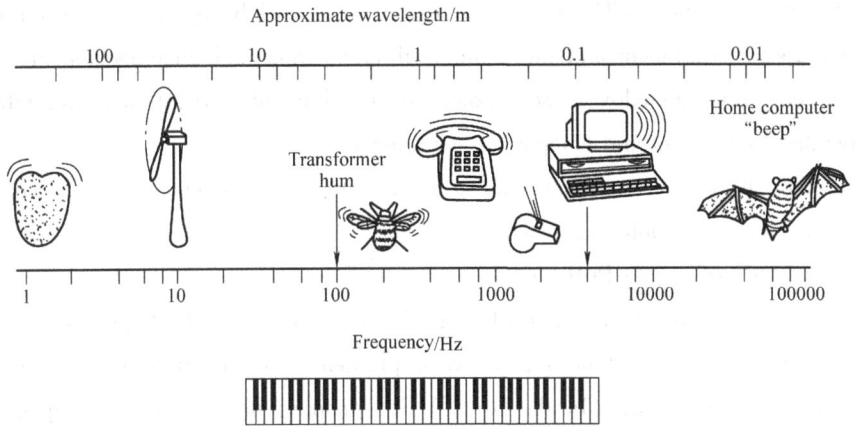

Fig. 2-5 Frequency and wavelength of everyday sound

frequencies.

Building services engineering design is primarily concerned with controlling the noise produced by items of plant such as boilers, supply air and exhaust air fans, refrigeration compressors, pumps etc.

2. Classification and Characteristics of the Room Noise

According to mechanical characteristics of sound source, noise can be classified as the following: noise generated by gas disturbance, noise generated by vibration of solid and liquid, impact-generated noise and electromagnetic noise generated by the electromagnetic effect.

According to the frequency of sound, noise can be divided into three categories: noise below 400Hz low-frequency, noise between 400~1000Hz and noise above 1000Hz high-frequency.

According to time-varying properties of sound, noise can be classified as steady-state noise, non-steady-state noise, rolling noise, intermittent noise and impulse noise.

3. The Main Source of Noise

(1) Traffic noise Traffic noise includes motor vehicles, ships, subways, trains, aircraft and other noise. With rapid increase of motor vehicle amount, traffic noise becomes the city's main noise source.

(2) Industrial noise Factory plant equipments make all types of industrial noise. Sound level of industrial noise is generally high with greater impact on workers and surrounding residents.

(3) Construction noise Construction noise comes mainly from the noise of construction machinery. Construction noise is characterized by high intensity, and mostly occurs in densely populated areas. Thus construction noise affects local residents life seriously.

(4) Air-conditioner noise Noise generated by air-conditioning systems is divided into aerodynamic noise and mechanical noise according to the generating form. Noise occurring positions can also be divided into two categories: equipments noise, air tubes and components noise. Air-conditioning systems include chillers, pumps, fans (including air-conditioning units, fan coil units and

fans), and cooling towers etc. The noise sources are generated by operation of compressors, motors, fan operation, equipment and mechanical vibration. Duct and duct components (mainly the supply-air outlet) generate eddy noise (noise generated by air swirl flow) and vibration noise (noise generated by air duct and components vibration).

(5) Community noise Community noise includes the noise made by people's social activities, household appliances and audio equipment.

4. The Hazards of Noise Pollution

The physical and psychological harm brought by noise is mainly the following:

(1) Damaging hearing Data shows that when people hear a continuous sound of motorcycles for 8 hours, hearing will be impaired. In the Rock Hall, people's hearing will be impaired after half hour's exposing to loud rock music. The possibility of deafness for people living in an environment of noise above 80 decibels is up to 50%.

(2) Impairing eyesight Noise would not only adversely affect the hearing organ but also could affect people's vision. There are delicate internal connection between the ears and eyes. When the noise acting on the auditory organ, the visual organs is also spread through the role of the nervous system, which can affect people's vision.

(3) Affecting cardiovascular system The urban noise and the resident's health survey carried out in China showed that if noise decibels increased by one, the incidence of hypertension would increase by 3%.

(4) Stimulating nervous system With long-term exposure in a noisy environment, people also get neurasthenia syndrome (such as headache, dizziness, tinnitus, memory loss, vision reduction etc.). Noise cause people impatient and irritable.

(5) Causing sleep problem With a sudden noise at 40dB, 10% of people would be waked up. Noise up to 60dB wake up 70% of the people.

2.3.2 Methods of Noise Control

1. The Basic Principle of Noise Control

(1) Control source of noise There are two ways to reduce the noise sources generally. First, we can control noise sources, such as improving equipment structure, machining precision parts and assembly quality, using reasonable operation methods, so as to reduce the incidence of noise power. Second, based on absorption, reflection, interference principles, we use sound absorption, sound insulation, shock absorption and vibration isolation techniques and make the muffler measures to control the sound source of the radiated power.

(2) Transmission control We can design rational layout plan guarding against noise source and cut off the transmission of noise. Make sure the noise source and the residential area, cultural and educational zones are separated. The slopes, hills or trees and other barriers can be used to build noise barriers.

(3) Personal protective　When the noise sources and transmission noise can not be controlled, personal protection methods can be used. Earplugs, anti-acoustic cotton, earmuffs and helmets etc. are used as personal protection. Shift operations could be used to shorten a person's exposure to the strong noise.

2. Control Methods

Noise control is most effective when it is considered at the design stage. Using alternatives in the design of a building and its construction methods can eliminate potentially noisy equipment and techniques.

(1) Sound-absorbing and noise-reducing　Sound-absorbing and noise-reducing are kind of methods to control noise intensity in the transmission way. The sound-absorbing function object is widespread, and the absorption effect not only varies with the sound-absorbing material, but also is related to sound-absorption structures. This technology is mainly used for interior space.

(2) Noise elimination　Muffler is one of the equipment which can make air pass through and reduce the noise effectively. Usually we can use it to reduce the noise of inlet and outlet of all kinds of aerodynamic equipments and noise along the pipe.

(3) Isolation　Noise of the machines is sealed in a small space to make it isolated with the surrounding environment, reducing its impact on environment. This approach is called sound insulation. Noise barriers and acoustic cladding are two main kinds of isolation design structure. Other sound insulation structures include sound booth, soundproof wall, sound insulation curtain and sound proof door.

3. Noise Pollution Control Methods for Air-conditioning System

There are several effective measures to reduce air-conditioning system noise in design and installation phase.

(1) Reduce the noise of air duct and its components

1) Duct design velocities should not be too high in order to reduce the noise generated by the air swirl. Generally, the fluid velocity is controlled to be less than 8m/s in main pipe, no higher than 3m/s in branch pipe and about 2m/s in outlet.

2) The piping is arranged artificially to alter airflow in the duct to attenuate noise rationally.

3) Air flow in each branch duct should be designed to achieve the natural balance.

4) Supply air volume and return air volume should be chosen to be equal to avoid the formation of significant indoor and outdoor pressure difference.

5) Duct diameter should be reduced or expanded gradually by using tapered pipe cross-section, without sudden change in diameter.

6) The distance between two elbows duct should not be too small. Otherwise, the noise will be generated because of eddy.

7) It cannot be rigid contacts between air duct and wall (floor). Vibration isolation treatment is needed shown as in Fig. 2-6 and Fig. 2-7.

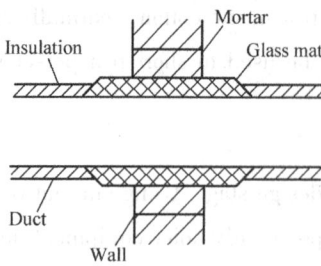 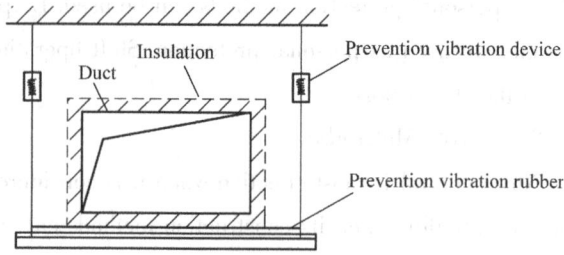

Fig. 2-6 Air duct design of vibration isolation through wall

Fig. 2-7 Designs of the air duct and floor vibration isolation

(2) Cooling tower noise reduction design

1) Cooling towers with reduced level of noise is preferred.

2) Cooling towers must have minimal impact on surrounding buildings, and should be located clear of main facades of buildings and main accesses.

3) Damping pads or shock absorbers should be located between the base of cooling tower and the concrete foundation.

4) Cooling towers can be equipped with mufflers.

5) Sound insulating wall could be built between cooling towers and surrounding buildings if necessary.

2.4 Architectural Luminous Environment

Vision is one of our most important humansenses. We use our sight to understand the environment, to move about and to carry out tasks. Light and the effects of light stimulate vision so the control of light from natural and artificial light sources is an important feature of the built environment and our comfort.

Light is energy in the form of electromagnetic radiation. Light is that particular electromagnetic radiation which can be detected by the human sense of sight. The range of electromagnetic radiation to which the eye is sensitive is just a very narrow band in the total spectrum of electromagnetic emissions, as is indicated in Fig. 2-8. The wavelengths of electromagnetic radiation that are visible to the eye range from approximately 380nm to 760nm.

Light is a basic element of nature. Vision is the detection of light. Light detection stimulates vision to eyes, proposed environmental perception. Light is necessary for human physiologically and psychologically. A better life needs better quality of light, as well as precise light control for different occasions. There is an increasingly high demand for decorative and artistic function of luminous environment.

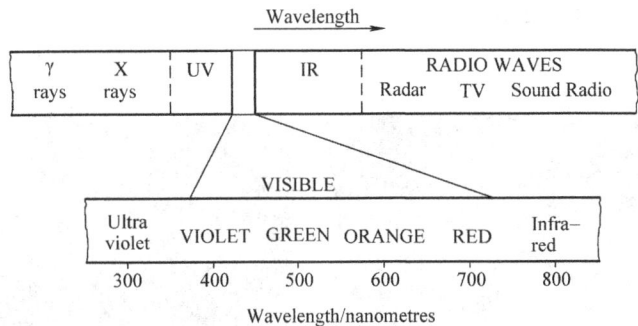

Fig. 2-8 Electromagnetic spectrum

2.4.1 Natural and Artificial Illumination

There are three main kinds of daylight sources in the built environment—diffuse sunlight (light coming from diffuse reflectance through cloudy or partially cloudy sky), direct sunlight (sunbeams coming from direct reflection through fine or partially cloudy sky), reflected light (light emitted by natural or artificial surface). Some crucial measures should be taken according to different light sources in order to obtain reasonable daylight in the buildings. An important design step for a building is to choose an appropriate form of lighting pattern corresponding to different building types (side lighting, top lighting, courtyard lighting). Side lighting forms are usually adopted in the office, sitting room and other small civilian and public rooms. Side lighting not only could enable indoor staff to see the external landscape, it can also make interior staff feel a sense of vertigo in certain positions. Partial separated blocks should be employed to reduce the possibility of glare production. Top lighting (especially at the low solar elevation angle) with low glaring rate, called roof skylight, could be used in warehouses, workshops and other buildings with less staff mobility. Atrium lighting technology should be adopted in shopping center, office building and other large-scale buildings because it not only lowers glare probability, but also lessens height restriction, resulting in perfect light depth penetration. However, not all architectures are qualified for atrium design because it results in large temperature difference between the ceiling and bottom floors under full sunlight, which in turn demands higher air-conditioner load. Thus atrium lighting is confined to certain building groups.

Though daylight has many advantages, its application is limited by time, location and exterior climate condition. Thus solar light pipes systems are designed as new types of nature lighting devices. Solar light pipes are a new kind of illuminating device, which could provide interior lighting during the day without conventional energy, reducing environmental pollution caused by conventional energy. Solar light pipe system is a green, healthy, energy saving and environmental protecting system. The solar light pipes systems in University of Science and Technology Beijing Gymnasium are indicated in Fig. 2-9 and Fig. 2-10.

Fig. 2-9　The solar light pipes systems in USTB Gymnasium (outside)

Fig. 2-10　The solar light pipes systems in USTB Gymnasium (inside)

　　Whenever daylight lighting is not able to meet specific needs of building illumination, artificial lighting should substantially remedy this disadvantage. For example, artificial light is needed for indoor buildings at night or for buildings with weaker daylight. Artificial light could be classified into two categories according to its employment: working lighting (functional lighting) and decoration lighting (artistic lighting). Many factors, such as light sources, luminaries, lighting power density, lighting quality and the corresponding power supply lines and equipments, should all be considered in artificial lighting designing. With development of light sources and decorative materials, artificial lighting is not only used for general indoor lighting, but also used for environment lighting and artistic lighting. It has become an indispensable element of indoor design when employed in commercial buildings, residential buildings, and large public buildings.

2.4.2　Design and Control of Luminous Environment

　　Daylight and artificial light should be integrated in the design process of architecture illumination. The combination mode of light sources and lamps should be taken into consideration. At the same time, attention should be paid to the mood of staff indoor. When designing of illumination, psychological effects brought by illumination should be fully taken into account. For example, bright environment makes one feel open. A uniform high-intensity white light makes one feel transparent. A high-illumination region in open space with uneven changes of lighting brightness (including extreme flashing, moving or flashing lights, and the surrounding environment formed by stimulus colors) gives one a sense of excitement and makes him or her in the mood to chat. One will feel unsafe and horrible when it is dark.

2.4.3 Energy Conservation Methods

(1) Sensible layout of the room To improve the daylight utilization efficiency and reduce artificial lighting time, rooms frequently used should face south or east. While rooms not frequently used, such as conference rooms, bathrooms, stairwells, are deployed in the north.

(2) Reasonable light source The energy-saving light source should be selected based on workplace characteristics and conditions. Development and application of high-efficiency lights and electrical accessories, especially energy-saving ballasts, should be emphasized. In office, employment of good color rendering light sources gives the same lighting effects while energy can be reduced by 25%. Energy-saving effect is remarkable.

(3) Appropriate illumination standard values The quantity of light on a certain surface is usually the primary consideration in the design of a lighting system. The quantity is specified by the density of luminous flux, or illuminance, and measured in lux. The illuminance needed for a particular task depends upon the visual difficulty of the task, the average standard of eyesight involved and the type of performance expected. The speed and accuracy of various types of work are affected by the level of illuminance supplied. For instance, the GB 50034—2004 "Architectural Lighting Design Standards" sets the standard value of illumination in general office and conference room as 300lux (work place 0.75m high), while that of high-grade office room as 300lux.

(4) Lighting control and energy efficiency To reduce energy consumption and easily utilizations, more attention should be paid to lighting control switch design. The following are requirements for switches layout:

1) Use of natural light as the first priority.
2) Turn off the lights automatically when there is no one in room.
3) Be centralized and manageable with automatic timer.
4) Group switches to light different sections for a large space to save energy.

Questions

1. What factors affect the human thermal comfort?
2. Write the human thermal comfort equations and explain the physical meaning of each item.
3. Explain what PMV index and PPD index are.
4. List typical indoor air pollutants.
5. What measures can be used to reduce indoor air pollutants?
6. Define the key terms used in lighting environment.
7. Sketch satisfactory arrangements for natural and artificial illumination in modern buildings and comment particularly on how glare and reflections are controlled.
8. How do you solve lighting pollutions in modern cities?

9. Calculate the room index for a classroom 15m × 10m in plan and 3m high, where the working plane is 0.75m above floor level.

10. Compare the energy efficiency and colour-rendering of different lamps and describe suitable applications for each lamp.

11. Propose three combinations of daylighting and artificial lighting and find the best overall lighting scheme for a large supermarket.

12. Please state how sound is transferred by the building structures.

13. List the sources of noise that could be found within an air-conditioned building.

14. Tell the performance and function of different kinds of absorption materials.

15. Five fans are installed in a building. The noise level of one fan is 50dB. What are the noise levels when two fans or five fans are operated at the same time?

16. How do you reduce the disturbances of noise according to your experience?

第 3 章 供　　热

本章要点：本章介绍了建筑热负荷的概念及计算方法，室内热水供热系统的分类及特征，室内热水供热系统的水力计算原理，集中供热系统的热源形式等内容。

知识点：热负荷；重力循环系统及机械循环系统的特点；垂直系统与水平系统的特点；上供下回、下供下回、上供上回及下供下回式系统的特点。

人们在日常生活和社会生产中都需要使用大量的热量。为了满足人们工作和生活的要求，应保持室内稳定的温度。因此，需要连续地向室内供热，补偿其热量损失，以保持其热平衡。将自然界的能源直接或间接地转化为热能，以满足人们需要的科学技术，称为热能工程。

3.1 热负荷

供热系统热负荷是指在某一室外温度下，为了达到要求的室内温度，供热系统在单位时间内向建筑物供给的热量。供热系统的设计热负荷是指，当室外空气温度为采暖设计计算温度时，为了保持室内所规定的温度所需要的供热量，称为供热热负荷。供热系统设计热负荷是系统散热设备计算、管道水力计算和系统主要设备选择计算的最基本依据。它直接影响着供热系统方案的选择，进而影响系统工程造价、运行管理以及使用效果。

3.1.1 供热系统设计热负荷计算

供热系统设计热负荷应根据房间得、失热量的平衡进行计算，即

$$房间设计热负荷 = 房间总失热量 - 房间总得热量$$

1. 房间的失热量
1) 围护结构传热耗热量 Q_1。
2) 加热由门、窗缝隙渗入室内的冷空气的耗热量 Q_2，简称冷风渗透耗热量。
3) 加热由门、孔洞及相邻房间侵入室内的冷空气的耗热量 Q_3，简称冷风侵入耗热量。
4) 水分蒸发耗热量 Q_4。
5) 加热由外部运入的冷物料耗热量 Q_5。
6) 通风耗热量 Q_6，即通风系统将空气从室内排到室外所带走的热量。
7) 其他耗热量 Q_7。

2. 房间的得热量

1）生产车间最小负荷班工艺设备散热量 Q_8。
2）非供热系统的热管道和其他热表面的散热量 Q_9。
3）热物料的散热量 Q_{10}。
4）太阳辐射进入室内的热量 Q_{11}。
5）其他得热量 Q_{12}。

对没有装置机械通风系统的建筑物，供热系统的设计热负荷可用式（3-1）表示。

$$Q' = Q'_1 + Q'_2 + Q'_3 - Q'_{11} \tag{3-1}$$

上标符号"'"均表示在设计工况下的各种参数。

围护结构的传热量是指当室内温度高于室外温度时，通过围护结构向外传递的热量。在工程设计中，计算供热是指当室内温度高于室外温度时，常把它分为围护结构传热的基本耗热量和附加耗热量两部分进行计算。基本耗热量是指在设计条件下，通过房间各部分围护结构（门、窗、墙、地板、屋顶等），从室内传到室外的稳定传热量的总和。附加耗热量是指包括风力附加、高度附加和朝向修正等的耗热量。朝向修正正是考虑围护结构的朝向不同，太阳辐射得热量不同而对基本耗热量进行的修正。因此，在工程设计中，供热系统的设计热负荷，一般可分为几部分进行计算。

$$Q' = Q'_{1,j} + Q'_{1,x} + Q'_2 + Q'_3 \tag{3-2}$$

式中 $Q'_{1,j}$——围护结构基本耗热量；
$Q'_{1,x}$——围护结构的附加耗热量。

围护结构基本耗热量 q'，可按式（3-3）计算。

$$q' = KF(t_n - t'_w)a \tag{3-3}$$

式中 K——围护结构的传热系数 $[W/(m^2 \cdot ℃)]$；
F——围护结构的面积（m^2）；
t_n——冬季室内计算温度（℃）；
t'_w——供暖室外计算温度（℃）；
a——围护结构的温差修正系数。

整个建筑物或房间的基本耗热量 $Q'_{1,j}$ 等于它的围护结构各部分基本耗热量的总和。

$$Q'_{1,j} = \sum KF(t_n - t'_w)a \tag{3-4}$$

在风力和热压造成的室内外压差作用下，室外的冷空气通过门、窗等缝隙渗入室内，被加热后逸出，把这部分冷空气从室外温度加热到室内温度所消耗的热量，称为**冷风渗透耗热量**。

按缝隙法计算冷风渗透耗热量公式为

$$\left.\begin{array}{l} Q'_2 = 0.278V\rho_w c_p(t_n - t'_w) \\ V = Lln \end{array}\right\} \tag{3-5}$$

式中 L——每米门、窗缝隙渗入室内的空气量，按当地冬季室外平均风速，采用表 3-1 所示的数据；

l——门、窗缝隙的计算长度（m）；

n——渗透空气量的朝向修正系数；

V——经门、窗缝隙渗入室内的总空气量（m³/h）；

ρ_w——供热室外计算温度下空气密度（kg/m³）；

c_p——冷空气的比定压热容，$c_p = 1$kJ/（kg·℃）；

0.278——单位换算系数，1kJ/h = 0.278W。

表3-1 每米门、窗缝隙渗入的空气量　　　　　　[单位：m³/（h·m）]

门窗类型	冬季室外平均风速/（m/s）					
	1	2	3	4	5	6
单层木窗	1.0	2.0	3.1	4.3	5.5	6.7
双层木窗	0.7	1.4	2.2	3.0	3.9	4.7
单层钢窗	0.6	1.5	2.6	3.9	5.2	6.7
双层钢窗	0.4	1.1	1.8	2.7	3.6	4.7
推拉铝窗	0.2	0.5	1.0	1.6	2.3	2.9
平开铝窗	0	0.1	0.3	0.4	0.6	0.8

在冬季受风压和热压作用下，冷空气由开启的外门渗入室内，把这部分冷空气加热到室内温度所消耗的热量称为**冷风侵入耗热量**。

冷风侵入耗热量，可按式（3-6）计算。

$$Q_4' = 0.278 V_w c_p \rho_w (t_n - t_w') \tag{3-6}$$

式中　V_w——流入的冷空气量（m³/h）。

3.1.2 高层建筑供热设计热负荷计算

高层建筑由于建筑物高度增加，热压作用不容忽视。因此，进行冷风渗透耗热量的计算时，应考虑风压和热压的共同作用。

高层建筑的冷风渗透耗热量可按式（3-7）计算。

$$Q' = 0.278 L l c_p \rho_w (t_n - t_w') m \tag{3-7}$$

$$L = a \Delta p^b \tag{3-8}$$

式中　L——不同类型门窗，每米缝隙渗入的空气量 [m³/（m·h）]；

Δp——室内外压力差；

a、b——修正系数，取决于门窗类型；

m——风压和热压共同作用下，考虑建筑体形、内部隔断和空气流通等因素后，不同朝向、不同高度的门窗冷风渗透压差综合修正系数。

3.2 热水供热系统

可分为室内热水供热系统与室外热水供热系统。

3.2.1 室内热水供热系统的分类

室内热水供热系统，可按下述方法分类：

1) 按系统循环动力的不同，可分为重力（自然）循环系统和机械循环系统。靠水的密度差进行循环的系统，称为重力循环系统；靠机械（水泵）力进行循环的系统，称为机械循环系统。

2) 按供、回水方式的不同，可分为单管系统和双管系统。热水经立管或水平供水管顺序地流过多组散热器，并顺序地在各散热器中冷却的系统，称为单管系统。热水经供水立管或水平供水管平行地分配给多组散热器，冷却后的回水自每个散热器直接沿回水立管或水平回水管流回热源的系统，称为双管系统。

3) 按系统管道敷设方式的不同，可分为垂直式和水平式系统。

4) 按热媒温度的不同，可分为低温水系统和高温水系统。

1. 重力（自然）循环热水供热系统

图 3-1 所示是重力循环热水供热系统的工作原理图。

假设图 3-1 所示的循环环路最低点的断面 A—A 处有一个假想阀门，若突然将阀门关闭，则断面 A—A 两侧受到不同水柱的压力。这两个不同的水柱压力的差就是驱使水在系统内进行循环流动的作用压力。

设 p_1 和 p_2 分别表示 A—A 断面右侧和左侧的水柱压力，则

$$p_1 = g(h_0\rho_h + h\rho_h + h_1\rho_g)$$
$$p_2 = g(h_0\rho_h + h\rho_g + h_1\rho_g)$$

断面 A—A 两侧之差值，即系统的循环作用压力为

$$\Delta p = gh(\rho_h - \rho_g) \quad (3\text{-}9)$$

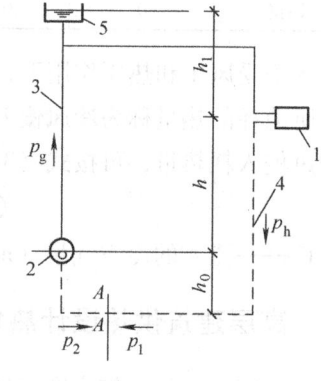

图 3-1 重力循环热水供热系统的工作原理
1—散热器 2—热水锅炉 3—供水管路
4—回水管路 5—膨胀水箱

式中 Δp——重力循环系统的作用压力（Pa）；

g——重力加速度（m/s²）；

h——冷却中心至加热中心的垂直距离（m）；

ρ_h——回水密度（kg/m³）；

ρ_g——供水密度（kg/m³）。

2. 机械循环热水供热系统

机械循环热水供热系统是应用最广泛的一种供热系统。机械循环热水供热系统主要有以下几种形式：

(1) 垂直式系统

1) 上供下回式双管和单管热水供热系统。图 3-2 所示为机械循环上供下回式热水供热系统。图左侧为双管式系统，图右侧为单管式系统。机械循环系统除膨胀水箱的连接位置与

重力循环系统不同外，还增加了循环水泵和排气装置。图左侧双管式系统，在管路与散热器连接方式上与重力循环系统没有差别。图右侧立管 3 是单管顺流式系统。单管顺流式系统特点是立管中全部的水量顺次流入各层散热器。顺流式系统形式简单、施工方便、造价低，是国内目前一般建筑广泛应用的一种形式。

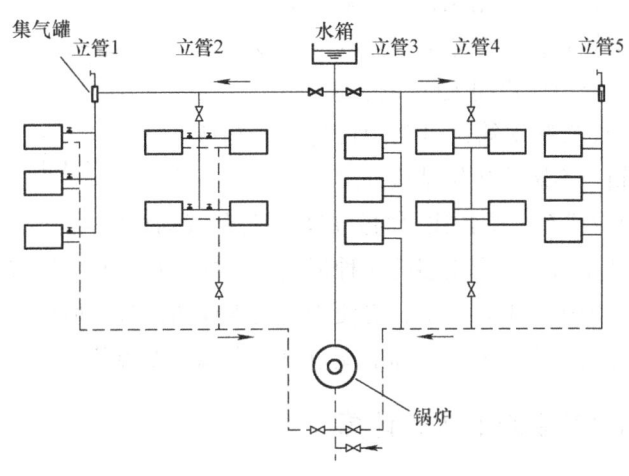

图 3-2　机械循环上供下回式热水供热系统

2）下供下回式双管热水供热系统。系统的供水和回水干管都敷设在底层散热器下面，称为下供下回式系统。与上供下回式系统相比，它有如下特点：在地下室布置供水干管，管路直接散热给地下室，无效热损失小；在施工中，每安装好一层散热器即可开始供热，给冬期施工带来很大方便；排除系统中的空气较困难。

3）下供上回式热水供热系统。系统的供水干管设在下部，而回水干管设在上部，顶部还设置有顺流式膨胀水箱。立管布置主要采用顺流式。

下供上回系统具有如下特点：水在系统内的流动方向是自下而上流动，与空气流动方向一致。可通过顺流式膨胀水箱排除空气，无须设置集气罐等排气装置；供水总立管较短，无效热损失小；对热损失大的底层房间，由于底层供水温度高，底层散热器的面积减小，便于布置。

4）混合式热水供热系统。混合式系统是由下供上回式和上供下回式两组串联组成的系统。如图 3-3 所示，Ⅰ区系统直接引用外网高温水，采用下供上回式系统。经散热器散热后，回水温度应满足Ⅱ区的供水温度要求，再引入Ⅱ区，Ⅱ区采用上供下回低温采暖系统，Ⅱ区回水水温降低至最低后，返回热源。该系统一般使用在民用建筑或生产厂房。

（2）水平式系统　水平式系统按供水管与散热器

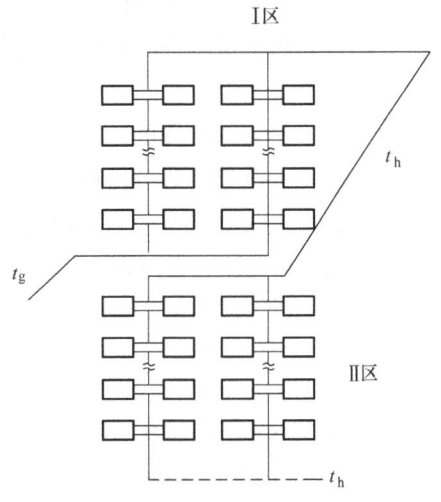

图 3-3　机械循环混合式热水供热系统

的连接方式分，同样可分为顺流式和跨越式两类。

水平式系统的排气方式要比垂直式上供下回系统复杂。它需要在散热器上设置冷风阀分散排气，如图3-4所示，或在同一层散热器上部串联一根空气管集中排气。

水平式系统与垂直式系统相比，具有如下优点：

1）系统结构形式简单，穿各层楼板的立管少，施工安装方便，且上下楼层住户间无噪声传递。

2）顶层不必专设膨胀水箱，可利用楼梯间、厕所等位置架设膨胀水箱，不影响建筑结构外形。

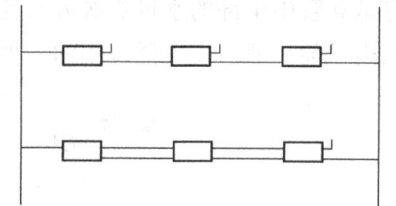

图3-4 单管水平串联式

3）水平单管跨越式系统使各住户的分户热量计量成为可能。

水平式系统也是在国内使用较多的一种形式。此外，对一些各层有不同使用功能和不同温度要求的建筑物，采用水平式系统，更便于分层管理和调节。但单管水平式系统串联散热器很多时，运行时易出现水平失调，即前端过热而末端过冷现象。

3.2.2 室内热水供热系统的水力计算

在供热系统中，管路是极其重要的组成部分。本章介绍了不可压缩流体管路流动的基本原理和水力计算过程。

根据流体力学理论，流体在管路中流动时，要克服流动阻力产生压力损失，压力损失有沿程压力损失和局部压力损失两种形式。

根据恒定流理论，流体伯努利方程为

$$\frac{p_1}{\rho_1 g} + \frac{v_1^2}{2g} + z_1 = \frac{p_2}{\rho_2 g} + \frac{v_2^2}{2g} + z_2 + h_f \tag{3-10}$$

式中 z_1、z_2——位置水头（m）；

h_f——压头损失（m）。

因此，热水供热系统中计算管段的压力损失，可用式（3-11）。

$$\Delta p = \Delta p_y + \Delta p_j \tag{3-11}$$

式中 Δp——计算管段的压力损失（Pa）；

Δp_y——计算管段的沿程损失（Pa）；

Δp_j——计算管段的局部损失（Pa）。

根据达西公式，沿程压力损失可用

$$\Delta p_y = \lambda \frac{l}{d} \cdot \frac{\rho v^2}{2}$$

式中 λ——沿程阻力系数；

d——管径（m）；

ρ——流体的密度（kg/m³）；

v——管中流体的速度（m/s）；

l——管段的长度（m）。

热媒在管内流动的摩擦阻力系数 λ 值取决于管内热媒的流动状态和管壁的粗糙程度，即

$$\lambda = f(Re, K/d) \qquad (3\text{-}12)$$

摩擦阻力系数 λ 是用实验方法确定的。根据实验数据整理的曲线，按照流体的不同流动状态，可整理出一些计算摩擦阻力系数 λ 的公式。在热水供热系统中，推荐使用的一些计算摩擦阻力系数 λ 值的公式如下：

1）层流流动。在此区域中，摩擦阻力系数 λ 值取决于雷诺数 Re 值，可按下式计算

$$\lambda = \frac{64}{Re}$$

2）湍流流动。整个湍流区还可以分为三个区域：

$$\lambda = \frac{0.3164}{Re^{0.25}} \qquad (3\text{-}13)$$

$$\lambda = \frac{1.42}{\left(\lg Re \dfrac{d}{K}\right)^2} \qquad (3\text{-}14)$$

$$\lambda = \frac{1}{\left(1.14 + 2\lg \dfrac{K}{d}\right)^2} \qquad (3\text{-}15)$$

3.3 集中供热系统的热源

热源是供热系统中三大重要组成部分之一。

3.3.1 热电厂

热电厂是电能和热能结合的产物，是目前各大中城市中最为常见的供热形式。联合生产电能和热能的方式，取决于采用供热汽轮机的形式。供热汽轮机主要分三大类型：

1. 背压式汽轮机

排气压力高于大气压力的供热汽轮机称为背压式汽轮机。机组工作原理如图 3-5 所示。

2. 抽汽式汽轮机

机组工作原理如图 3-6 所示。

3. 凝汽机组改造成供热系统

热电厂提供的高温水温度一般为 110～150℃，回水温度为 60～70℃，系统一般需经换热站进行热交换，将二次水转换为 95℃/70℃ 的热水，提供给民用建筑使用，一次水放热后返回热电厂。

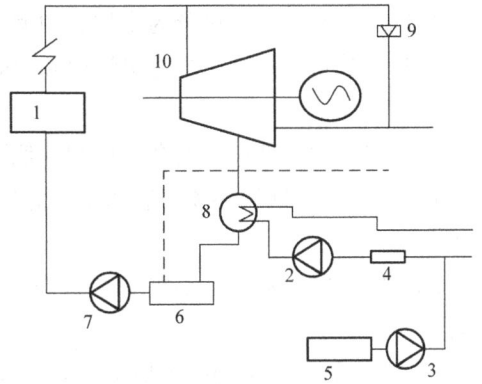

图 3-5 背压式热电厂供热系统
1—蒸汽锅炉 2—热水循环水泵 3—补给水泵
4—除污器 5—软水处理装置 6—凝结水回收装置
7—锅炉给水泵 8—热网水换热器
9—减压装置 10—背压式汽轮发电机组

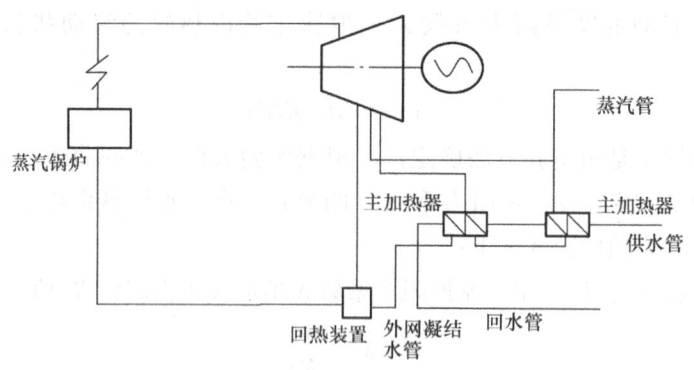

图 3-6 抽汽式热电厂供热系统

3.3.2 区域锅炉房

区域锅炉房是城镇集中供应热能的热源。

1. 锅炉的组成和分类

通常，把用于发电和提供动力方面的锅炉，称为动力锅炉；把用于工业及供暖方面的锅炉，称为供热锅炉，又叫工业锅炉。

1) 锅炉是由"燃烧部分——炉子"和"换热部分——汽锅"两大部分组成。以燃煤锅炉为例，炉子是由煤斗、炉排、炉膛、除渣板、送风装置等组成的燃烧设备。汽锅是由锅筒、对流管束、水冷壁、集箱和下降管等组成的一个封闭汽水系统。

2) 锅炉的分类方法。

锅炉按燃烧的燃料不同，可分为燃煤锅炉、燃气锅炉、燃油锅炉和电锅炉等。

按生产的热媒不同，可分为蒸汽锅炉和热水锅炉。

按热水在锅中的压力高低，可分为低压锅炉、中压锅炉和高压锅炉。

按热媒的温度高低，可分为低温锅炉和高温锅炉。

按锅炉容量大小，可分为小型、中型和大型锅炉。

按炉筒数目不同，可分为单炉筒和双炉筒等。

2. 锅炉的附件

常见锅炉的附件包括安全附件和其他附件。

1) 水位计。锅炉必须安装两个彼此独立的水位计，司炉人员可通过水位计来监视汽炉里的水位。

2) 压力表。压力表是锅炉的安全附件之一，司炉人员根据压力表来调节炉内燃烧情况。

3) 安全阀。安全阀是锅炉重要的安全部件，当锅炉由于某种原因使炉内压力超过允许值时，安全阀自动开启，排汽泄压，从而保证锅炉安全运行。蒸发量大于 0.5t/h 的锅炉，至少装设两个安全阀（不包括省煤器安全阀）。

4) 锅炉的其他附件。为了保证锅炉能正常工作，锅炉还必须装设如下配件：①温度计：在锅炉上需要进行温度测量的有蒸汽温度、给水温度、空气温度、烟气温度和炉膛温度等。②调节阀：用来调节并联运行的热水锅炉的水量。③给水阀：给水阀用来开关锅炉的给水管。为防止热水循环泵或锅炉给水泵突然停转，使炉水汽化。④止回阀：安装在锅炉的手动给水阀前，防止锅炉内的水倒流入给水管中。在循环水泵出口，一般也装有单向阀。⑤排污阀：排污阀装在排污管上，用来排除锅中污垢，保证锅炉中的水质符合要求。

3.3.3 其他热源形式

其他热源，如工业余热、地热供热、太阳能和核能也可以作为系统的热源。

1. 工业余热

工业余热是指工业生产过程的产品和排放物料所含的热或设备的散热。工业余热的利用，根据余热的载能不同，可分为气态余热利用、液态余热利用和固态余热利用集中类型。

2. 地热供热

地热通常是指陆地地表以下 5000m 深度内的热能。利用地热与其他热源供热相比，它具有节省燃料和不造成城市大气污染的特殊优点。

3. 太阳能

太阳能的利用已日益广泛，它包括太阳能的光热利用，太阳能的光电利用和太阳能的光化学利用等，人类依赖这些能量维持生存。

太阳能是一次能源、可再生能源，它资源丰富，对环境无污染。但太阳能有两个缺点：一是能流密度低；二是其强度受到各种因素（季节、地点、气候等）的影响不能维持常量。

4. 核能

核能供热是解决城市能源供应、减轻运输压力和消除烧煤造成环境污染的一种新能源。从安全角度，核热电站应该建造在城市郊区。

习　　题

1. 建筑热负荷的概念是什么？建筑热负荷的计算方法是什么？
2. 分别论述重力循环系统的水力特征和机械循环系统的水力特征。
3. 论述上供下回、下供下回、上供上回及下供下回式供热系统的优缺点。
4. 室内热水系统水力计算步骤是什么？
5. 集中供热系统的热源形式有哪些？

Chapter 3
Heating

Abstract: This chapter introduces the concept of heating load and the design process of an indoor heating system respectively. This chapter briefly describes characteristics and categories of indoor heating systems. Principles of hydraulic calculation which are suitable for both indoor and outdoor heating system are discussed. Different kinds of heating sources are also summarized in the last section of this chapter.

Key points: heating load, gravity heating system, mechanical heating system, vertical heating system, horizontal deflection heating system, up-feed system, feed-up system, mixing heating system.

Buildings are enclosures for benefits of human habitation, work or recreation. The primary purpose of a heating system is to supply heat to the occupied space at a rate equal to that at which heat is lost from that space to the colder outdoors.

3.1 Heating Loss Calculation

Heat loss occurs by convection and radiation from the outside of the building, and by infiltration of outdoor air. Heating equipment is sized on the basis of steady-state heat flows through the building fabric, with an estimation of effect of non-steady influences rating to the thermal storage capacity of the structure, adventitious heat gains from people, lighting and machines, and the intermittency of heating system operation.

3.1.1 Design Heating Loss Calculation of Heat System

The surrounding rooms will steadily transfer heat into the target room and then this heat will escape through the one external wall by natural ventilation. Design heating loss is combined by heat flow in and heat flow out as the following:

Design heating loss = Total heat flow out-Total heat flow in

1. Heat Flow Out of Building

1) Offset transmission losses through the floor, walls and ceiling Q_1.

2) Temper such air as passes through the space as a result of either natural infiltration of me-

chanical ventilation Q_2.

3) Temper such air invasion through the doors or windows Q_3.

4) Provide the latent heat of vaporization for such amount of water as may be evaporated during the process of humidification Q_4.

5) Temper the cold material entering from outside Q_5.

6) Offset ventilation loss Q_6 is determined as the introduction of outside air into enclosure, the resultant increased heat requirements.

7) Other heat loss Q_7.

2. Heat flow in of building

1) Heat flow in through equipment of workshop Q_8.

2) Heat flow in through non-thermal heating system pipes and other heat surface Q_9.

3) Conductive transfer in hot material Q_{10}.

4) Solar radiation Q_{11}.

5) Other heat flow in Q_{12}.

The basic equation for the heat load of building is the form

$$Q' = Q'_1 + Q'_2 + Q'_3 - Q'_{11} \qquad (3\text{-}1)$$

Superscript symbols "'" mean that they are parameters at the design condition.

Heat transfers from the wall of the building: Normal heat transfers from indoor to outdoor through wall, windows, ceiling etc., when the temperature of indoor is higher than out door. Theoretically we often divide the heat to two parts such as the basic heating loss and the appendix heating loss in system design. Thus, the basic equation is the following form

$$Q' = Q'_{1,j} + Q'_{1,x} + Q'_2 + Q'_3 \qquad (3\text{-}2)$$

Where $Q'_{1,j}$—Basic heating loss;

$Q'_{1,x}$—Appendix heating loss.

Normal heat transfer through walls

$$q' = KF(t_n - t'_w)a \qquad (3\text{-}3)$$

Where K—Coefficient of transmission [W/ (m² · ℃)];

F—Net area of wall (m²);

t_n—Inside temperature (℃);

t'_w—Outside temperature (℃);

a—Additional coefficient of temperature.

Total heating loss of all heat transfer surface

$$Q'_{1,j} = \sum KF(t_n - t'_w)a \qquad (3\text{-}4)$$

Infiltration through wall or windows: Infiltration is the flow of outside air through cracks, crevices or porous walls into an enclosure. Since infiltration involves flow, it must depend on the existence of some type of potential acting in the direction of flow.

The equation of infiltration loss is

$$Q'_2 = 0.278 V \rho_w c_p (t_n - t'_w) \\ V = Lln$$ (3-5)

Where L—Ventilation rate. According to local air velocity, ventilation rate varied with different situation as in Table 3-1;

l—Calculation length of door or window (m);

n—Additional coefficient of orientation;

V—Total ventilation rate infiltration through wall or windows (m³/h);

ρ_w—Density of outdoor air (kg/m³);

c_p—Specific heat at constant pressure, $c_p = 1$ kJ/(kg·℃);

0.278—1kJ/h = 0.278W.

Table 3-1 Ventilation rate [unit: m³/(h·m)]

Description	Air velocity/(m/s)					
	1	2	3	4	5	6
Single wood glass	1.0	2.0	3.1	4.3	5.5	6.7
Double wood glass	0.7	1.4	2.2	3.0	3.9	4.7
Single steel window	0.6	1.5	2.6	3.9	5.2	6.7
Double steel window	0.4	1.1	1.8	2.7	3.6	4.7
Fixed or opening windows	0.2	0.5	1.0	1.6	2.3	2.9
Opening type (Closed) window	0	0.1	0.3	0.4	0.6	0.8

Invasion through the doors or windows: The difference in velocity and density between outside air and warm inside air is responsible for two pressure differences which influence infiltration.

The equation of this loss is

$$Q'_4 = 0.278 V_w c_p \rho_w (t_n - t'_w)$$ (3-6)

Where V_w—Ventilation rate (m³/h).

3.1.2 Heat Loss Calculations for High Buildings

With the increase of building height, the effect of hot pressure to heat loss is more obviously. We must consider the wind pressure and the hot pressure together during the hot loss calculations for high buildings.

The equation of infiltration loss of high building is

$$Q' = 0.278 L l c_p \rho_w (t_n - t'_w) m$$ (3-7)

$$L = a \Delta p^b$$ (3-8)

Where L—Ventilation rate [m³/(h·m)];

Δp—Differential pressure between the door and the window (Pa);

a, b—Coefficients, depended on the types of door and window;

m—Correlation coefficient under the both effects of wind pressure and hot pressure.

3.2 Hot-water Systems

Hot-water system includes indoor heating system and outdoor hot-water supply system.

3.2.1 Indoor Heating System

According to different methods, the indoor heating system can be classified as:

1) Gravity system or mechanical system. In gravity system, hot water flows naturally from boiler to emitters without the need from a pump. In the mechanical system a positive displacement pump is used to lift hot water into boiler.

2) One-pipe system and two-pipe system. Radiators of one-pipe system are separately attached to the water distribution pipe with a diverter, which is used to regulate the amount of hot water entering it. Two-pipe system uses separate pipes for supply and return water, which ensures a small temperature differential between radiators, regardless of their location.

3) Vertical system and horizontal system.

4) Low temperature heating system and hot water heating system.

1. Gravity Heating System

Fig. 3-1 illustrates the operation principle of gravity heating system.

Imaging a valve at the A—A plane in Fig. 3-1, we shut the valve suddenly. The different pressures are generated between the A—A plant. The pressure differential is the circulation power of this system.

p_1 and p_2 are pressures of A—A plant, then

$$p_1 = g(h_0\rho_h + h\rho_h + h_1\rho_g)$$
$$p_2 = g(h_0\rho_h + h\rho_g + h_1\rho_g)$$

We got the circulation power

$$\Delta p = gh(\rho_h - \rho_g) \qquad (3\text{-}9)$$

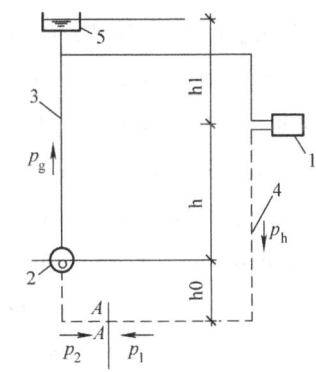

Fig. 3-1 Gravity heating system
1—Heat emitter 2—Boiler 3—Hot water flow
4—Return flow 5—Water tank

Where Δp—Circulation pressure (Pa);

g—Gravity acceleration (m/s^2);

h—Vertical height between cooling center to heating center (m);

ρ_h—density of return flow (kg/m^3);

ρ_g—density of hot flow (kg/m^3).

2. Mechanical Heating System

The most comprehensive system is mechanical heating system. It can be divided into the following types:

(1) Vertical system

1) Two-pipe up-feed system and one-pipe up-feed system. Fig. 3-2 illustrates the mechanical up-feed system. Different from the gravity system, mechanical systems have the circulating water pump and air exhaust device. The junction types of pipe and radiator with two-pipe up-feed systems have no difference between gravity systems. Simple types, convenient construction and low cost are the advantages of one-pipe up-feed system, so it is the most common system of current mechanical system.

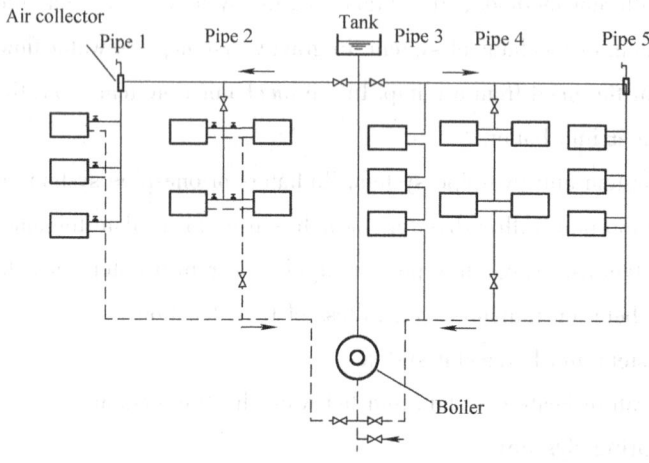

Fig. 3-2 Mechanical heating system

2) Two-pipe feed-feed system. Compared with two-pipe up-feed system, it has the following characteristics: Flow pipes are laid out at basement; Invalid heat loss decreases; During the building construction, the radiators of every floor are installed then they can start to heat; It's more difficult to remove air of the system.

3) Two-pipe feed-up system. Compared with two-pipe up-feed system, it has the following characteristics: Due to the common flow direction between air and water, the air exhaust device is not needed in the system; The flow pipe is shorter than other system, so the invalid heat loss decreases; The higher temperature of flow pipe, the less radiator area of first floor.

4) Mixing heating system. The system is composed of feed-up system and up-up system. Fig. 3-3 illustrates the mixing heating system. High-temperature water is quoted from area I directly; the temperature of backwater must meet the demand of area II. The system is generally used in civil and factory building.

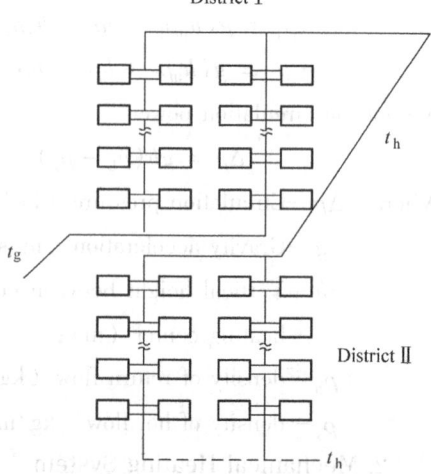

Fig. 3-3 Mixing heating system

(2) Horizontal system. According to the junction types of flow pipe and radiator, the system can be classified into right-left system and great-leap-forward system.

Air exhaust system of horizontal is a more complex vertical system. Fig. 3-4 illustrates the situation of air exhaust valve.

Compared with vertical system, horizontal system has the following advantages:

1) Simple types, convenient construction and no noise transfer between each floor.

2) The expansion tank can be placed at stairwell, toilet, which doesn't effect the outward appearance of construction.

3) The system makes household metering possible.

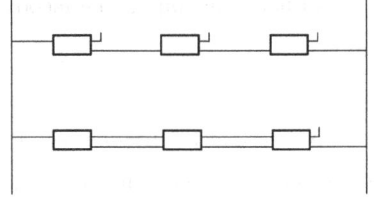

Fig. 3-4 Horizontal system

Horizontal system is the most common and widely used form of distribution, which can control and manage the temperature and flow layer-by-layer. However, this system needs more radiators than other systems.

3.2.2 Hydraulics of Indoor Hot Water Heating System

The distribution of fluids by pipes is essential to all heating system. This chapter deals with the fundamentals of incompressible flow of fluids in conduits, and develops simple design procedures for water piping system.

According to fluid dynamics theory, fluid flowing in pipeline needs to overcome the resistances, which include pipe loss and local loss.

The adiabatic, steady flow of a fluid in a pipe is governed by the first law of thermodynamics, which leads to the equation

$$\frac{p_1}{\rho_1 g} + \frac{v_1^2}{2g} + z_1 = \frac{p_2}{\rho_2 g} + \frac{v_2^2}{2g} + z_2 + h_f \tag{3-10}$$

Where z_1, z_2—elevation (m);

h_f—lost head (m).

The basic equation for the loss is

$$\Delta p = \Delta p_y + \Delta p_j \tag{3-11}$$

Where Δp—pressure loss (Pa);

Δp_y—pipe loss (Pa);

Δp_j—local (Pa).

For incompressible flow in pipes and ducts the lost head is expressed as

$$\Delta p_y = \lambda \frac{l}{d} \cdot \frac{\rho v^2}{2}$$

Where λ—moody friction factor;

l—length of the pipe or duct (m);

d—diameter of the pipe or duct (m);

v—average velocity in the conduit (m/s);

ρ—density of fluid (kg/m^3).

In hot water pipe, the moody friction factor λ depends on flow state and the roughness of pipe, so

$$\lambda = f(Re, K/d) \tag{3-12}$$

Notice that the friction factor can be read directly from figure, if the Reynolds number and relative roughness are sufficiently large for the flow to be considered as in a fully turbulent regime.

1) When the pipe flow is laminar state, the friction factor λ is

$$\lambda = \frac{64}{Re}$$

2) When the pipe flow is turbulent state, the friction factor λ has three equations:

$$\lambda = \frac{0.3164}{Re^{0.25}} \tag{3-13}$$

$$\lambda = \frac{1.42}{\left(\lg Re \frac{d}{K}\right)^2} \tag{3-14}$$

$$\lambda = \frac{1}{\left(1.14 + 2\lg \frac{K}{d}\right)^2} \tag{3-15}$$

3.3 Heating Source of Central Heating Systems

Heating source is one of three big important constituents of heating system.

3.3.1 Heating Power Station

The heating power station is joint product of electricity and thermal power, which is the most common heating form in large and medium-sized cities. The utilization rate of heat resource is governed by the form of heating gas turbine. Steam turbine for cogeneration is divided into three types:

1. Back-pressure steam turbine

The heating gas turbine whose exhaust pressure is higher than the atmospheric pressure is called the back pressure type gas turbine. Fig. 3-5 illustrates the operation principle of back-pressure steam turbine.

2. Extraction steam turbine

Fig. 3-6 illustrates the operation principle of extraction steam turbine.

3. Modified condensing turbine

Generally, the temperature of heating flow is 110~150℃ and return flow is 60~70℃ of this system. Hot water with 95℃/70℃ is generated by heating exchanger.

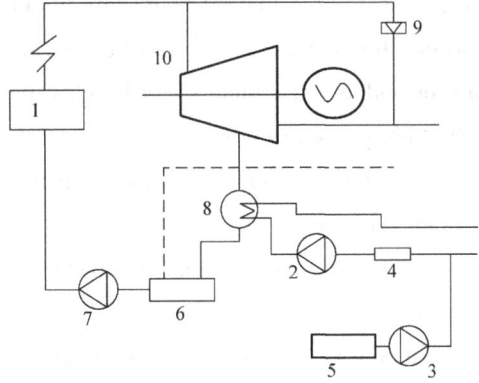

Fig. 3-5 Back-pressure steam turbines

1—Steam boiler 2—Hot water circulating water pump 3—Supplies water pump
4—Trash-cleaning machine 5—Water treatment equipment
6—Condense water recovery installment 7—Pump 8—Heat interchanger
9—Decompression equipment 10—Back-pressure steam turbine power set

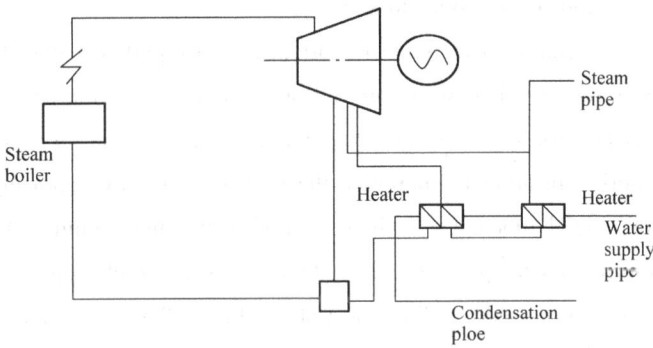

Fig. 3-6 Extraction steam turbine

3.3.2 District Boiler

District boiler is the heating source of town district heating.

1. Types of Boilers

In terms of their design and function, boilers can be classified and described as follows: power boiler and industrial boiler.

1) The two parts "combination-stove" and "heat transfer-steam boiler" build up a boiler. Take a fire tube boiler as the example, the stove is composed by the coal scuttle, the fire grate, the chamber, slag removal system, the blast installment and so on. The steam boiler is composed by boiler barrel, the convection tube, the water cooling wall, the collection box and the gas down tube and so on.

2) Classified methods of boilers. According to the burning fuel, the boilers can be classified as

coal-burning boiler, the fuel gas boiler, the fuel oil boiler and the electric boiler and so on.

According to the heat carrier, the boilers can be classified as steam boiler and hot water boiler.

According to the pressure of boilers, the boilers can be classified as the low-pressure boiler, mid-pressure the boiler and the high-pressure boiler.

According to the temperature of heat carrier, the boilers can be divided into the low temperature boiler and the high temperature boiler.

According to the boiler capacity, the boilers can be divided into small-, medium- and the large-scale boiler.

According to the stove tube number, the boilers can be divided into one stove tube and double stove tube.

2. Boiler Accessories

The common appendices of boiler are security appendix and other appendices.

1) Stage recorder. Two independent stage recorders must be installed in a boiler, which are necessary for the staff to monitor the water level of boiler.

2) Pressure gauge. Pressure gauge is one of the security appendices of boiler, which can supply the combustion situation in the boiler to staff.

3) Safety valve. The safety valve is the important security part of boiler. It can open automatically to exhaust decompression when stove internal pressure surpasses the permissible value. At least two safety valves must be installed when the evaporation capacity is bigger than 0.5t/h.

4) Other accessories. In order to guarantee the normal work, the following fittings must be installed on the boiler: ①Thermometer, which can give the temperature of steam temperature, water-supply temperature, air temperature, haze temperature, the chamber temperature and so on. ②Regulating valve, which is used to adjust the water volume. ③The feed water valve, which is installed on the water supply pipe, can prevent water vaporization when pump power failed. ④Check valve, which is used to prevent the water flows backwards into the service pipe. The exportation of a circulation water pump is also loaded with a one-way valve generally. ⑤Blow-off valve, which is installed in the sewage pipe to guarantee the water quality request of boiler.

3.3.3 Other Heat Sources

Other heat sources such as afterheat of industrial, terrestrial heat, solar energy and nuclear energy also can be used in central heating system.

1. Afterheat of Industrial

Afterheat of industrial refers to the heat which is produced during the industrial production process and the emissions of material. According to different afterheat carrier, it can be classified into gaseous state, liquid state and solid state.

2. Geothermal Heat Supply

It usually refers to the heat energy 5000m depth below land surface. Compared with other heat energies, an advantage of using this energy is that it won't create any pollution.

3. Solar Energy

Solar energy has been brought into wide use, which includes light heat utilization, photo electricity use and photochemistry use and so on.

As primary energy, solar energy has the obvious comparative advantages as renewable energy, resources rich, no pollution to environment. However, it has also two disadvantages as follow: One is the low energy density, the other is the inconstant intensity which is effected by season, place, and climate and so on.

4. Nuclear Energy

It is one kind of new energy, which solves the city energy supply, reduces the transportation pressure and eliminates the environmental pollution caused by coal bunking. On the safety issue, nuclear heating power station should be constructed in city suburb.

Questions

1. What is the heating load of a building and how to calculate it?
2. Please briefly describe the characteristics of gravity heating system and mechanical heating system.
3. Please analyse the advantages and disadvantages of different heating system such as up-feed system, feed-up system and mixing heating system.
4. What is hydraulic calculation procedure for an indoor heating system?
5. How many kinds of central heating sources are existed usually?

第 4 章
空气调节与制冷

本章要点：本章介绍了空调系统的基本原理和分类。湿空气的特性，全空气、空气—水、冷剂式空调系统的组成，最后介绍了制冷系统的基本原理和设备。

知识点：空气调节，舒适性空调系统，工艺性空调系统，湿空气，冷/热负荷，全空气系统，气流组织，空气—水系统，冷剂式系统，制冷，蒸气压缩式制冷系统，吸收式制冷系统。

4.1 空气调节与空调系统

4.1.1 空气调节的概念和空调系统的作用

空气调节是一个能同时实现多种功能的复杂过程，包括对空气的处理和输送并最终分配到空调区域。空调系统由实现上述过程的一系列设备部件构成，通常具有以下功能：

1) 提供需要的冷量和热量。
2) 调节送风，也就是对空气加热/冷却、加湿/去湿、净化，降低空调设备造成的噪声。
3) 将处理后的空气（包含足够的新风）输送到空调区域。
4) 将室内环境参数如室内空气的温度、湿度、洁净度、流速、声级以及室内外压差，控制并维持在预先设定的范围内，以达到人们对室内环境舒适和健康的要求，或者满足一定的生产过程需要。

4.1.2 空调系统的分类

空调系统按其用途可分为舒适性空调和工艺性空调。

舒适性空调（简称"舒适空调"）是为室内人员创造舒适健康环境的空调系统，主要用于商业建筑（如办公大楼、超市、商场、购物中心、餐厅等）、居住建筑（如宾馆、汽车旅馆、酒店、公寓、别墅等）、公共建筑（如中小学、大学、图书馆、博物馆、室内体育馆、医院、疗养院、影剧院、会堂等）、交通工具（如飞机、汽车、火车、轮船等）。

工艺性空调（又称"工业空调"）是为工业生产或科学研究提供特定室内环境的空调系统。例如，在纺织厂，适当的湿度控制能增加纱线的强度。相对湿度过高在纺纱过程中会产生问题，而相对湿度过低会产生静电从而影响纺纱过程；因为许多电子元件的质量都受空气微粒的影响，所以电子元件都要求在洁净厂房中制造；精密仪器制造业需要精确的温度和湿度控制，一般要求空气温度的变化范围为±（0.1~0.5）℃，相对湿度的变化范围不超过±5%；药品工业不仅要求一定的空气温湿度，还需要控制空气洁净度。

此外，按承担室内热负荷、冷负荷和湿负荷的介质种类不同，空调系统可分为全空气系统、全水系统、空气-水系统和冷剂系统。

4.2 湿空气的物理性质

进行空调系统的设计，必须先了解湿空气的物理性质。

4.2.1 湿空气

包围着地球的空气层称为大气层。从通风空调技术的角度看，大气是由干空气（包括各种污染物）和水蒸气组成的混合物，又称为湿空气。

在通常情况下，干空气的组成是不变的，仅随地理位置和时间略有变化。干空气的组成成分（以体积百分数表示）见表4-1。

表4-1 干空气的组成成分

组成成分	体积百分数（%）
氮	78.13
氧	20.90
氩	0.93
二氧化碳	0.03
其他气体（如氖、氦、二氧化硫等）	0.01

湿空气中水蒸气的含量很少，但它对湿空气的状态变化影响却很大，因此水蒸气含量不能忽略。湿空气中都含有一定量的污染物，它们对空调区域内人员的健康有很大影响；但是由于污染物的质量浓度很低，对湿空气物理性质影响很小。因此，在分析和计算湿空气物理性质时，通常将其简化为由干空气和水蒸气构成的二元混合气体。

4.2.2 湿空气的状态参数

湿空气的状态通常可以用压力、温度、湿度等参数来度量和描述，因此，这些参数称为湿空气的状态参数。

1. 压力

根据道尔顿定律，对于体积和温度一定的混合气体而言，其总压力等于组成该混合气体的各种气体的分压力之和，即

$$p = p_1 + p_2 + \cdots \tag{4-1}$$

式中　　p——混合气体的总压力（Pa）；

$p_1, p_2, \cdots$——各种气体的分压力（Pa）。

混合气体中每种气体的分压力不受其他气体的分压力影响。

将道尔顿定律应用于湿空气,有

$$p_{at}(B) = p_g + p_q \tag{4-2}$$

式中 $p_{at}(B)$——大气压或湿空气总压力(Pa);
p_g——干空气分压力(Pa);
p_q——水蒸气分压力(Pa)。

2. 温度

物质的温度反映了物质的冷热程度。温度的高低用"温标"来衡量。国际上常用的三种温标有开氏温度K、摄氏温度℃、华氏温度℉。

绝对温标(又称开氏温标),符号为T,单位为K;摄氏温标,符号为t,单位为℃;华氏温标,符号为t,单位为℉。华氏温标和摄氏温标的换算关系为

$$t℃ = \frac{5}{9}(t℉ - 32) \tag{4-3}$$

开氏温标和摄氏温标的换算关系为

$$T = 273.15 + t℃ \tag{4-4}$$

3. 含湿量和相对湿度

含湿量d是指湿空气中与1kg干空气同时并存的水蒸气质量,即

$$d = \frac{m_q}{m_g} \tag{4-5}$$

式中 m_q——水蒸气质量(kg);
m_g——干空气质量(kg)。

湿空气的相对湿度定义为空气中水蒸气分压力p_q和同温度下饱和水蒸气分压力$p_{q,b}$的百分比,用符号φ或RH表示。定义式为

$$\varphi = \frac{p_q}{p_{q,b}} \times 100\% \tag{4-6}$$

4. 比体积和密度

在湿空气的计算中往往以含1kg干空气的湿空气作为计算基础。所以空气的比体积定义为当湿空气中干空气质量为1kg时湿空气的体积,单位为m^3/kg(干空气),即

$$v_g = \frac{V}{m_g} \tag{4-7}$$

式中 V——湿空气的体积(m^3);
m_g——干空气质量(kg)。

相应地,空气密度定义为干空气质量和湿空气体积之比,单位是kg(干空气)/m^3,即

$$\rho_g = \frac{m_g}{V} = \frac{1}{v_g} \tag{4-8}$$

5. 露点温度

露点温度在数值上等于与湿空气的含湿量和大气压均相等的饱和湿空气的温度。含湿量

和水蒸气分压力相等时，湿空气的露点温度也相等。因此，当大气压一定时，露点温度与湿空气的含湿量和水蒸气分压力相关。湿空气被冷却时，当冷却温度低于空气的露点温度时，就会出现结露现象，因此，露点温度是空气结露与否的临界温度。

6. 焓

对于理想气体，在定压过程中，焓差等于热交换量，即

$$\Delta h = c_p(t_2 - t_1) \tag{4-9}$$

式中　c_p——比定压热容 [kJ/ (kg·K)]；

t_1、t_2——理想气体在状态点 1 和 2 的温度（℃）。

因为湿空气可以近似认为是干空气和水蒸气的混合物，因此湿空气的焓可以表示为

$$h = h_g + h_q \tag{4-10}$$

式中　h_g、h_q——干空气和水蒸气的焓 [kJ/kg（干空气）]。

7. 显热和潜热

湿空气的焓可以分成两部分：显热和潜热。显热是与空气温度变化相关的热量，潜热与水蒸气的状态变化相关。汽化潜热是指将液态的水蒸发成水蒸气所需要的热量，而冷凝潜热是指将水蒸气凝结成液态的水所放出的热量。在湿空气的处理过程中，总是存在水的蒸发或水蒸气的冷凝，因此，包括了一定量的潜热。

8. 湿球温度

湿球温度是确定空气状态的又一个独立参数，是空调工程中经常利用的一个重要状态参数。干湿球温度计通过测量空气的干球温度和湿球温度来反映空气的相对湿度。干湿球温度计由两个温度计构成：其中一支温度计的感温包（干球）裸露在空气中，它所测得的温度称为干球温度，也就是实际的空气温度；另一支温度计的感温包（湿球）裹上脱脂棉纱布，纱布的下端浸入盛有蒸馏水的玻璃杯中，纱布始终处于润湿状态，当不饱和空气流过湿球表面时，纱布表面的水蒸发使得纱布和湿球表面温度都降低，此时湿球温度计所显示的读数为空气的湿球温度。

4.2.3　典型空气状态变化过程

空气处理的方法有加热、冷却、加湿和去湿等。

（1）等湿（干式）加热过程　空气调节中常用表面式空气加热器或电加热器来加热空气。当湿空气通过加热器时获得了热量，提高了温度，但含湿量并没有变化。

（2）等湿（干式）冷却过程　当用表面式空气冷却器处理空气时，如果表冷器的进水温度和盘管表面温度都比空气露点温度高，则空气将在含湿量不变的情况下冷却，其焓值必相应减少。

（3）等焓减湿过程　用固体吸附剂（例如硅胶）处理空气时，由于吸附剂表面存在水蒸气压力差和电场使得水蒸气被吸附，空气的含湿量降低，空气失去潜热而得到水蒸气凝结时放出的汽化热使温度升高，但焓值基本不变。

（4）等焓加湿过程　用喷水室喷循环水处理空气时，水吸收空气中的热量而蒸发为水蒸气，使得空气温度降低而含湿量增加，并且趋于饱和。此时，循环水温将稳定在空气的湿

球温度上。

（5）等温加湿过程　向空气中喷蒸汽，空气吸收水蒸气后，其焓和含湿量都将增加。

（6）减湿冷却（冷却干燥）过程　如果用表面冷却器处理空气，当表冷器的进水温度和盘管表面温度低于空气的露点温度时，空气中的水蒸气将凝结为水，从而使空气冷却并干燥。如果用喷水室处理空气，当喷水温度低于空气露点温度时，也能实现减湿冷却（冷却干燥）过程。

4.3　负荷计算

进行空调系统设计的第一步是负荷计算。热负荷、冷负荷与湿负荷是暖通空调工程设计的基本依据，决定了暖通空调设备容量的大小。

4.3.1　室内外空气计算参数

热负荷、冷负荷与湿负荷的计算以室外气象参数和室内要求保持的空气参数为依据。

1. 室内空气设计参数

室内空气设计参数直接影响空调房间的室内环境，具体包括以下三类参数：

1）基本设计参数：室内空气温度、室内空气相对湿度、室内风速。
2）室内空气品质：空气污染物、换气次数、空气洁净度。
3）特殊设计参数：声级、室内外压差。

根据 GB 50019—2003《采暖通风与空气调节设计规范》中的规定，舒适性空调室内计算参数如下：

夏季：温度，24~28℃；相对湿度，40%~65%；风速，小于或等于0.3m/s。
冬季：温度，18~22℃；相对湿度，40%~60%；风速，小于或等于0.2m/s。

2. 室外空气计算参数

室外空气计算参数的取值，直接影响室内空气状态、房间冷负荷以及空调设备的选择。如果以一年当中的最高和最低气温作为室外空气计算参数，会因空调设备庞大、运行费用高而造成浪费。室外空气计算参数一般是由多年（30年）气象数据的统计分析得到。GB 50019—2003《采暖通风与空气调节设计规范》中规定了空调室外空气计算温度。

4.3.2　冷负荷计算

1. 冷负荷特点

为了维持空调房间内的温度，就必须及时排除进入室内的热量。房间得热量是指某一时刻由室内和室外热源进入房间的热量总和。冷负荷是指维持室内温度、湿度恒定，在某一时刻应从室内除去的热量。

瞬时得热中的显热部分包括以对流方式传递的热量和以辐射方式传递的热量。以对流方式传递的显热得热和潜热得热部分，直接散发到房间空气中，立刻构成房间瞬时冷负荷；而以辐射方式传递的显热得热量，首先被围护结构和室内设备所吸收并贮存于其中。当围护结构和室内设备表面温度高于室内温度时,所贮存的热量再借助于对流方式逐时放出,从而形成冷负荷。由此可见,任一时刻房间瞬时得热量的总和未必等于同一时刻的瞬时冷负荷。

2. 室内冷负荷

室内冷负荷包括内部负荷和外部负荷:

(1) 外部冷负荷　形成外部冷负荷的得热来源于通过建筑物外围护结构的太阳辐射和室内外温差传热。

(2) 内部冷负荷　内部冷负荷来源于室内的人员、家具和设备的潜热和显热得热。

室内冷负荷是确定空调房间送风量以及空气处理设备容量的依据之一。

3. 制冷系统的冷负荷

制冷系统的冷负荷是指制冷系统中制冷剂在蒸发器中所吸收的热量。对于集中式空调水系统,制冷系统的冷负荷等于盘管负荷加上冷冻水管得热、水泵得热以及蓄水罐得热。对于大部分商业建筑的空调水系统而言,冷冻水管和水泵的得热量是盘管负荷的5%～10%。对于直接膨胀式空调系统,制冷系统的冷负荷就等于盘管负荷。

盘管负荷是制冷负荷的主要部分,是指流过盘管(表冷器)的冷冻水所带走的热量,或者是盘管(直接膨胀式系统)中的制冷剂所吸收的热量。如果忽略盘管与周围环境的传热量,盘管负荷主要包括:

1) 房间冷负荷(包括显热和潜热负荷)。

2) 新风(满足室内人员卫生要求)所形成的显热和显热冷负荷。

3) 送风系统得热(包括送风机得热和送风管得热)所形成的冷负荷。

4) 回风系统得热(包括顶棚或照明灯具得热、回风机得热、回风管得热)所形成的冷负荷。

4.3.3 热负荷计算

空气调节房间热负荷的计算在原理上与采暖热负荷的计算是相同的,即按稳定传热计算法,将耗热量作为房间的热负荷,室外计算温度采用冬季空调计算温度。由于空调建筑通常保持室内为正压,一般情况下可以不计算冷风渗透引起的热负荷,除非窗户密闭性很差或者室外风速很高。具体计算方法参见文献。

4.4　全空气系统

全空气系统通常由冷热源(锅炉和冷水机组)、水系统(将冷热源提供的热水和冷冻水输送到空气处理单元)、空气系统(在空气处理机组中将新风和回风的混合空气处理后送到空调房间)以及控制系统构成。此外,根据空气调节的具体要求,可以增加回风系统(用于热回收)、防排烟系统或机械排风系统。

4.4.1　空气处理机组

对空气进行各种热、湿、净化等处理的设备称为空气处理机组。空气处理机组主要有两大类：组合式空调机组和整体式空调机组。组合式空调机组由各种功能的模块（称为功能段）组合而成，用户可以根据自己的需要选择不同的功能段进行组合。组合式空调机组最基本的功能段包括混合段、风机段、表冷段、空气过滤段和控制段。组合式空调机组（图4-1）使用方便灵活，是目前应用比较广泛的一种空气处理机组。整体式空调机组在工厂中组装成一体，具有固定的功能。这种机组结构紧凑、体型较小，适用于需要对空气处理的功能不多，机房面积较小的场合。

下面介绍空气处理机组中的主要功能段。

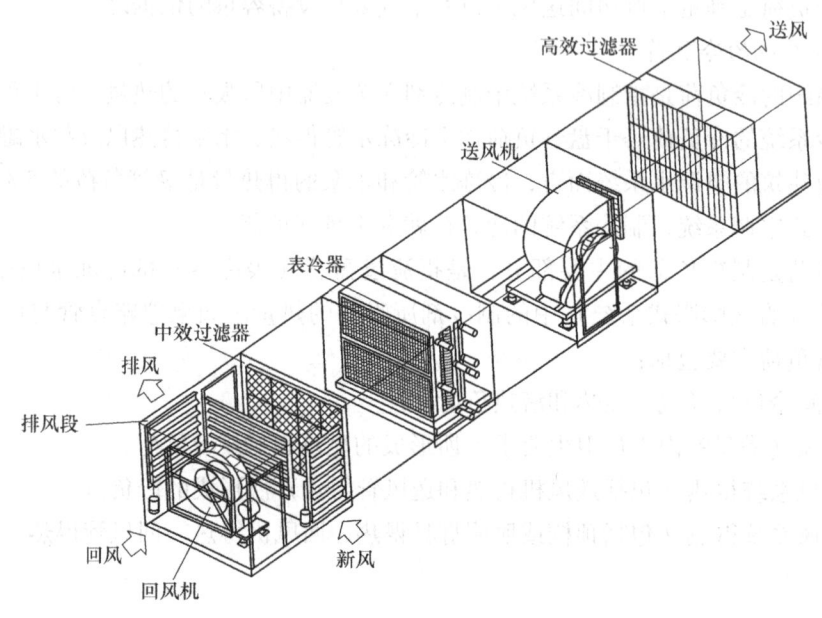

图 4-1　组合式空调机组

1. 混合段

混合段通常由新风口、回风口、风阀以及混合箱构成。由于新风口的位置直接影响室内空气品质（IAQ）；因此，应设在挡风避雨的地方并且尽可能远离排风口。为了更好地控制新风量，较大的空调机组可以采用两个新风阀：一个是最小新风阀，另一个是按全新风设计的调节风阀。合理设置新风口和回风口的位置，能够保证新风和回风充分混合。

2. 空气过滤段

空气过滤器是获得合适室内空气品质的重要设备。空调工程中常用的过滤器按效率可分为低效过滤器、中效过滤器、高效过滤器和超高效过滤器四类。低效过滤器有平板式、折叠式和袋式过滤器三种，如图4-2所示。低效过滤器广泛用于商业建筑中的空调机组、生产车间以及要求较高的住宅。中效过滤器通常制成袋式或抽屉式，主要用于对空气品质有一定要求的商业和工业建筑。

3. 喷水室

喷水室是最早的空气处理设备（1904年），已经广泛用于空气的加湿、冷却和净化处理。图4-3所示为应用较多的卧式喷水室的构造。喷水室主要由喷嘴与排管、前后挡水板、

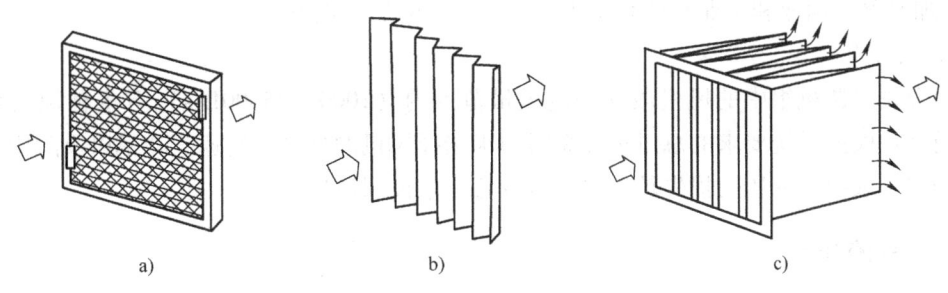

图 4-2 过滤器类型
a) 平板式过滤器 b) 折叠式过滤器 c) 袋式过滤器

外壳、底池（或水箱）以及管路系统等组成。喷水室可以实现多种空气处理过程，包括对空气进行冷却加湿、冷却除湿以及洗涤和净化，因此，在空调房间的温湿度要求较高的场合，如纺织厂、卷烟厂等工艺性空调系统中，得到了广泛应用。

4. 表冷器

水冷式表冷器以冷冻水作为冷媒。当空气经过盘管和翅片的外表面时，被冷冻水冷却或冷却除湿，如图 4-4 所示。为了获得更好的传热效果，表冷器中空气和水一般是按逆流布置，也就是冷空气遇冷水，热空气遇热水。盘管通常是用直径为 15mm、壁厚为 0.25～0.5mm 的铜管加工而成。盘管沿气流方向按顺排或叉排形式布置成 4 排、6 排或 8 排，以供用户选择。采用叉排布置的表冷器可以提高换热效率，并且增大空气的压降。

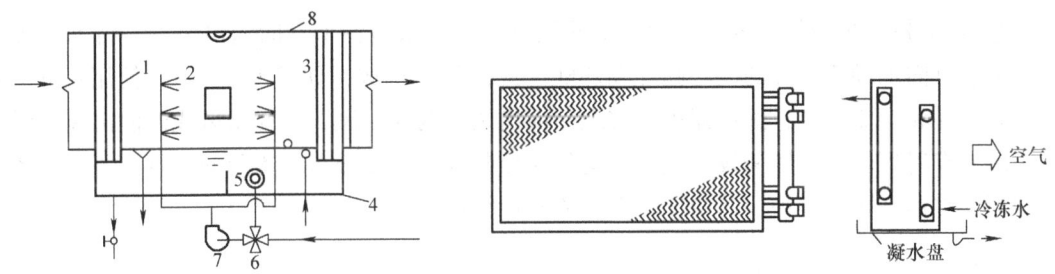

图 4-3 卧式喷水室的构造
1—前挡水板 2—喷嘴与排管
3—后挡水板 4—底池 5—滤水器
6—三通阀 7—水泵 8—外壳

图 4-4 水冷式表冷器

5. 空气加热段

空气加热器主要有热水空气加热器和蒸汽空气加热器两类。热水空气加热器的结构与水冷式表冷器相似，二者的主要区别在于：加热器盘管中的介质是热水，而表冷器中是冷冻水；热水加热器的盘管排数比表冷器少，一般为 1 排、2 排或 4 排，热水温度不超过 120℃。

6. 空气加湿段

对于舒适性空调，空气处理机组中一般不需要设加湿段；只有在冬季室外空气特别干燥的情况下才设置加湿段。对用于医疗房间和生产过程的工艺性空调（如制药车间、半导体生产车间、纺织厂、计算机房等），空气处理机组中必须设置加湿器。干蒸汽加湿器和电热

（极）加湿器是商业和工业空调系统中应用最广泛的加湿设备。

7. 风机段

组合式空调机组中的风机段在一定风量范围内（1000～25000L/s）有多种规格可供选择。通常是根据系统要求的总风量和总阻力来选择风机的型号、转速、功率以及配用电动机等。当回风系统的总压力损失较大时，可以考虑增设回风机。

4.4.2 气流组织

气流组织就是根据室内人员的要求，将处理过的空气以一定形式送入空调房间。合理的气流组织能够将处理过的空气均匀地送出，以最经济的方式获得健康舒适的室内环境，或满足一定工艺要求的环境。由于气流组织是空气调节的最后一个过程，并且发生在空调房间内，因此，气流组织是否合理，不仅直接影响房间的空调效果，还影响空调系统的能耗。

1. 送风口和回风口

（1）送风口　送风口形式对射流的发展及流型的形成有直接影响；因此，在进行气流组织设计时，应根据房间的装修、需要的气流形式、室内环境设计要求和空调负荷等方面的要求选择合适的送风口形式。

1）格栅送风口和百叶送风口。格栅送风口和百叶送风口是最常用的侧送风口。安装在侧墙上部向房间内横向送出气流的风口叫侧送风口。格栅型风口用于一般空调工程的送风，也可用作回风口和排风口。带有风量调节阀和活动叶片的百叶风口是侧送风口中用得最多的。单层百叶送风口如图4-5所示。

2）散流器。散流器是安装在顶棚上的送风口，可以向各个方向送出空气。普通散流器由一组装有固定导流叶片的同心圆环和外框（或外壳）构成，如图4-6所示。使用不同类型的同心圆环和导流叶片，散流器可以实现一面出风、两面出风、三面出风或四面出风。散流器送风具有射程较短、风速较低且分布均匀、控制区内温度分布较均匀的特点。普通散流器有圆形、方形和矩形三种，其中，方形散流器用得最多。

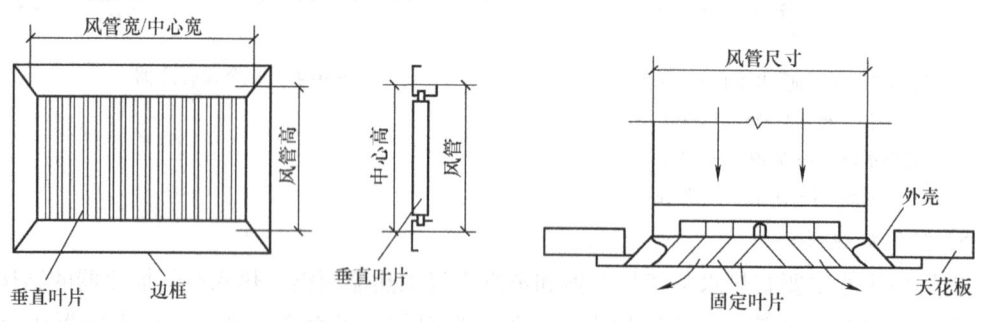

图4-5　单层百叶送风口（垂直叶片）　　　　图4-6　散流器

（2）回风、排风口　由于回风、排风口的汇流场对房间气流组织影响比较小，因此其形式比较简单，有的只在孔口加一金属网格，也有装格栅和百叶的。回风口的形状和位置根据气流组织要求而定，通常要与建筑装饰相配合。回风、排风口形式可以简单，但要求有调节风量的装置。

2. 典型气流分布模式

气流分布模式决定了室内工作区空气的分布情况。而气流分布模式主要取决于送风口形式、位置，送风参数（送风温度、速度），室内空气的温度、湿度和速度，对室内空气品质的要求，以及建筑物的结构特点。下面介绍三种常见的气流分布模式。

（1）侧送风　这种送风方式是把侧送风口布置在房间侧墙或风道侧面上，空气由送风口横向送出，送风射流贴附在顶棚表面流动，气流吹到对面墙上折转下落到工作区以较低速度流过工作区，再由回风口排出。根据房间跨度大小，可以布置成单侧送单侧回和双侧送双侧回多种形式，如图 4-7 所示。上侧送风常用的送风口有格栅送风口、百叶送风口和条缝形送风口。

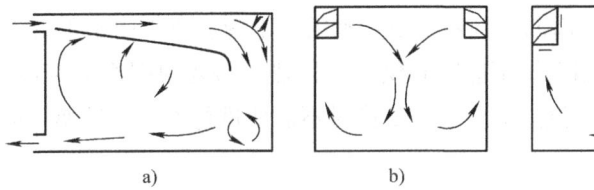

图 4-7　上侧送风的气流流型

（2）散流器送风　散流器送风有平送和下送两种形式。散流器平送风的主要特点是射流扩散快、射程短，工作区具有较均匀的温度和速度分布。对于变风量系统，通常选用高诱导比的散流器作为送风口。

（3）下送风　对于室内余热量大的场合，如计算机房、演播大厅等，常采用地板送风、顶棚回风的下送风系统，气流流型如图 4-8 所示。采用地板送风，地面需架空，下部空间布置送风管，把空气分配到地板送风。送出的气流卷吸下部的部分空气，在工作区形成许多小的混合气流。工作区内人体和热物体周围的空气变热而形成热射流，卷吸周围空气向上升，污染的热气流通过上部回风口排出房间。这种气流模式保证工作区有

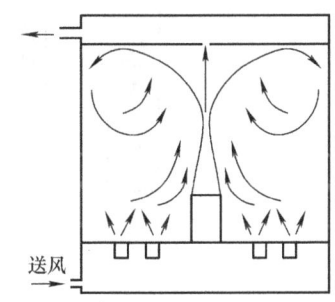

图 4-8　地板送风的下送风气流流型

较高的空气品质，称为置换通风。此外，由于从顶部排风，可以带走荧光灯产生的热量，从而降低房间冷负荷。

4.4.3　水系统

水系统是空调系统的一个重要组成部分，把冷热源、空气处理机组以及末端设备连接起来的设备和管路系统称为冷、热水系统。空调水系统包括冷冻水系统、冷却水系统和热水系统。热水系统详见第 3 章，这里不作介绍。

1. 冷冻水系统

空调冷冻水的参数范围：冷冻水供水温度 5~9℃，一般为 7℃；冷冻水供回水温差 5~10℃，一般为 5℃。空调冷冻水系统有以下几种分类方式：

1）根据系统的运行特点，空调冷、热水系统可分为闭式和开式两种形式。在闭式系统

中，冷、热水在盘管、加热器、冷水机组、锅炉以及其他换热器中流动，形成一个封闭的环路，环路中的水不与大气接触。在开式系统中，管路中的水与大气相通。

2）根据末端设备的水流程可分为异程式系统和同程式系统。异程式系统应用较多，但要注意流量分配和压力平衡的问题。同程式系统可以较好地解决流量分配和压力平衡的问题，但是管路系统较复杂，使得系统的初投资大。

3）按水量特性划分为定流量系统和变流量系统。在系统运行期间，定流量系统中各主要干管在任意截面处的流量保持不变，三通阀作为水量调节阀；对于变流量系统，水流量随着系统负荷的改变而变化，二通阀作为水量调节阀。

4）根据供回水管的数目，可分为两管制和四管制系统。两管制系统由供水干管和回水干管组成，如图 4-9 所示；而四管制系统由热水供水干管、热水回水干管、冷水供水干管和冷水回水干管组成。两管制系统不能同时供冷、供热，需要根据季节变换进行冷、热转换。四管制系统可以同时供冷、供热，在季节变换时不需要进行冷、热转换；但是四管制系统的初投资高。

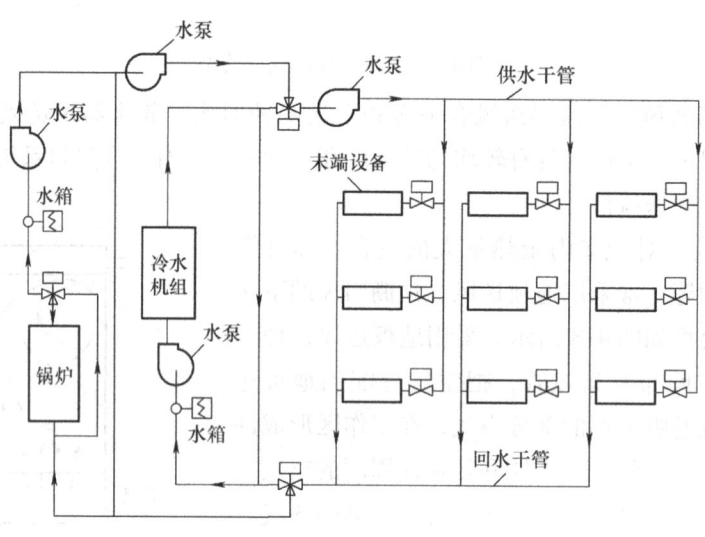

图 4-9 两管制水系统

2. 冷却水系统

在冷水机组中，用温度较低的水带走制冷剂冷凝时放出的热量，从而把冷凝器中高温高压的气态制冷剂冷凝为低温高压的液态制冷剂。冷却水通常来自于冷却塔或天然冷源（河水、湖水、海水、井水），冷却水的温度与当地气候条件相关。机械循环式冷却水系统主要由冷却塔、冷却水泵和冷却水管路等组成，如图 4-10 所示。在机械循环式冷却水系统中，采用冷却塔把在冷凝器中吸热升温的冷却水重新冷却，再送入冷凝器中循环使用。商业建筑用制冷机组或工业用空调中采用的冷却塔大多数是机械通风冷却塔，即利用风机将空气吸入塔内。有关冷却水

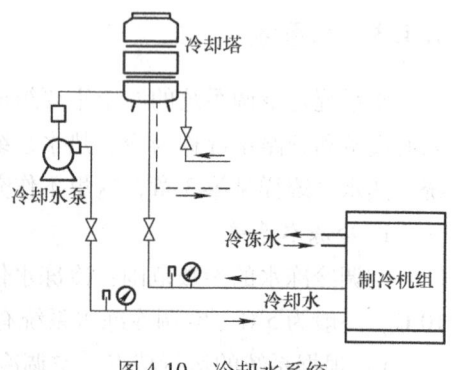

图 4-10 冷却水系统

系统的系统形式、设计方法参阅空调工程的制冷技术专著或空调设计手册。

4.4.4 常见全空气系统

根据系统特点，集中式空调系统有以下四种分类方法：

（1）单区域和多区域系统 单区域系统中没有末端设备，室内温度、相对湿度和送风量直接由空气处理单元或空调机组控制。多区域系统中，每个区域的温度和送风量由末端设备控制。

（2）单风道和双风道系统 单风道系统中，处理后的空气由一根风道送入空调房间。双风道系统有两根送风道，一根送热风，另一根送冷风。在空调区域的外区一般由冷、热风道同时送风，内区仅需要冷风道。

（3）定风量（CAV）和变风量（VAV）系统 定风量系统通过调节送风温度来满足负荷的变化。变风量系统保持送风温度不变，而通过改变送风量来满足负荷的变化。

（4）单风机和双风机系统 单风机系统只有一个送风机。常用的双风机系统有：送风机和排风机的组合、送风机和回风机的组合。

1. 定风量单风道系统

单区域单风道定风量系统（图4-11）是最典型的全空气空调系统，也是到目前为止使用最广泛的空调系统。定风量是指在空调系统运行期间送风量始终保持不变，通过调节送风温度来满足负荷的变化。单区域是指空调系统服务于对温度、湿度、洁净度等参数控制要求相同的某一特定空间（可以是房间中的某个区域、单独的一个房间或多个房间）。单区域单风道定风量系统适用于空调热/冷负荷分布均匀的场合，广泛用于居住建筑和超市等商业建筑。

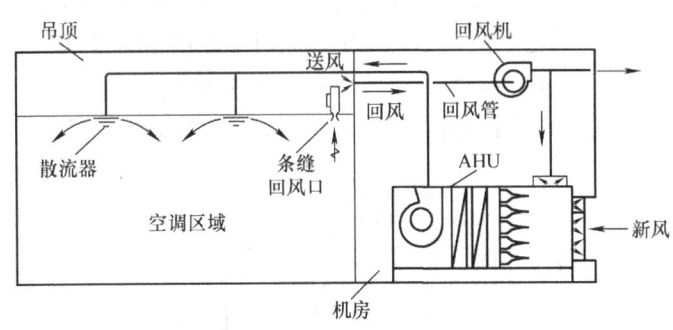

图4-11 单区域单风道定风量系统

2. 变风量单风道系统

变风量（VAV）系统是利用改变送入室内的空气量来实现对室内温湿度调节的全空气空调系统。负荷变化时系统的送风状态保持不变，只是调节风机改变送风量。单区域单风道变风量系统（图4-12）一般由空气处理机组、单风道送风管、变风量末端装置、柔性风管、送回风口、回风管以及回风机等组成。其空气处理机组与定风量系统一样，集中处理的空气送入空调区域的末端装置。当负荷变化时，变风量末端装置根据室内温度调节送风量，以维持室内温度。单区域变风量系统主要用于室内体育场馆、候机厅以及某些工业系统。

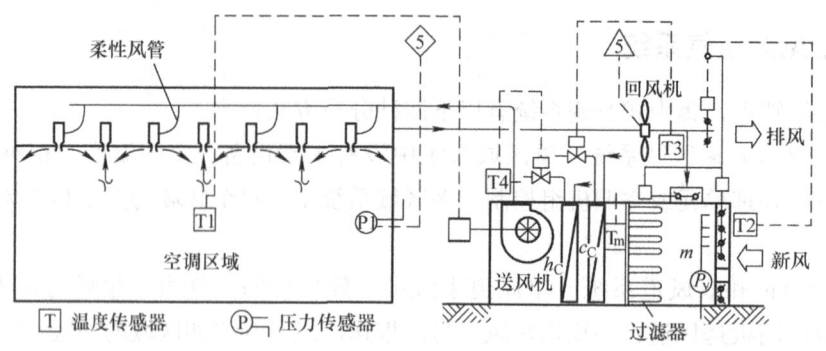

图 4-12　单区域单风道变风量系统

4.5　空气-水系统

目前使用的空气-水系统有风机盘管系统、诱导器系统和辐射供冷系统。

空气-水系统一般是由带加热或冷却盘管的末端装置以及独立的新风系统构成。末端装置（如风机盘管、诱导器）通常安装在离空调区域很近的地方，对室内空气进行循环处理，承担部分或全部室内负荷。新风系统是为了保证人体健康和维持室内正压，给房间补充新风量的设施，还可以承担部分室内负荷。空气-水系统中没有回风管，新风管是系统中唯一的干管；因此，节省了建筑空间。各区域或房间单独控制，不存在交叉污染。此外，空气-水系统的运行能耗比集中式空调系统低。但是末端装置中通常只安装低效过滤器，甚至不装过滤器；因此，室内空气品质难以保证。由于末端装置安装在空调区域附近，会产生噪声问题。此外，独立新风系统的送风量较小，发生火灾时不能用于防排烟，需要另设系统。

空气-水风机盘管系统包括冷热源（锅炉和冷水机组）、水系统（为风机盘管提供冷、热水）、风机盘管机组（循环处理室内空气）以及独立的新风系统，如图 4-13 所示。

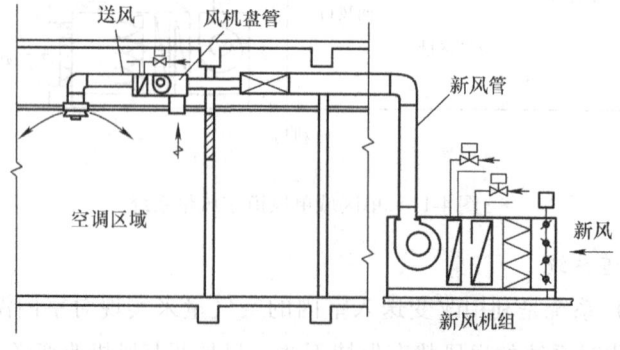

图 4-13　风机盘管加新风系统

1. 风机盘管机组

风机盘管机组简称风机盘管，是一种末端装置，直接安装在空调区域中或空调区域的顶棚中。风机盘管主要由一个离心风机或两个平行连接的风机、盘管、过滤器、控制器和外壳组成，如图 4-14 所示。从结构形式看，常用风机盘管有立式、卧式和柱式。

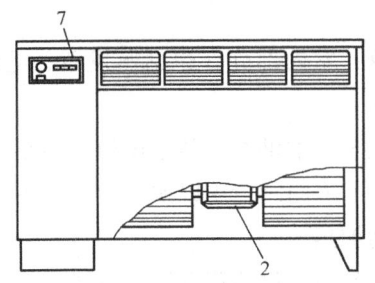 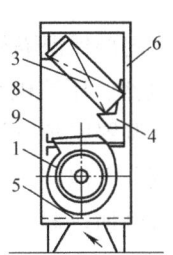

图 4-14　立式风机盘管构造

1—风机　2—发动机　3—盘管　4—凝结水盘　5—进风口
6—出风格栅　7—控制器　8—吸声材料　9—箱体

2. 独立新风系统

独立新风系统用于满足室内人员对新鲜空气的需求以及补偿排风。室外空气在独立的新风机组中冷却除湿、加热或加湿。集中处理过的新风输送到风机盘管机组中，与室内回风混合并进行二次处理。处理后的新风也可由送风管直接送入空调房间，在室内与经风机盘管处理后的回风混合。

3. 风机盘管水系统

风机盘管水系统分为双管制系统、三管制系统和四管制系统。

双管制系统包括供、回水管各一根。夏季向盘管提供冷水对空气进行冷却除湿，冬季向盘管提供热水对空气进行加热。盘管进口处通常设有双向阀，根据负荷变化调节供水量。双管制系统要求按季节进行冷热转换，因此其应用受到限制。

三管制系统包括两根供水管（冷冻水和热水）、一根回水管。盘管进口处设有三通阀，按需要供应冷水或热水。由于供冷、供热均使用同一根回水管，存在冷热量的混合损失。

四管制系统包括两根供水管（冷冻水和热水）和两根回水管。供冷、供热可使用同一盘管；也可设两个盘管，一个冷却盘管，一个加热盘管。四管制系统的初投资高，管路系统较复杂。但是系统无需冷、热工况的转换，易于操作，且运行费用比双管制系统少。因此，四管制系统的应用日趋增加，特别是带独立新风的系统已广泛用于宾馆、汽车旅店和医院。

4.6　冷剂式空调系统

冷剂式空调系统，也称机组式系统。空调工程中最常见的机组式系统有：房间空调器系统、单元式空调系统和水环热泵空调系统。

4.6.1　房间空调器

房间空调器是国内使用最广泛的空调机组，可以分为三类：窗式空调器、热泵式空调器、分体式空调器。目前,房间空调器的冷量一般在 1.5~10kW;常用的制冷剂为 HCFC-22,HFC-407C 和 HFC-410A 是 2020 年以后的替代工质。房间空调器的平均使用寿命是 10 年左右。

窗式空调器由内部保温隔板分成两部分:室内部分(包括蒸发器、毛细管和风机)、室外部分(包括冷凝器、压缩机和风机电动机)。

热泵式窗式空调器属于空气源热泵,用于夏季供冷、冬季供热。热泵式窗式空调器的结构与普通窗式空调器类似,只是多了一个四通换向阀,用以实现冷、热工况的切换。热泵式空调器中通常设有电加热器,冬季用于辅助加热。

分体式空调器由室内机和室外机构成:室内机包括蒸发器、进风口、送风口、风机和过滤器,室外机包括压缩机、冷凝器和风机。分体式空调器安置方便,并且有利于减少空调房间的振动和噪声。

4.6.2 单元式空调机组

单元式空调系统是中小型商业建筑和工业建筑中经常选用的空调系统形式。一个典型的单元式空调系统由送风管、回风管、散流器、回风口、单元式空调机组以及控制系统构成。其中,最主要的是单元机组,根据其结构特点可分为屋顶式空调机组、室内空调机组以及变制冷剂流量(VRV)系统;根据其运行工况可以分为单冷型和热泵型两类。热泵型单元机组多为空气源热泵,通过四通换向阀改变制冷剂流向,实现供冷工况和供热工况的切换。

屋顶式空调机安装在空调区域的屋顶上,如图 4-15 所示。在单元式机组中,屋顶式空调机广泛应用于低层商业建筑。一个典型的屋顶式空调机主要由机壳、室内风机、直接膨胀式蒸发器、过滤器、混合箱、活塞式/螺杆式压缩机、风冷冷凝器以及控件构成。还可根据空调需求增设燃气加热器、回风机或加湿器。

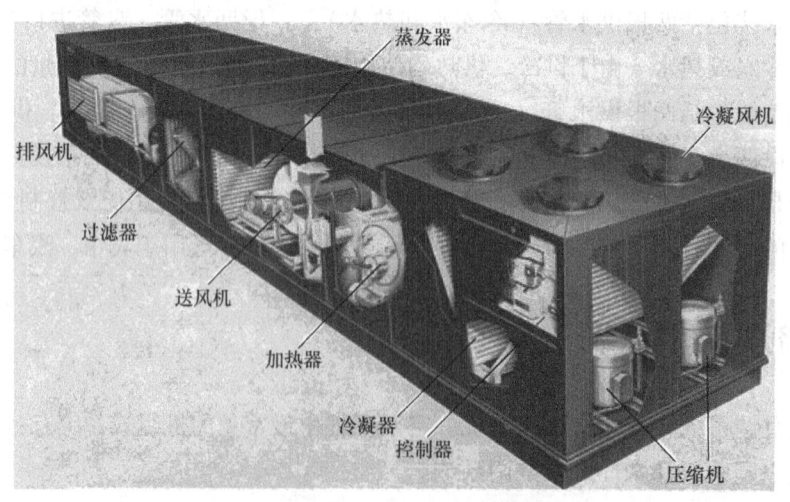

图 4-15 屋顶式空调机

室内空调机组一般安装在机房或设备间内。室内空调机和屋顶式空调机的最大区别在于其冷凝器的布置：如果是风冷冷凝器，采用分体式，冷凝器放在室外；如果是水冷式冷凝器，采用整体式。中小型室内空调机组也可以直接安装在地板上，利用风管送风或直接送风，例如用于计算机房的室内空调机组。

4.6.3 水环热泵空调系统

水环热泵系统就是小型的水/空气热泵机组的一种应用方式，即用水环路将小型的水/空气热泵机组并联在一起，构成一个以回收建筑物内余热为主要特点的热泵供暖、供冷的空调系统。在过渡季节和初冬，大型建筑周边区域的热泵机组从水环路吸热以供暖，内区热泵机组向水环路放热以供冷，通过水环路将内区的热量传递给周边区域。因此，水环热泵系统比常规空调系统节能。典型的闭式水环热泵系统由室内水源热泵、闭式冷却塔、加热设备、两台循环水泵（一用一备）、蓄热容器、控制系统、管道以及必要的附件构成。

4.7 制冷设备与系统

为了使某一物体或空间达到并维持所需要的低温，就得不断地从它们中间取出热量并转移到环境介质中去，这个不断地从被冷却对象取出并转移热量的过程就是制冷过程，简称制冷。这里所说的环境介质，就是指自然界的空气和水。制冷系统由一系列设备部件组合而成，以实现制冷过程。常见的空调用制冷系统有三类：蒸气压缩式制冷系统、吸收式制冷系统和气体喷射式制冷系统。其中，蒸气压缩制冷广泛用于舒适性和工艺性空调系统中。

4.7.1 制冷剂和冷媒

1. 制冷剂

制冷剂是在制冷装置中进行制冷循环的工作物质，也称为制冷工质。它吸收空间或物体（直接膨胀式系统中的空气或冷水机组中的冷冻水）的热量后，在制冷装置中循环，通过冷凝器把热量释放到周围环境介质中。制冷剂在制冷系统中循环流动，不断地从被冷却对象中吸收、转移并释放热量。

目前使用的制冷剂归纳起来可分为四类：无机化合物、烃类、卤代烃以及混合工质。

2. 冷媒

冷媒（也称载冷剂）是将制冷装置的制冷量传递给被冷却介质的媒介物质。在间接供冷系统中，它是必不可少的。常用的冷媒有空气、水、盐溶液、乙二醇等。水是空调用制冷系统中常用的冷媒，在空调工程中称其为冷冻水。

4.7.2 蒸气压缩式制冷系统

蒸气压缩式制冷系统广泛用于家用冰箱/冰柜、汽车空调、超市用制冷以及大多数的住宅、商业和工艺用空调中。

1. 理想蒸气压缩制冷循环

单级理想蒸气压缩制冷的具体工作流程如图 4-16 所示。压缩机排出的高温高压气体进入冷凝器，将热量传递给冷却水或空气而冷凝成液体（放热过程）。液体经过节流机构（膨胀阀）节流降压（节流过程），成为低压气液混合物进入蒸发器，吸收冷冻水热量而全部汽化（吸热过程）。然后，气体被吸进压缩机压缩（压缩过程），完成制冷循环。

2. 制冷系统主要设备部件

蒸气压缩式制冷系统的四大部件是：压缩机、冷凝器、蒸发器和节流机构。

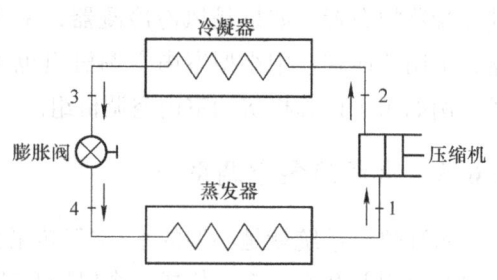

图 4-16　单级理想蒸气压缩制冷工作流程

1）压缩机是蒸气压缩式制冷机的核心组成部分，起着压缩和输送制冷剂的作用。根据压缩过程的特点，压缩机分为容积式和非容积式（速度式）两类。常见的容积式压缩机有活塞式、涡旋式、螺杆式和滚动转子式；而离心式压缩机是应用最广的非容积式压缩机。

2）冷凝器是制冷系统的主要设备，是一个间接接触的换热器。从压缩机出来的过热制冷剂蒸气，进入冷凝器后，向冷却介质（通常是空气或水）放热，过热蒸气在冷凝压力下变成饱和液体或过冷液体。冷凝器按其冷却介质和冷却方式，可以分为水冷式、空气冷却式（或称风冷式）和蒸发式三种类型。

3）蒸发器是制冷系统的主要部件，也是一个间接接触的换热器，制冷剂从环境介质（空气、冷冻水等）中吸热蒸发。蒸发器按照被冷却介质的种类，可分为三类：冷却液体载冷剂的蒸发器、冷却空气的蒸发器以及用于冰蓄冷的制冰机。

3. 常见蒸气压缩制冷机组

根据蒸发器中放热介质的不同，压缩制冷机组可分为两大类：

1）冷风机组：机组中的压缩机通常为活塞式、螺杆式和转子式。

2）冷水机组：风冷压缩式冷水机组的压缩机通常为活塞式和螺杆式两大类。根据压缩机类型不同，常见的水冷压缩式冷水机组有离心式冷水机组、螺杆式冷水机组和活塞式冷水机组三类。

4.7.3　吸收式制冷系统

吸收式制冷和蒸气压缩式制冷一样，都是利用制冷剂液体在汽化时要吸收汽化热这一物理特性来实现制冷的。所不同的是蒸气压缩式制冷是靠消耗机械功或电能，使热量从低温热源转移到高温热源的；而吸收式制冷则是依靠消耗热能来完成这种非自发过程的。吸收式制冷使用的工质是两种物质组成的二元溶液，称为"工质对"。溴化锂—水溶液是空调用吸收式制冷系统常用的工质对，水为制冷剂，溴化锂为吸收剂。

吸收式制冷系统（图 4-17）主要由四部分组成，即发生器、冷凝器、蒸发器和吸收器。它们组成两个循环环路：制冷剂循环和吸收剂循环。制冷剂循环由蒸发器、冷凝器和膨胀阀组成。高压气态制冷剂在冷凝器中向冷却水放热被凝结为液态后，经节流机构（膨胀阀）减压降温进入蒸发器。在蒸发器，该液体被汽化为低压制冷剂蒸气，同时吸取被冷却介质的热量产生制冷效应。这些过程与蒸气压缩式制冷是一样的。吸收剂循环主要由吸收器、发生器和溶液泵组成。在吸收器中，用液态吸收剂吸收蒸发器产生的低压气态制冷剂，以达到维持蒸发器内低压的目的。吸收剂吸收制冷剂蒸气而形成的制冷剂—吸收剂溶液，经溶液泵升压后进入发生器。在发生器中，该溶液被加热至沸腾，其中沸点低的制冷剂汽化形成高压气态制冷剂，又与吸收剂分离，然后前者去冷凝器液化，后者则返回吸收器再次吸收低压气态制冷剂。

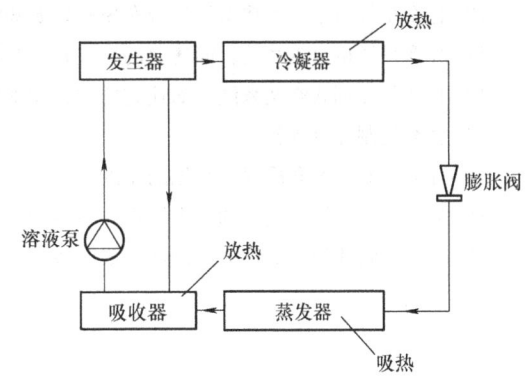

图 4-17　吸收式制冷系统

目前，常用的吸收式制冷机组有三类：
1）吸收式冷水机组，利用热能进行制冷。
2）吸收式冷热水机组，利用热能进行供冷或供热。
3）吸收式热泵机组，向低温热源吸热，供应热水或蒸汽或向空间供热。

4.7.4　热泵

热泵机组在冬季消耗少量的功由低温热源（空气或水）取热，向需热对象供应更多的热量，夏季系统消耗少量的功将需冷对象中的热量带走，释放到高温热汇（空气或水）中。热泵机组不但效率高，而且可以夏季供冷、冬季供热，实现一机两用。热泵机组包括了房间空调器或单元式空调机组中的主要部件，即风机、过滤器、压缩机、蒸发器、冷凝器、毛细管以及控制设备；热泵机组比普通压缩式制冷系统主要增加了四通换向阀。当机组从制冷工况转换到制热工况时，换向阀把制冷剂从冷凝器转换到蒸发器，蒸发器的空气通道相应地转换到冷凝器。根据低温热源的特点，通常把热泵分为空气源热泵、水源热泵和土壤源热泵。

习　　题

1. 什么是空气调节？空调系统的主要功能是什么？
2. 什么是湿空气？湿空气的基本物理性质有哪些？
3. 典型的空气状态变化过程有哪些？
4. 什么是舒适性空调和工艺性空调？分别举例说明。
5. 什么是冷负荷？冷负荷的特点是什么？
6. 如何计算空调负荷？
7. 什么是全空气系统？简述它的构成和主要特点。
8. 常见的全空气系统有哪些？
9. 什么是空气处理机组？空气处理机组的主要功能段有哪些？

10. 什么是气流组织？典型气流分布模式有哪些？
11. 什么是风机盘管系统？简述它的构成和主要特点。
12. 什么是冷剂式空调系统？简述它的构成和主要特点。
13. 什么是制冷过程？
14. 什么是制冷剂和冷媒？常见的制冷剂和冷媒有哪些？
15. 简述蒸气压缩式制冷的基本原理和主要设备。
16. 简述吸收式制冷的基本原理和主要设备。
17. 什么是热泵？

Chapter 4
Air Conditioning & Refrigeration

Abstract: This chapter introduces the basic functions and main components of air conditioning systems. This chapter briefly describes the classification of air conditioning systems. The characteristics of moist air are summarized. The configuration of all-air system, air-water system and refrigerant air conditioning system are introduced respectively. The basic principles and main components of refrigeration systems are introduced at last.

Key points: air conditioning, comfort air conditioning system, process air conditioning system, moist air, cooling/heating load, all-air system, space air diffusion, air-water system, refrigerant air conditioning system, refrigeration, vapor compression refrigeration systems, absorption refrigeration systems.

4.1 Air Conditioning and Air Conditioning Systems

4.1.1 The Concept of air Conditioning and the Function of Air Conditioning Systems

Air conditioning is a combined process that performs many functions simultaneously. It conditions the air, transports it, and introduces it to the conditioned space. An air conditioning system is composed of components and equipment, and often performs the following functions:

1) Provide the cooling and heating energy required.

2) Condition the supply air, that is, heat or cool, humidify or dehumidify, clean and purify, and attenuate any objectionable noise produced by the HVAC&R equipment.

3) Distribute the conditioned air, containing sufficient outdoor air, to the conditioned space.

4) Control and maintain the indoor environmental parameters-such as temperature, humidity, cleanliness, air movement, sound level, and pressure differential between the conditioned space and surroundings-within predetermined limits for the comfort and health of the occupants of the conditioned space or for the purpose of product processing.

4.1.2 Classification of Air Conditioning Systems

Air conditioning systems can be classified according to their applications into comfort air conditioning systems and process air conditioning systems.

Comfort air conditioning systems provide occupants with a comfortable and healthy indoor environment in which to carry out their activities. The various sectors of the economy using comfort air conditioning systems are as follows: the commercial sector includes office buildings, supermarkets, department stores, shopping centers, restaurants, and others; the residential and lodging sector consists of hotels, motels, apartment houses, and private homes; the institutional sector includes such applications as schools, colleges, universities, libraries, museums, indoor stadiums, hospitals, nursing homes, cinemas, theaters, concert halls, and recreation centers; the transportation sector includes aircraft, automobiles, railroad cars, buses, and cruising ships.

Process air conditioning systems provide needed indoor environmental control for manufacturing, product storage, or other research and development processes. The following areas are examples of process air conditioning systems. In textile mills, proper control of humidity increases the strength of the yarn and fabric during processing. A too high value of the relative humidity can cause problems in the spinning process. On the other hand, a lower relative humidity may induce static electricity which is harmful to the production processes. Many electronic products require clean rooms for manufacturing such things as integrated circuits, since their quality is adversely affected by airborne particles. Precision manufacturers always need precise temperature and relative humidity control during production of precision instruments, tools, and equipment. Pharmaceutical products require temperature, humidity, and air cleanliness control.

Air conditioning systems can also be classified into all-air systems, air-water systems, all-water systems, and refrigerant systems according to their media for cooling or heating.

4.2 Thermodynamic Properties of Moist Air

The design of air conditioning systems relies on an understanding of the properties of moist air.

4.2.1 Moist Air

The surface of the earth is surrounded by a layer of air called the atmosphere. From the point of view of psychrometrics, the lower atmosphere, or homosphere, is a mixture of dry air (including various contaminants) and water vapor, often known as moist air.

The composition of dry air is comparatively stable. It varies slightly according to geographic location and from time to time. The approximate composition of dry air by volume percent is listed in the Table 4-1.

Table 4-1 The approximate composition of dry air

Composition	Volume percent
Nitrogen	78.08

(续)

Composition	Volume percent
Oxygen	20.95
Argon	0.93
Carbon dioxide	0.03
Other gases such as neon, krypton, sulfur dioxide, etc.	0.01

The amount of water vapor present in moist air is fairly small. However, it has a significant influence on the characteristics of moist air. Although air contaminants may seriously affect the health of occupants of the air conditioned space, they have little effect on the thermodynamic properties of moist air since their mass concentration is low. For simplicity, moist air is always considered as a binary mixture of dry air and water vapor during the analysis and calculation of its properties.

4.2.2 Properties of Moist Air

The thermodynamic state of moist air can be characterized by many parameters, such as pressure, temperature, humidity, and so on. These parameters are called as state parameters of moist air.

1. Air Pressure

Dalton's law shows that for a mixture of gases occupying a given volume at a certain temperature, the total pressure of the mixture is equal to the sum of the partial pressures of the constituents of the mixture, i.e.,

$$p = p_1 + p_2 + \cdots \tag{4-1}$$

Where p—total pressure of mixture (Pa);

$p_1, p_2, \cdots$—partial pressure of constituents 1, 2, ... (Pa).

The partial pressure exerted by each constituent in the mixture is independent of the existence of other gases in the mixture.

Applying Dalton's law for moist air, we have

$$p_{at}(B) = p_g + p_q \tag{4-2}$$

Where $p_{at}(B)$—atmospheric pressure or pressure of the outdoor moist air (Pa);

p_g—partial pressure of dry air (Pa);

p_q—partial pressure of water vapor (Pa).

2. Air Temperature

The temperature of a substance is a measure of how hot or cold it is. The temperature scale is used to measure the temperature of various substances. Three kinds of temperature scales commonly used in the world are Kelvin scale, Celsius scale and Fahrenheit scale.

Absolute scale, or Kelvin scale, is denoted by T, with the unit of K. Celsius scale is denoted by t, with the unit of ℃. Fahrenheit scale is denoted by t, with the unit of ℉. The conversion from

Fahrenheit scale to Celsius scale is as follows:

$$t°C = \frac{5}{9}(t°F - 32) \tag{4-3}$$

Conversion between Kelvin and Celsius systems is

$$T = 273.15 + t°C \tag{4-4}$$

3. Humidity Ratio and Relative Humidity

The humidity ratio of moist air d is the ratio of the mass of water vapor to the mass of dry air contained in the mixture of the moist air. The humidity ratio can be calculated as

$$d = \frac{m_q}{m_g} \tag{4-5}$$

Where m_q—mass of water vapor (kg);

m_g—mass of dry air (kg).

The relative humidity of moist air φ, or RH, is defined as the ratio of the partial pressure of water vapor p_q in a moist air sample to the water vapor pressure of saturated moist air $p_{q,b}$ at the same temperature and pressure. This relationship can be expressed as

$$\varphi = \frac{p_q}{p_{q,b}} \times 100\% \tag{4-6}$$

4. Moist Volume and Density

Since the calculation and analysis of moist air are always related to a unit mass of dry air, for the sake of convenience, moist volume of moist air v_g, in m³/kg (a), is defined as the volume of the mixture of the dry air and water vapor when the mass of the dry air is exactly equal to 1 kg, that is

$$v_g = \frac{V}{m_g} \tag{4-7}$$

Where V—total volume of mixture (m³);

m_g—mass of dry air (kg).

Accordingly, air density ρ_g, in kg (a) /m³, should be defined as the ratio of the mass of dry air to the total volume of the mixture, i.e., the reciprocal of moist volume, or

$$\rho_g = \frac{m_g}{V} = \frac{1}{v_g} \tag{4-8}$$

5. Dew-point Temperature

The dew-point temperature is the temperature of saturated moist air of the same moist air sample, having the same humidity ratio, and at the same atmospheric pressure of the mixture. Two moist air samples at the same dew-point temperature will have the same humidity ratio and the same partial pressure of water vapor. At a specific atmospheric pressure, the dew-point temperature determines the humidity ratio and the water vapor pressure of the moist air. During the cooling process, when the cooling temperature is lower than the dew-point temperature of moisture, the dew will occur in moist air. Dew-point temperature is the critical temperature for whether dew or not.

6. Enthalpy

The difference in specific enthalpy Δh for an ideal gas, in kJ/kg, at a constant pressure can be defined as

$$\Delta h = c_p(t_2 - t_1) \tag{4-9}$$

Where c_p—specific heat at constant pressure $[kJ/(kg \cdot K)]$;

t_1、t_2—temperature of ideal gas at points 1 and 2 (℃).

As moist air is approximately a binary mixture of dry air and water vapor, the enthalpy of the moist air can be evaluated as

$$h = h_g + h_q \tag{4-10}$$

Where h_g, h_q—enthalpy of dry air and total enthalpy of water vapor $[kJ/kg (a)]$.

7. Sensible and Latent Heat

The enthalpy of moist air can be divided into two parts: sensible heat and latent heat. Sensible heat is the heat energy associated with the change of air temperature between two state points, and the latent heat of vaporization denotes the latent heat required to vaporize liquid water into water vapor. Also, the latent heat of condensation indicates the latent heat to be removed in the condensation of water vapor into liquid water. When moisture is added to or removed from a process or a space, a corresponding amount of latent heat is always involved, to vaporize the water or to condense water vapor.

8. Wet-bulb Temperature

The wet-bulb temperature is another unique property of a given moist air sample; hence, it is an important state parameter usually used in air conditioning engineering. A psychrometer is an instrument that permits one to determine the relative humidity of a moist air sample by measuring its dry-bulb and wet-bulb temperatures. A psychrometer consists of two thermometers. The sensing bulb of one of the thermometers is always kept dry. The temperature reading of the dry bulb is called the dry-bulb temperature. The sensing bulb of the other thermometer is wrapped with a piece of cotton wick, one end of which dips into a cup of distilled water. The surface of this bulb is always wet. When unsaturated moist air flows over the wet bulb of the psychrometer, liquid water on the surface of the cotton wick evaporates, and as a result, the temperature of the cotton wick and the wet bulb drops. At this time, the temperature reading of the wet bulb is called the wet-bulb temperature.

4.2.3 Basic Psychrometric Processes

Treatment of air is based on heating, cooling, humidification and dehumidification.

(1) Sensible heating processes   The sensible heating process occurs when moist air flows through a heating coil in which heat is transferred from the hot water inside the coil tubes to the moist air, or through an electric heater. A sensible heating process is a process in which heat is added to

the moist air, resulting in an increase in its temperature, while its humidity ratio remains constant.

(2) Sensible cooling processes The sensible cooling process occurs when moist air flows through a water cooling coil and the temperature of the entering chilled water in the coil and the outer surface temperature of the coil's tubes are higher than the dew point of entering air. A sensible cooling process removes heat from the moist air to the chilled water inside the cooling coil, resulting in a drop in its temperature while maintaining a constant humidity ratio of the moist air.

(3) Constant-enthalpy dehumidifying processes Absorption occurs when moist air flows over a bed of solid desiccant, at the bed of adsorbents. Solid adsorbents such as silica gels attract moisture because of the vapor pressure difference and the electric field at the desiccant's surface. During the desiccant dehumidification process, the humidity ratio of the leaving moist air is decreased. Although there is a heat loss through the outer casing of the dehumidifier to the ambient air, it is rather small compared with the release of the heat of sorption.

(4) Constant-Enthalpy Humidifying Processes An air washer is a device that sprays water into air to humidify, to cool and dehumidify, and to clean the air. When moist air flows through an air washer sprayed with recirculating water, the moist air is humidified and evaporatively cooled, tending to approach saturation. The temperature of recirculating water then approaches the wet-bulb temperature of the air entering the air washer.

(5) Constant-Temperature Humidifying Processes In a humidifying process using the steam injection, steam is often supplied from the main line to a grid-type humidifier and then injected directly into the air through small holes.

(6) Cooling and Dehumidifying Processes If the temperature of the entering chilled water in a water cooling coil and the outer surface temperature of the coil's tubes are lower than the dew point of entering air, condensation occurs on the outer surface of the coil tubes on water cooling coils. In air washer, if chilled water or a mixture of chilled water and recirculating water is used for spraying water, and its temperature is lower than the dew point of the entering air, the air is cooled and dehumidified.

4.3 Load Calculations

The first step in the design of air conditioning systems is to calculate loads. Cooling load calculations for air conditioning system design are mainly used to determine the volume flow rate of the air system as well as the coil and refrigeration load of the equipment—to size the HVAC&R equipment.

4.3.1 Indoor and Outdoor Design Conditions

In principle, the capacity of air conditioning equipment is selected so that indoor design conditions can be maintained when the outdoor weather does not exceed the design values.

1. Indoor Design Conditions

Indoor design parameters are those that influences directly to produce a required conditioned indoor environment in buildings. They are grouped as follows:

1) Basic design parameters: indoor air temperature, indoor relative humidity and indoor air movement.

2) Indoor air quality: air contaminants, outdoor ventilation rate provided and air cleanliness for processing.

3) Specific design parameters: sound level, and pressure differential between the space and surroundings.

According to GB 50019—2003 "Code for design of heating ventilation and air conditioning", indoor design parameters for comfort air conditioning systems are as follows:

Summer: dry-bulb temperature, $24 \sim 28 ℃$; relative humidity, $40\% \sim 65\%$; air speed, $\leqslant 0.3$ m/s.

Winter: dry-bulb temperature, $18 \sim 22 ℃$; relative humidity, $40\% \sim 60\%$; air speed, $\leqslant 0.2$ m/s.

2. Outdoor Design Conditions

The outdoor weather affects the space cooling load and the capacity of the air system to condition the required amount of outdoor air. It is not economical to choose the annual maximum or annual minimum values as the design data. Outdoor design conditions are usually determined according to statistical analysis of the weather data of the previous 30 years. GB 50019—2003 "Code for design of heating ventilation and air conditioning" gives summer and winter outdoor design conditions.

4.3.2 Cooling Load Calculation

1. Cooling Load Characteristics

To maintain the preset space air temperature, the heat that has been convected or released to the conditioned space should be removed from the space instantaneously. Space heat gain represents the rate at which heat enters a conditioned space from an external source or is released to the space from an internal source during a given time interval. Space cooling load, often simply called the cooling load, is the rate at which heat must be removed from a conditioned space so as to maintain a constant temperature and acceptable relative humidity.

The instantaneous sensible heat gains of the conditioned space can be classified into two categories: convective heat and radiative heat. The instantaneous space latent heat gain and convective sensible heat gain will be the same as the instantaneous space latent cooling load. The instantaneous radiative heat gain is absorbed by the slab, furnish and equipment. After absorption, the outer surface temperatures of the slab, furnish and equipment increase. The stored heat is released to the space air when surface temperatures of the slab, furnish and equipment are higher than the indoor air temperature. Such phenomenon results in a smaller instantaneous cooling load than that of the heat gain when it is at its maximum value during a diurnal cycle. To sum up, the instantaneous heat gain of a conditioned space is not equal to the instantaneous cooling load because of storage of part of the radiative heat inside the building structures, furnish and equipment.

2. Components of Cooling Load

Cooling load usually can be classified into two categories: external and internal.

(1) External cooling loads These loads are formed because of heat gains in the conditioned space from external sources through the building envelope or building shell and the partition walls.

(2) Internal cooling loads These loads are formed by the release of sensible and latent heat from the heat sources inside the conditioned space.

Cooling load is mainly used to determine the volume flow rate of the air system and to size the air handling equipment.

3. Components of Refrigerating Load

Refrigerating load is the rate at which heat is absorbed by the refrigerant at the evaporator. For central hydronic systems, the refrigerating load is the sum of the coil load plus the chilled water piping heat gain, pump power heat gain, and storage tank heat gain. For most water systems in commercial buildings, the water piping and pump power heat gain is only about 5 to 10 percent of the coil load. In an air conditioning system using DX coil (s), the refrigerating load is equal to the DX coil load.

Coil load is the rate of heat transfer at the coil. The cooling coil load is the rate at which heat is removed by the chilled water flowing through the coil or is absorbed by the refrigerant inside the coil. If the conductive heat gain from the coil's framework and the support is ignored, the cooling coil load consists of the following components:

1) Space cooling load including sensible and latent load.

2) Sensible and latent load because of the outdoor ventilation rates to meet the requirements of the occupants and others.

3) Supply system heat gain because of the supply fan heat gain, and supply duct heat gain.

4) Return system heat gain because of heat gains of recessed electric lights and ceiling plenum, of return duct, and return fan, if any.

4.3.3 Heating Load Calculation

The design heating load, or simply the heating load, is always the maximum heat energy that might possibly be required to supply the conditioned space at winter design conditions to maintain the winter indoor design temperature. All heating losses are instantaneous heating loads. Infiltration can not be considered exceptwhen the exterior window is not well sealed and there is a high wind velocity. The detailed calculation procedures for heating loads are referenced to documents.

4.4 All-air Systems

An all-air system consists of: a central plant in which a boiler and chillers are located, a water system to transport hot and chilled water from the central plant to the air handling units, and an air system often with air handling units to condition the mixture of outdoor and recirculating air and distribute the conditioned supply air to the conditioned space. Also, a return air system for energy saving, smoke control systems for multistory buildings according to fire codes, and mechanical exhaust systems may be required.

4.4.1 Air-Handling Units

An air handling unit (AHU) is the primary equipment in an air system to handle and condition the air. Air handling units may be classified into custom-built (or field-built) AHUs and factory-fabricated (or standard fabricated) AHUs. Custom-built AHUs are modular so that they have the flexibility to add components as required. A custom-built AHU (Fig. 4-1) basically consists of an outdoor air intake and mixing box section, a fan section including a supply fan and a fan motor, a coil section with a water cooling coil, a filter section, and a control section. Custom-built AHUs provide more flexibility in structure, system component arrangements, dimensions, and specialized functions than standard fabricated units, and are therefore widely used. Factory-fabricated AHUs own fixed functions.

In AHUs, main function sections in serial order are dedicated as follows.

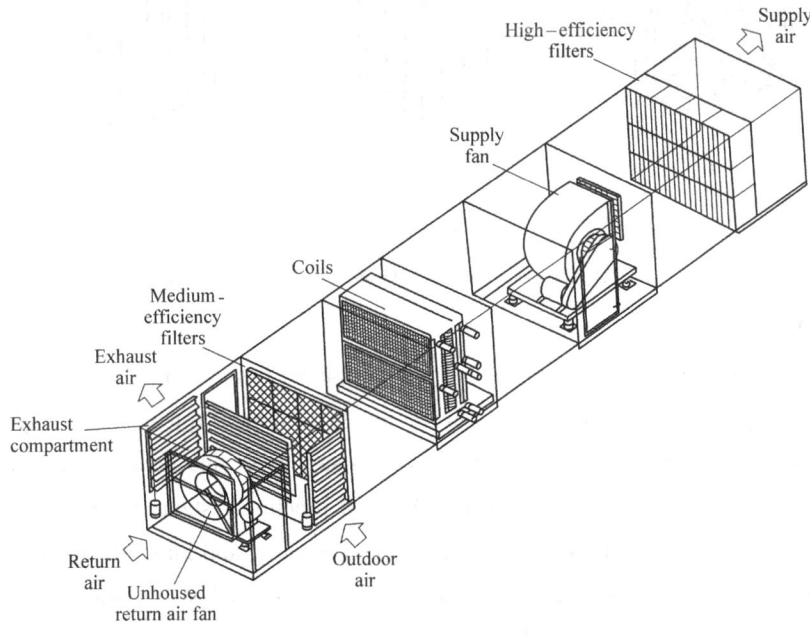

Fig. 4-1 Structure of a typical custom-built unit

1. Mixing Section

A mixing section usually includes an outdoor air intake, a return air intake, dampers, and a mixing box. The location of outdoor air intake has a direct impact on space IAQ. The outdoor air intake for each AHU should install with wind shield and louvers to prevent rain and birds. The outdoor air intake must be located as far away from the exhaust outlets. For better outdoor ventilation air control, an outdoor damper should split into two dampers: a minimum outdoor ventilation damper and an economizer damper of 100 percent outdoor air free cooling except in small AHUs. Poor mixing, such as parallel outdoor and recirculating airstreams in the mixing box, causes stratification of the mixture.

2. Filter

Air filtration is an important component to achieve an acceptable indoor air quality. In air conditioning engineering, air filters can be classified according to their efficiency as low-efficiency air filters, medium-efficiency air filters, high-efficiency air filters, and ultrahigh-efficiency filters. Low-efficiency air filters are often flat panel filters, pleated filters, bags, or sometimes automatic renewable rolling filters, as shown in Fig. 4-2. Low-efficiency filters are widely used in packaged units and air-handling units in commercial and institutional buildings, industrial workplaces, and more demanding residential applications. Medium-efficiency air filters are often bag and box filters with pleated mat. Medium-efficiency air filters are used in demanding commercial building and industrial applications.

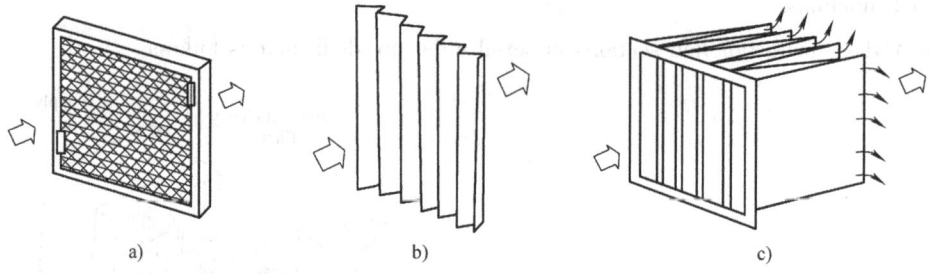

Fig. 4-2 Types of air filters
a) Flat panel filter b) Pleated filter c) Bag filter

3. Air Washer

The air washer was the first air conditioning equipment developed in 1904, and it is still used today to humidify, cool, and clean the air in many factories. Typical single-stage horizontal air washers are illustrated in Fig. 4-3. An air washer consists of spraying banks with nozzles, a bank of guided baffles, eliminators, casing, water tank, and pipeline systems. Currently, air washers are used to perform one or more of the following functions: cooling and humidification; cooling and dehumidification; washing and cleaning. Air washes are widely used in demanding industrial applications, such as textile industry and tobacco industry.

4. Cooling Coil

A water cooling coil uses chilled water as the coolant inside the tubes. The chilled water cools or cools and dehumidifies the moist air that flows over the external surface of the tubes and fins, as shown in Fig. 4-4. To maintain a higher rate of heat transfer, the air and water normally follow a counterflow arrangement; i.e., coldest air meets the coldest water and the warmest air meets the warmest water. The water tubes are usually copper tubes of 15 mm diameter with a thickness of 0.25 to 0.5 mm. The tubes may be arranged along the airflows in 4, 6, or 8 rows, in either staggered or aligned form. The staggered arrangement provides better heat transfer and a higher air pressure drop.

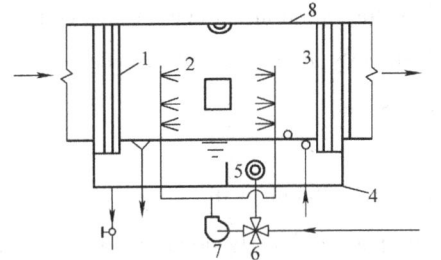

Fig. 4-3   Schematic diagrams of horizontal air washers

1—Baffle   2—Nozzles   3—Eliminator
4—Water basin   5—Water strainer
6—3-way valve   7—Pump   8—Casing

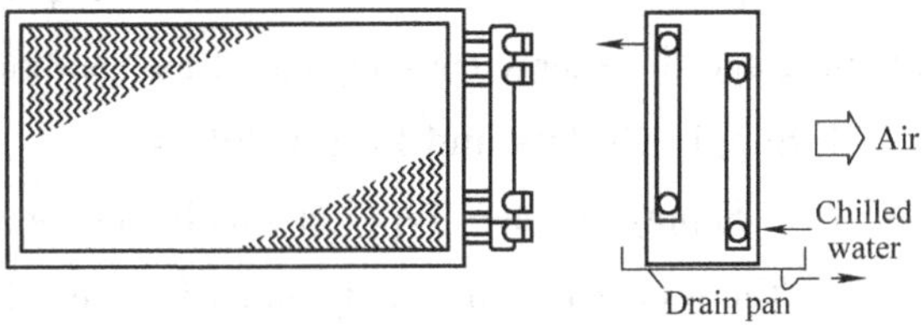

Fig. 4-4   Water cooling coil

5. Heating Coils

Heating coils can be classified into water heating coils and steam heating coils. The water heating coil is similar in construction to the water cooling coil. There are two main differences between them. Hot water, instead of chilled water, is used as the heating medium in a water heating coil. Also, there are fewer rows in the water heating coil than in the water cooling coil. Generally, one-, two-, or four-row water heating coils are available on the market. Water heating coils are rated at temperatures up to 120℃.

6. Humidifier

Usually, there is no humidifier installed in the AHU for comfort air conditioning systems; but the outdoor climate is very cold in winter so that if a humidifier is not employed, the winter indoor relative humidity may be too low. Humidifiers are necessary for health care facilities and processing systems in pharmaceutical, semiconductor, textile, communication centers, and computer rooms. Steam humidifiers or electric heating element humidifiers, are widely used in AHUs for commercial and industrial applications.

7. Fans

Supply volume flow rates of AHUs vary from 1000 to 25000 L/s. Selection of a fan for a given air system actually is done in two stages: selection of fan type and determination of fan size. An axial relief fan or an unhoused centrifugal return fan may be added as an optional system component when the total pressure loss of the return system is considerable.

4.4.2 Space Air Diffusion

Space air diffusion distributes the conditioned air containing outdoor air to the occupied zone (or a given enclosure) in a conditioned space according to the occupants' requirements. A satisfactory space air diffusion evenly distributes the conditioned and outdoor air to provide a healthful and comfortable indoor environment for the occupants or the appropriate environment for a specific manufacturing process, at optimum cost. Because space air diffusion is the last process of air conditioning and takes place entirely within the conditioned space, it directly affects the effectiveness of air conditioning and the energy consumption of air conditioning system.

1. Supply Outlets and Return Inlets

(1) Supply outlets Types of supply outlets are directly influenced the air jet and the airflow pattern. The proper type of supply outlet for a conditioned space is largely determined by the architectural setup of the room, the airflow pattern needed, the indoor environmental requirements, and the load conditions.

1) Grilles and registers. Grilles and registers are commonly used high side outlets. A high side outlet may be a sidewall outlet mounted at the high level of a conditioned space. A grille is an outlet for supply air or an inlet for return air or exhaust air. Grilles are generally used for air conditioning projects. Registers with volume control dampers or adjustable vanes are the most widely used in high side outlets. Fig. 4-5 shows a single-deflection grille.

2) Ceiling diffusers. Ceiling diffusers are often mounted at the ceiling of the conditioned space and discharge air in all directions. A ceiling diffuser consists of a series of concentric rings or inner cones made up of vanes arranged in fixed directions and an outer shell or frame, as shown in Fig. 4-6. Supply air is discharged through the concentric air passages or directional passages in one, two, three, or in all directions by using different types of inner cone and vanes. Ceiling diffusers produce a better surface effect, a shorter throw, a lower and more even distribution of air velocity,

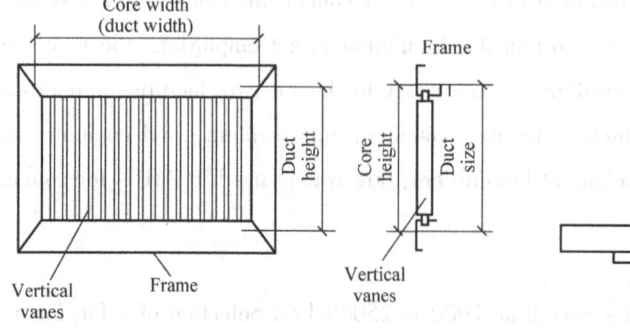

Fig. 4-5 Single-deflection (vertical vanes)

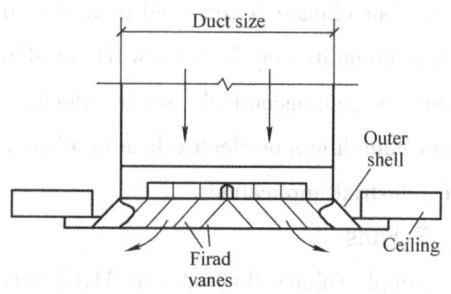

Fig. 4-6 Ceiling diffusers

and a more even temperature in the occupied zone. Ceiling diffusers can be round, square, or rectangular. Square diffusers are most widely used.

(2) Return and exhaust inlets   In return and exhaust inlets, air velocity decreases very sharply as the distance from the surface of the inlet increases. This phenomenon is the major difference in airflow characteristics between a return inlet and a supply outlet. Return grilles and registers, similar in shape and construction to supply grilles and registers, are widely used in commercial applications.

2. Typical Airflow Patterns

Airflow pattern determines the performance of space air diffusion in the occupied zone of commercial buildings or in the working area of a factory. The optimum airflow pattern for an occupied zone depends mainly on types and locations of supply outlets; the supply air temperature and air velocity; the indoor temperature, relative humidity, and indoor air quality requirements; and characteristics of the building. Three types of airflow patterns are currently used in air conditioned space.

(1) Air supply using high sidewall outlets   A high side outlet may be a sidewall outlet mounted at the high level of a conditioned space, or an outlet mounted directly on the supply duct. Several airflow patterns using high side outlets are shown in Fig. 4-7. As the air jet discharges from the high sidewall outlet horizontally, the surface effect tends to keep the air jet in contact with the ceiling. During cooling, the air jet is deflected downward by the opposite wall, and enters the occupied zone with excessive air velocity. Grilles, registers and slot diffusers are widely used as high side outlets.

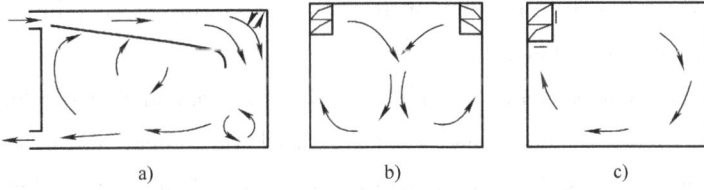

Fig. 4-7   Airflow patterns of air supply using high side outlets

(2) Air supply using ceiling diffusers   Airflow patterns of air supply using ceiling diffusers include horizontal airflow and downward airflow. Ceiling diffusers with horizontal airflow produce a better surface effect, a shorter throw, a lower and more even distribution of air velocity, and a more even temperature in the occupied zone than sidewall outlets. Many ceiling diffusers are designed to have a high induction ratio and to produce a very good surface effect. These ceiling diffusers are often used in variable-air-volume systems.

(3) Upward flow   Upward flow from a raised floor has been successfully used for space air diffusion in computer rooms and other industrial applications with high cooling load density. Fig. 4-8 shows an upward flow space air diffusion from a raised floor plenum—an underfloor air distribution system. For this airflow pattern, conditioned air (including outdoor ventilation air) is supplied to

the occupied zone directly, which results in a better indoor air quality. Usually there is no stagnant air in the occupied zone. Upward airflow carries most of the lighting heat gains at high level to the ceiling plenum; this results in a higher return air temperature and, therefore, a higher space diffusion effectiveness factor and a low space cooling load.

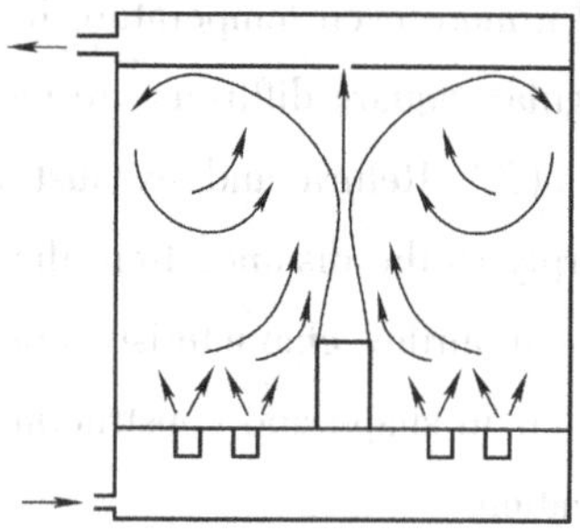

4.4.3 Water Systems

Fig. 4-8 Upward flow: upward flow underfloor air distribution

Water systems that are part of an air conditioning system and that link the central plant, chiller/boiler, air-handling units (AHUs), and terminals may be classified into chilled water system, hot water system and condenser water system. Hot water systems are covered in greater detail inChap. 3.

1. Chilled Water System

Chilled water is first cooled in the water chiller to a temperature of 5 to 9℃, mostly 7℃. It is then pumped to the water cooling coils in AHUs and terminals. After flowing through the coils, the chilled water increases in temperature by 5℃ to 10℃, usually 5℃, and then returns to the chiller. Chilled water systems may be classified in different ways.

1) Chilled water systems can be classified according to their operating characteristics into closed system and open system. In a closed system, chilled or hot water flowing through the coils, heaters, chillers, boilers, or other heat exchangers forms a closed recirculating loop. In a closed system, water is not exposed to the atmosphere during its flowing process. In an open system, the water is exposed to the atmosphere.

2) Closed water systems can be classified into direct return and reverse return according to water loops. The direct-return system is more commonly used. The system must be carefully analyzed to avoid flow-balancing problems. The reverse-return system is preferable from a control and balancing point of view, since it provides closely balanced flow rates. However, the additional piping for a reverse-return system is usually not economical.

3) Closed water systems can also be classified into constant-flow and variable-flow systems. A constant-flow water system is a system for which the volume flow at any cross-sectional plane in the supply or return mains remains constant during the operating period. Three-way mixing valves are used to modulate the water flow rates to the coils. In a variable-flow system, all or part of the volume flow varies when the system load changes during the operating period. Two-way valves are used to modulate the water flow rates to the coils or terminals.

4) According to the number of supply mains and return mains, water systems may be classified into two-pipe systems and four-pipe systems. The water piping can be either a two-pipe system, with a supply main and a return main, as shown in Fig. 4-9; or a four-pipe system, with a hot water supply main, a hot water return main, a chilled water supply main, and a chilled water return

main. For a two-pipe system, it is impossible to heat and cool two different coils or terminals in the same zone simultaneously. Changeover from summer cooling mode operation to winter heating mode operation is required. A four-pipe system does not need changeover operation. Chilled and hot water can be supplied to the coils or terminals simultaneously. However, a four-pipe system requires a greater installation cost.

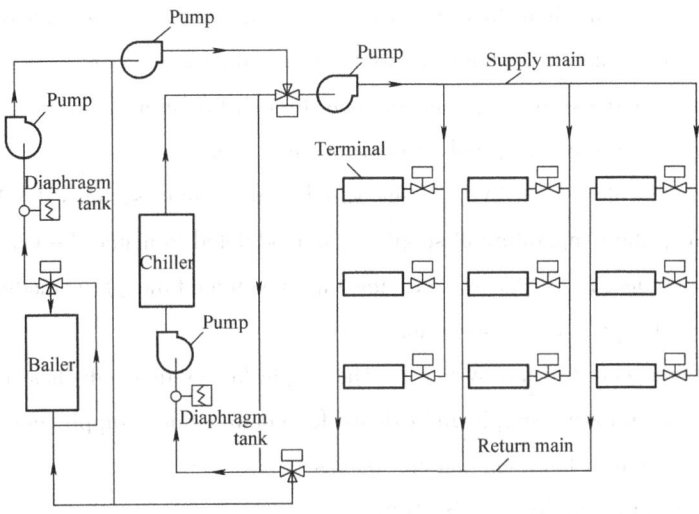

Fig. 4-9 Two-pipe systems

2. Condenser Water System

In a condenser water or cooling water system, the latent heat of condensation is removed from the refrigerant in the condenser by the condenser water. This cooling water either is from the cooling tower or is surface water taken from a lake, river, sea, or well. The temperature of the cooling water depends mainly on the local climate. The mechanical cooling water system consists of a cooling tower, a condenser water pump, and water loops, as shown in Fig. 4-10. A cooling tower is a device in which recirculating condenser water from a condenser or cooling coils is evaporatively cooled by contact with atmospheric air. Most cooling towers used in refrigerating plants for commercial buildings or industrial applications for air conditioning are mechanical draft cooling towers which uses fan (s) to extract atmospheric air. Great detail about cooling water systems should be referred to documents.

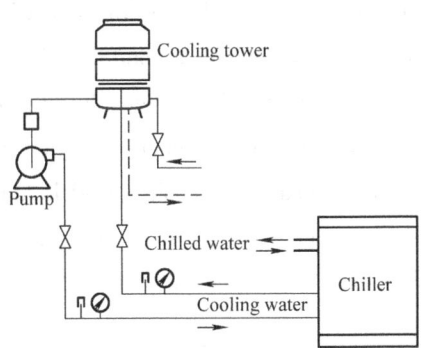

Fig. 4-10 Cooling water systems

4.4.4 Commonly Used All-air Systems

Central air conditioning systems, in a narrower sense, can be classified into the following categories according to their system characteristics:

(1) Single-zone versus multizone systems   In a single-zone system, there is no terminal. Space temperature, relative humidity, and volume flow rate are controlled directly by the coils, humidifiers, and inlet vanes or ac inverter in the air-handling unit or packaged unit. In a multizone system, zone temperature or zone supply volume flow rate is controlled by terminals.

(2) Single-duct versus dual-duct systems   In a single-duct system, conditioned air is supplied to the conditioned space by a single supply duct. In a dual-duct system, conditioned air is supplied to the conditioned space in the perimeter zone through two supply ducts: a warm air duct and a cold air duct. In the interior zone, only a cold air duct is needed.

(3) Constant-air-volume (CAV) versus variable-air-volume systems (VAV)   In a constant-volume system, the temperature of supply air is modulated to match the variation of space load during part-load operation. In a VAV system, the supply volume flow rate is modulated to maintain a predetermined space temperature as space load varies.

(4) Single-fan versus two-fan systems   The single-fan system only has a supply fan. Three two-fan systems are often used: supply and exhaust fan combination, supply and relief fan combination, and supply and return fan combination systems.

1. Constant-volume Single-duct System

A single-zone, single-duct, constant-volume, and outdoor air and recirculating air mixing system is a basic all-air system used in a temperature-controlled area (Fig. 4-11). A constant-volume system means that there is a constant volume of supply air throughout the operating period. Supply air temperature is varied when the space load reduces in part-load operation. Single-zone state indicates that the system serves a conditioned space which is controlled to maintain a unique indoor temperature, relative humidity, cleanliness, and other parameters, either a volume or a site without a partition or a partitioned room or group of rooms. This system will maintain comfort conditions in an area where the heating or cooling load is fairly uniform throughout the space. Therefore, single-zone single-duct, constant-volume systems have been widely used in residential buildings and small retail stores in commercial buildings.

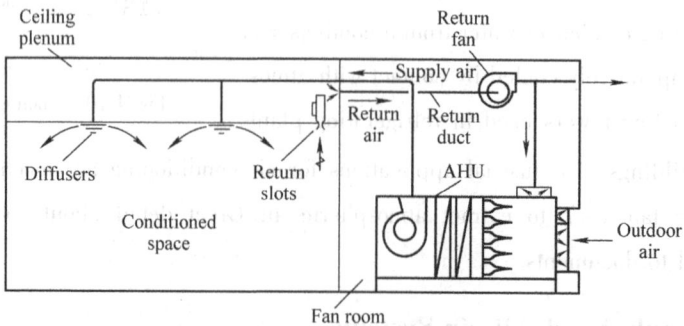

Fig. 4-11   Single-duct constant-volume system

2. VAV Single-duct System

A single-zone variable-air-volume (VAV) system (Fig. 4-12) is an air system that varies its supply air volume flow rate to match the reduction of space load during part-load operation to maintain a predetermined space parameter, usually air temperature, and to conserve fan power at reduced volume flow. The system typically consists of a central air-handling unit with heating and cooling coil, single-duct supply system, VAV box, supply duct with air diffuser, return air duct, and return air fan. Constant-temperature air is provided from the central air-handling unit through a single-supply air duct to the individual VAV box which regulates supply air to zone to offset cooling load requirements. Single-zone VAV systems are widely used in arenas, indoor stadiums, airport terminals, and many industrial applications.

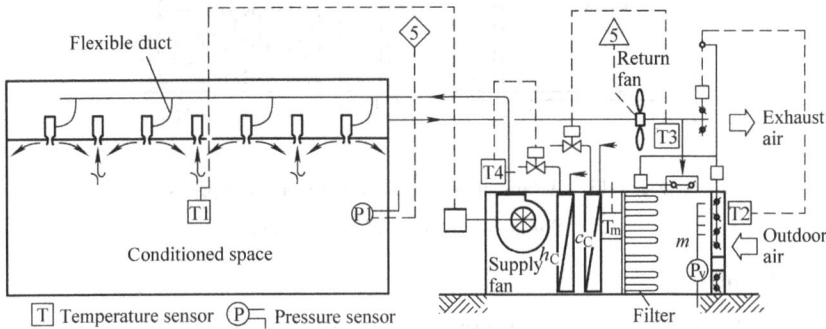

Fig. 4-12 Single-zone VAV system

4.5 Air-water Systems

Currently used air-water systems can be subdivided into fan-coil air conditioning systems, induction unit air conditioning systems, and panel cooling systems.

An air-water system includes terminals with a heating or cooling coil and a separately dedicated outdoor ventilation system. Both heating and cooling terminals, such as fan coils or induction units, are installed very near to the conditioned space in order to condition the recirculating air. The separately dedicated outdoor ventilation system is always required to provide ventilation air for occupants as well as the necessary exhaust air. There is no return duct in a space conditioning system. The outdoor ventilation air duct is probably the only main duct with comparatively less headroom required than in the supply duct that crosses under the beams in the ceiling plenum. There is less cross-contamination between rooms and control zones. The energy use of an air-water system is less than other air conditioning systems, such as VAV or CAV systems. However, only low-efficiency filters are used in terminals, even no filters. Because fan coils and induction units are often mounted directly above or near the conditioned space, they may create a noise problem. In addition, the volume flow rate of outdoor ventilation air is not sufficient to prevent smoke contamination in case of a building fire.

A fan-coil system includes boilers and chillers in the central plant, water system supplying chilled or hot water to the fan coils, a space recirculating system using fan coils to condition the space recirculating air, and a dedicated outdoor ventilation air system using an outdoor air AHU to condition the outdoor air, as shown in Fig. 4-13.

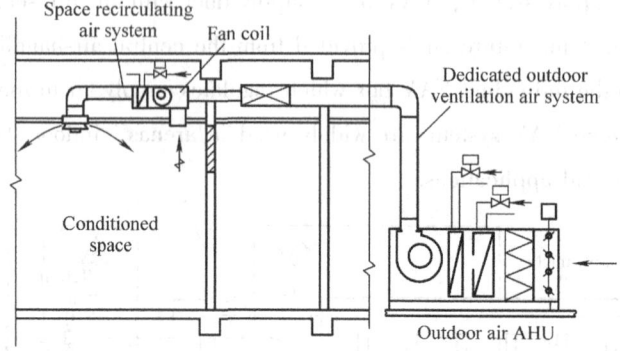

Fig. 4-13　A fan-coil system with outdoor air supplied to the mixing plenum of fan-coil unit

1. Fan-coil Units

A fan-coil unit, or a fan coil, is a terminal unit installed directly inside the conditioned space or in the ceiling plenum just above the conditioned space. A fan-coil unit includes a small motor driven centrifugal fan or two small centrifugal fans connected in parallel, a finned coil, a filter, an outer casing, and controls, as shown in Fig. 4-14. A fan-coil unit can be a horizontal unit installed inside the ceiling plenum, or a vertical unit mounted on the floor under the windowsill, or a stack unit installed vertically along the two sides of the window.

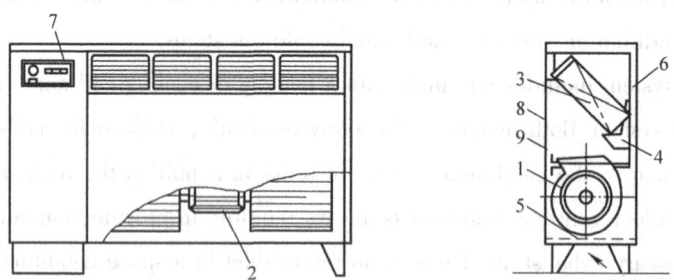

Fig. 4-14　Schematic diagrams of vertical fan-coil units

1—Centrifugal fan　2—Motor　3—Coil　4—Drain pan　5—Inlet with a filter
6—Outlet　7—Controller　8—Inner lined layer　9—Casing

2. Dedicated Outdoor Ventilation Air Systems

The dedicated outdoor ventilation system is always required to provide ventilation air for occupants as well as the necessary exhaust air. Outdoor air is often cooled and dehumidified, heated, or sometimes even humidified in a separate outdoor air or makeup AHU. The outdoor air is then transported to the fan coils where outdoor air is mixed with the recirculated air and conditioned. If the conditioned outdoor air is supplied directly to the conditioned space via supply ducts in the dedicated ventilation system, then it is mixed with the conditioned recirculating air from the fan coil of the space recirculating system in the space.

3. Water Systems

Water systems for fan-coils may be classified into two-pipe systems, three-pipe systems, and four-pipe systems.

A two-pipe system is equipped with a supply pipe and a return pipe. In such a system, chilled water is supplied to the coil to cool and dehumidify the air during cooling mode operation. In heating mode operation, chilled water is changed over to hot water and then supplied to the coil to heat the air. A two-way valve is usually installed before the coil inlet, and saves pump power at part-load operation when the water flow rate is reduced. Because of the waste of energy and the difficulties in changeover operations, the applications of two-pipe fan-coil systems are comparatively less.

A three-pipe system is equipped with a hot water supply pipe, a chilled water supply pipe, and a common return pipe. A three-way valve is usually installed before the coil inlet. The three-pipe system has been discontinued because of the energy loss in the common return pipe.

A four-pipe fan-coil system is equipped with two supply mains: a chilled water supply and a hot water supply. There are also two return mains: a chilled water return and a hot water return. The finned coil may be a common coil or two separate coils, a cooling coil and a heating coil. A four-pipe system has a higher initial cost, and many pipes must be squeezed into the ceiling plenum. On the other hand, it is more flexible, easy to operate because there are no troublesome changeover problems, and lower in operating cost than a two-pipe system. Four-pipe fan-coil systems with a dedicated ventilation and space recirculating air system are widely used in hotels, motels and hospitals.

4.6 Refrigerant Air Conditioning Systems

Refrigerant air conditioning systems can be called individual air conditioning systems. Individual systems can be subdivided into: room air conditioning systems, unitary packaged air conditioning systems, and water-source heat pump systems.

4.6.1 Room Air Conditioning Systems

Room air conditioning systems are the most widely used individual air conditioning system in China. Window-mounted or through-the-wall types of room air conditioners, room heat pumps, and split air conditioners are three kinds of equipment used in room air conditioning systems. The cooling capacity of currently available room air conditioners ranges between 1.5 and 10 kW. Refrigerant

HCFC-22 and alternative refrigerants HFC-407C and HFC-410A are the refrigerants used now and after 2020. The average service life of a room air conditioner is about 10 years.

Window-mounted air conditioner is divided into indoor and outdoor compartments which are separated by insulated wall to reduce the heat transfer. The DX coil, capillary tube, and indoor fan are in the indoor compartment. The outdoor compartment contains the compressors, condensers, outdoor fan, and fan motor.

A room heat pump, a kind of air-source heat pumps, is used to provide both heating in winter and cooling in summer. It has a similar configuration to a room air conditioner except that a four-way reversing valve is added to change from cooling mode to heating mode, and vice versa. Electric resistance heating is often used in room heat pumps to supplement the winter heating when the outside weather is cold.

A split air conditioner is a room air conditioner separated into two split units, namely an outdoor condensing unit with compressor and condenser and an indoor air handler for the sake of greater flexibility in location of the air handler as well as isolation of compressor noise outdoors.

4.6.2 Unitary Packaged Air Conditioning Systems

Unitary packaged air conditioning systems can be called, in brief, packaged systems. It is the most widely used system in small- and medium-size air conditioning systems in both commercial and industrial buildings. A typical packaged system consists of supply ducts, return ducts, diffusers, return inlets, controls, and a packaged unit. The primary equipment of unitary packaged systems are integrated, factory-assembled, and ready-to-use packaged units, which can be subdivided according to their configuration and operating characteristics into rooftop packaged units, indoor packaged units, and VRV systems. A packaged unit can also be a packaged heat pump. Most of them are air-source heat pumps. In a packaged heat pump, in addition to the fan, DX coil, filters, compressors, condensers, expansion valves and controls, there are four-way reversing valves to reverse the refrigerant flow when cooling mode operation is changed to heating mode operation.

A rooftop packaged unit is mounted on the roof of the conditioned space, as shown in Fig. 4-15. Among packaged units, rooftop packaged units are most widely used in low-rise commercial buildings. A typical rooftop packaged unit consists of mainly a casing, an indoor fan, DX coils, filters, a mixing box, a reciprocating or scroll compressor, a outdoor condenser, and controls. A gas-fired heater, a relief or return fan, and a humidifier are optional.

An indoor packaged unit is usually installed indoors inside a fan room or a machinery room. An indoor packaged unit differs from a rooftop packaged unit in condensing arrangements. Usually there are two alternatives in indoor packaged units: an air-cooled condenser located on the rooftop, a water-cooled condenser installed inside the unit. A small- or medium-size indoor packaged unit may sometimes be floor-mounted directly inside the conditioned space with or without connected ductwork, such as the indoor packaged unit in computer rooms.

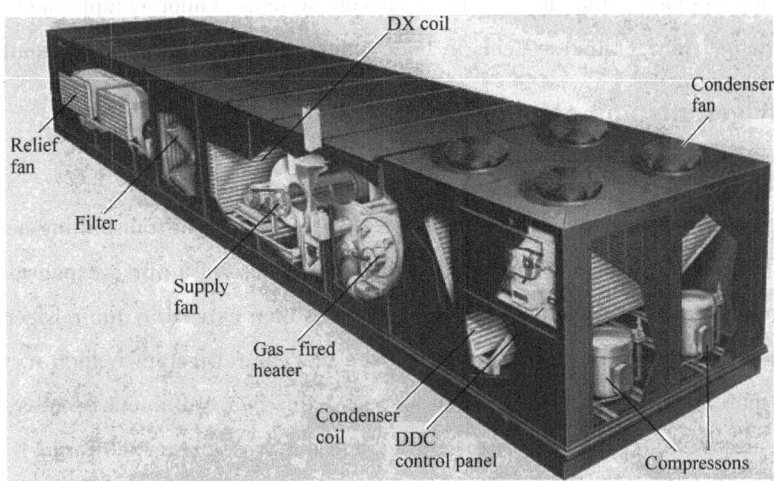

Fig. 4-15 A typical rooftop packaged unit

4.6.3 Water-source Heat Pump Systems

In a water-source heat pump system, some water-source heat pumps located in the shady side of the perimeter zone of a building may extract heat from a water loop to heat the supply air, and other water-source heat pumps in the core part of the building may reject heat to the water loop to cool the supply air. Excess heat is therefore transferred from the core of the building to the perimeter zone of the building. A water-source heat pump system conserves more energy than many other air conditioning systems only when simultaneous heating and cooling occur in a building and therefore excessive heat from the core part is recovered and transferred to the perimeter zone of the building. A typical closed-circuit water-source heat pump system consists of water-source heat pumps, an evaporative water cooler, a boiler or water heater, two water circulating pumps, an expansion tank, piping, necessary accessories, and controls. One of the water circulating pumps is the lead pump, the other is a standby.

4.7 Refrigeration Equipment and Systems

Refrigeration is defined as the process of extracting heat from a lower-temperature heat source, substance, or cooling medium and transferring it to a higher-temperature heat sink. Refrigeration maintains the temperature of the heat source below that of its surroundings while transferring the extracted heat, and any required energy input, to a heat sink, atmospheric air, or surface water. A refrigeration system is a combination of components and equipment connected in a sequential order to produce the refrigeration effect. The refrigeration systems commonly used for air conditioning can be classified by the type of input energy and the refrigeration process as follows: vapor compression systems, absorption systems, and air or gas expansion systems. Vapor compression systems are the most widely adopted refrigeration systems in both comfort and process air conditioning.

4.7.1 Refrigerants and Cooling Media

1. Refrigerants

A refrigerant is the primary working fluid used for absorbing and transmitting heat in a refrigeration system. They absorb heat from the medium (air in the case of a direct expansion air conditioner or water for a chiller) to be cooled. The absorbed heat is then carried by the refrigerant to a heat rejector, e.g. condenser, where the heat can be given up. The refrigerant is then recycled in the system to absorb more heat. In most refrigeration systems, this is a continuous process, so heat is continually being absorbed and rejected as the refrigerant is moved around the cycle.

Chemicals suitable for use as refrigerants can be broadly broken down into four major classifications: inorganic refrigerants, hydrocarbons, halocarbons, and refrigerant blends.

2. Cooling Media

A cooling medium is the working fluid cooled by the refrigerant to transport the cooling effect between a central plant and remote cooling units and terminals. Air, water, brine, and glycol are used as cooling media in many refrigeration systems. Water is the commonly used cooling media in most air conditioning systems, therefore is often called chilled water.

4.7.2 Vapor Compression Refrigeration Systems

Vapor compression systems are the most widely adopted refrigeration systems in household refrigerator/freezers, automobile air conditioning, most residential, commercial and institutional air conditioning and commercial (supermarket) refrigeration.

1. Ideal Vapor Compression Cycle

Fig. 4-16 shows an ideal single-stage vapor compression cycle. In vapor compression systems, compressors activate the refrigerant by compressing it to a higher pressure and higher temperature level after it has produced its refrigeration effect. The compressed refrigerant transfers its heat to the sink (usually water or air) and is condensed to liquid form. This liquid refrigerant is then throttled in the throttling device to a low-pressure, low-temperature vapor to produce refrigerating effect by evaporation in the evaporator. The vapor compression cycle is the most common type of refrigeration cycle.

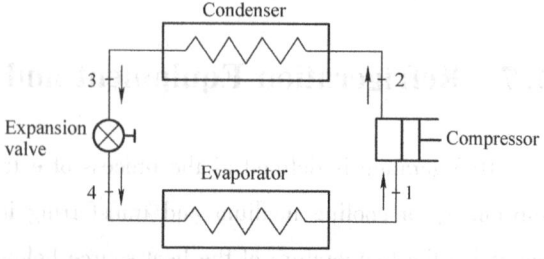

Fig. 4-16 Schematic diagram of single-stage ideal vapor compression cycle

2. Main Components of Refrigeration Systems

Vapor compression systems consist of four main components, namely compressors, condensers, evaporators, and throttling devices.

1) Refrigeration compressors. A refrigeration compressor is the heart of a vapor compression refrigeration system. Its function is to raise the pressure of the refrigerant and provide the primary force to circulate the refrigerant. According to the characteristics of the compression process, currently used refrigeration compressors can be classified as positive displacement compressors and non-positive displacement compressors. Positive displacement compressor mainly includes reciprocating, scroll, screw, and rotary compressors. The only type of non-positive displacement refrigeration compressor widely used in refrigeration systems is the centrifugal compressor.

2) Condensers. A condenser is a major system component of a refrigeration system. It is also an indirect-contact heat exchanger in which the total heat rejected from the refrigerant is removed by a cooling medium, usually air or water. As a result, the gaseous refrigerant is cooled and condensed to liquid at the condensing pressure. Based on the cooling medium used, condensers used in refrigeration systems can be classified into water-cooled condensers, air-cooled condensers and evaporative condensers.

3) Evaporators. The evaporator is one of the main components of a refrigeration system, in which refrigerant evaporates for the purpose of extracting heat from the surrounding air, chilled water, or other substances. In vapor compression refrigeration systems, the evaporator is also an indirect-contact heat exchanger. Evaporators can be classified into three categories, depending on the medium or substance to be cooled: air coolers, liquid coolers, and ice makers for ice storage systems.

3. Commonly Used Refrigeration Systems

Vapor compression refrigeration systems can therefore be primarily classified as follows:

1) Air, or direct-expansion cooler (DX) systems: air-cooled reciprocating DX coolers, air-cooled screw DX coolers, air-cooled rotary DX coolers.

2) Chillers: Air-cooled reciprocating or screw chillers, water-cooled centrifugal, screw, or reciprocating chillers.

4.7.3 Absorption Refrigeration Systems

The absorption cycle has similarities with the vapor compression refrigeration cycle. During both refrigeration processes, heat is transferred from the relatively warm system water (which is flowing through the evaporator tubes) to the cooler refrigerant by evaporating. In absorption cycle, heat is used to produce refrigerant vapor while electric or mechanical used in vapor compression refrigeration. The absorption cycle utilizes an absorbent (usually a salt solution) and a refrigerant. Aqueous lithium bromide (LiBr) is often used to absorb the refrigerant, the water vapor, and provides a higher coefficient of performance.

An absorption refrigeration system consists of four main components, namely generator, condenser, evaporator, and absorber, as shown in Fig. 4-17. In the absorption cycle, energy in the form of heat is added to the generator, and the solution pump (which can be compared to the compressor of the mechanical system) pumps the lithium bromide solution from the low-pressure absorber to the relatively higher-pressure generator. In both sections, heat is used to produce refrigerant vapor. The refrigerant vapor is cooled and condensed into liquid by the cooling water flowing through the condenser tubes. Liquid refrigerant from the condenser is metered through a metering orifice (similar to the expansion valve of the mechanical system) and is pumped by the refrigerant pump to the evaporator, where it is sprayed over the evaporator tubes. The extremely low vacuum in the evaporator causes some of the refrigerant to evaporate. During this process, heat is transferred from the relatively warm system water (which is flowing through the evaporator tubes) to the cooler refrigerant. In the absorber, the spray solution absorbs the refrigerant vapor and the resultant heat of absorption is removed by the condenser water (from the cooling tower) flowing through the tubes. In this system, note that heat is removed in both the condenser and the absorber sections by the cooling water and that it is finally rejected to the atmosphere by the cooling tower in the same manner as in the mechanical system.

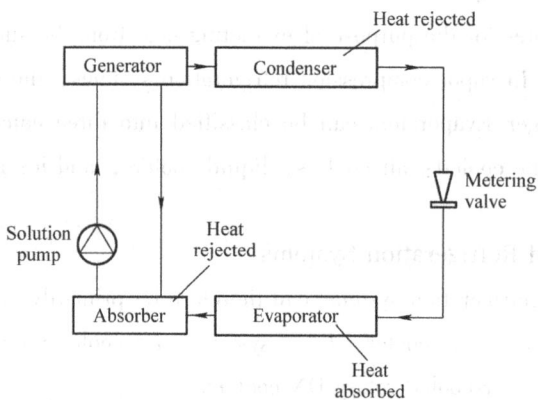

Fig. 4-17　Schematic diagram of absorption refrigeration system

Current absorption systems can be divided into the following categories:

1) Absorption chillers use heat energy to provide refrigeration.

2) Absorption chiller-heaters use heat energy to provide cooling or heating.

3) Absorption heat pump extracts heat energy from the evaporator through the absorber, adds to the heat input in the generator, and releases it both to the hot water in the condenser for heating.

4.7.4　Heat Pumps

A heat pump extracts heat from a heat source and rejects heat to air or water at a higher temperature. During summer, the heat extraction, or refrigeration effect, is the useful effect for cooling, whereas in winter the rejected heat alone, or rejected heat plus the supplementary heating from a heater, forms the useful effect for heating. A heat pump is a packaged air conditioner or a packaged unit with a reversing valve or other changeover setup. A heat pump has all the main components of an air conditioner or packaged unit: fan, filters, compressor, evaporator, condenser, short capillary tube, and controls. The apparatus for changing from cooling to heating or vice versa is often a reversing valve, in which the refrigerant flow to the condenser is changed to the evaporator. Alternatively, air passage through the evaporator may be changed over to passage through the condenser. According to the types of heat sources from which heat is absorbed by the refrigerant, currently used heat pump systems can be mainly classified into three categories: air-source heat pump, ground-coupled heat pump and water-source heat pump systems.

Questions

1. What's air conditioning? What's the main function of air conditioning systems?
2. What's the concept of moist air? What are the state parameters of moist air?
3. What are the basic psychrometric processes?
4. What are the comfort air conditioning system and process air conditioning system? Give examples of them respectively.
5. What's cooling load? What are the characteristics of cooling load?
6. How do you calculate the cooling load of a building?
7. What's all-air system? Introduce the main components and configuration of all-air systems.
8. What are the commonly used all-air systems?
9. What's air-handling unit? Name the main function sections of an air-handling unit.
10. What's space air diffusion? How many typical airflow patterns do we have?
11. What's the fan-coil system? Describe the main components and configuration of different air-water systems.
12. What's refrigerant air conditioning system? Introduce the main components and configuration of refrigerant systems.
13. What's refrigeration process?
14. What are refrigerants and cooling media? Give examples of them respectively.
15. Introduce the principles of a vapor compression refrigeration system and its main components.
16. Introduce the fundamentals of an absorption refrigeration system and its main components.
17. What's a heat pump?

第 5 章
燃 气 工 程

本章要点：本章介绍了燃气气源的种类和特性，燃气输配系统的组成，燃气输配系统的压力机制和常见燃烧器的种类和特性。

知识点：燃气的种类，燃气的热值和密度，燃气管道的七种压力范围，用气负荷的计算，灶具前的允许压力范围，燃气的储存方式，三种燃烧器的燃烧特点和应用。

燃气是一切可以燃烧的气体的总称。通常所见的可燃的气体有 H_2、CO、CH_4、H_2S 等。但燃气中也有一些不可燃成分，如 CO_2、N_2、稀有气体等。几种常见城市燃气有天然气、煤制气、液化石油气和沼气。城市燃气工程是向民用、商业及工业用户供应燃气作为炊事、热水、采暖空调和生产加工燃料的工程。燃气工程最初起源于将煤转化成煤气并将煤气供应给用户使用的工业过程。1812 年，英国建成了世界上第一座煤气厂。1865 年上海建造了我国第一座煤制气工厂，产量小，只用于街道照明。此后我国燃气工业发展缓慢，1949 年我国仅有 9 个城市有煤气厂，1950 年后开始对原有煤气工业进行改造和扩建。在冶金工业带动下，焦化工业有了很大发展，从而促进了用焦炉气作为气源的煤气事业的发展。同时建造了大量发生炉和水煤气炉来制造气化煤气供给工业用户作为燃料气和原料气。随着石油化工的发展，20 世纪 60 年代开始采用油制燃气及液化石油气作为城市燃气气源。20 世纪 80 年代以来，城市燃气工业得到了飞速发展，各个城市纷纷上马燃气工程，不仅煤制气技术有了很大提高，气源种类也得到了丰富。天然气的大力开发和应用使燃气工业从最开始以煤制气为主转化为现在以天然气为主。中国的城市燃气工程进入了史无前例的蓬勃发展的新阶段。

国外的燃气工业发展也大体经历了同样的过程，从煤制气为主阶段，发展到煤、油制气混合应用阶段，随后发展到天然气为主的阶段。

天然气、煤制气和油制气是对基本资源的高效利用。国家正在大力发展天然气等的应用。

燃气易点燃，易控制，燃烧效率高，燃烧后没有残渣，燃烧产物中有害物含量少。燃气比煤、油的碳含量少，燃烧产生的 CO_2 也少，是清洁燃料。天然气比人工煤气、液化石油气含碳量低，是公认的绿色燃料。

燃气工程得到大力发展是社会进步的表征，是历史的必然。首先，现代社会不同于原始社会，拢火取暖烧饭，人们生活水平的提高对能源的质量提出了更高的要求，方便、快捷、清洁的燃气是人们的喜爱，必然取代使用不便、污染很重的固体燃料。高质量的工业民用产品生产过程中对燃料也有更高的要求，传统的固液体燃料未必能满足要求。其次，燃气工大力发展是保护全球能源避免世界能源危机的需要。固体和液体能源使用过程中能源利用效率较低，燃气的使用提高了能源利用率。我国面临着常规能源资源约束，能源利用效率低等问题。我国能源消费总量已经位居世界第二，约占世界能源消费总量的11%，而我国人均煤炭、石油、天然气资源量仅为世界平均水平的60%、10%和5%。我国每吨标准煤的产出效率仅相当于日本的10.3%、欧盟的16.8%。在这种严峻的情况下，减少能源效率低的燃煤量，增加能源效率高的燃气量，实为必然。最后，在全球环境恶化，大气环境亟须保护的今天，燃气工程的发展成为减轻污染的第一重要措施。尤其我国过分依赖煤炭，大气污染严重，主要呈现为煤烟型污染特征。城市大气环境中总悬浮颗粒物含量普遍超标；二氧化硫污染保持在较高水平；环境亟须控制和改善。全国90%的二氧化硫排放，大气中70%的烟尘是燃煤造成的。近几年，北京市对大气污染进行了积极的治理。坚决落实燃煤锅炉改清洁能源任务。使北京城市能源结构明显改善，城市燃煤逐年减少，代之以天然气等清洁能源，粉尘等污染物的排放量大量减少，空气质量明显好转。因此，扩大燃气（特别是天然气）在能源结构中的比例是十分重要的。

我国21世纪的能源战略以发展城市燃气作为重要内容。20世纪90年代开始的陕甘宁天然气进京工程解决了京津用气问题。21世纪初开始的西气东输工程堪称中国能源大动脉。西气东输的输气管道西起新疆轮南，东至上海市，途经10个省、自治区、直辖市，线路全长约4200km，是中国目前距离最长、管径最大、投资最多、输气量最大、施工条件最复杂的天然气管道。年设计输量$120 \times 10^8 m^3$；供气范围覆盖中原、华东、长江三角洲地区。并将与陕京二线等其他管线连接，在未来一二十年内形成天然气网络体系，使新疆、陕甘宁、青海、川渝四大气区实现互联，它们与下游市场的京津唐、长三角、华中及珠三角地区也全部实现互联互供。具备世界上主要输气管线所遵循的多气源、联网、有大的地下储气库等几项重要的保障条件。社会对天然气的认识也发生了变化。在陕京工程和西气东输工程建成前，下游用户对使用天然气采取推托甚至冷眼态度，随着工程建设及建成投产，下游市场的用气需求迅速膨胀，多数实际用气量都不断突破"原计划"，显现出对清洁高效能源的惊人渴求。

中国的天然气产业是一个处于发展初期、快速发展的产业，LNG（液化天然气）将在其中扮演重要的角色。当前中国经济持续快速的发展势头仍在继续，但是保障经济的能源动力却极度紧缺。中国的能源结构以煤炭为主，石油、天然气只占很小的比例，远远低于世界平均水平。在国际石油价格节节升高的情势之下，中国的能源危机越发显得严重。随着国家对能源需求的不断增长，引进LNG将对优化我国的能源结构，有效解决能源供应安全、生态环境保护的双重问题，实现经济和社会的可持续发展发挥重要作用。

燃气工程通常包括三大部分：燃气生产（气源），燃气输配和燃气燃烧与应用。下面对这三部分进行简要叙述。

5.1 燃气气源

城市燃气的种类大致分为天然气、人工燃气、液化石油气、生物质气等。当前城市燃气主要采用的燃气种类是天然气、液化石油气。某些中小城市目前还用人工燃气。生物质气主要指的是沼气，在小城镇和农村有所采用。

5.1.1 天然气

天然气一般可分为四种：从气井开采出来的气田气或称纯天然气；伴随石油一起开采出来的石油气，也称石油伴生气；含石油轻质馏分的凝析气田气；从井下煤层抽出的煤矿矿井气。

在还没有人类的时期，地球上气候温暖潮湿，生长着茂密的森林，同时还有各种陆上走兽和水中游鱼。大批生物自生自灭，它们的遗体堆积在地球低洼的地方，经过地壳变动，海洋突起为高山，丘陵变成湖泊，把这些动植物遗体埋在地下。在隔绝氧及一定压力、温度作用下，经过复杂的变化，形成可燃物质，其中树木大部分变为固体燃料（煤），其他有机体遗体，在细菌的作用下，发生生物化学作用，有机物分解，形成不同形式的碳水化合物。当它们呈液态时为液体燃料（石油），呈气态时为气体燃料（天然气）。以固体燃料为主的矿床为煤矿，煤矿有时伴有可燃气体，在采煤时取出，称为矿井气。以液体燃料为主的矿床称为石油矿，伴随石油常有一定数量的可燃气体，这种天然气称为石油伴生气（1t 原油可获得 60~150m^3 伴生气）。以气体燃料为主的矿床称为天然气矿，这种天然气矿生产的可燃气体称为气井气或称气田气。凝析气田气是一种深层的富天然气。在 1500m 以下的地下是以液相存在的。开采时气液发生分离而得的气体称为凝析气田气。

纯天然气（简称天然气）的组分以甲烷为主，含有少量的二氧化碳、硫化氢、氮气等。每个气田的天然气热值不尽相同，但热值都在 35000kJ/m^3 以上。石油伴生气的甲烷含量为 80% 左右，并含有丙烷、丁烷和少量稀有气体，热值在 40.5MJ/m^3 以上。凝析气田气除了含有大量甲烷外，还含有 2%~5% 的戊烷和戊烷以上的碳氢化合物。矿井气的主要可燃成分是甲烷，其组分随采气方式而变化。

开采天然气由三个步骤完成：钻井、完井及安装井口设备。钻井是用钻头破坏地壳岩层，并把碎石引上地面。完井是为了保护井壁不塌陷，在钻井过程中加导向管，该管与井壁间灌水泥。每个气井的出口都有分离设备，以除去天然气中的固态与液态杂质，然后经过计量后送入集气网，一个天然气矿有许多气井，用集气网将气井联合起来。当天然气中硫化氢、二氧化碳、凝析油的含量和含水量超过管道输气规定标准时，需设置天然气净化处理厂。来自集气管线或天然气净化厂的天然气进入起点站，进行除尘、调压，计量后进入长距离输气干线。在长距离输气干线上，根据需要设置中间压气站、清管球收发装置、阴极保护站、阀室等设施。输气干线上压气站的数量和出口压力，与输气管道的管径和加压成本之间的关系极大，要通过技术经济计算确定，也由此决定两个压气站的合理距离。管线末端的压力要根据储气设备的种类及城市管网的压力要求决定。长输管线或支线末端就是城市燃气供应系统。燃气分配站，也称城市门站，设在长输管线末端，是长输管线的终点站和城市管网系统的气源站，该站内接受长输管线送来的燃气，经调压、除尘，将燃气压力降至城市管网系统所需的压力，计量、加嗅后送入城市管网。

5.1.2 人工燃气

1. 固体燃料干馏及焦炉气

固体燃料煤是一种复杂的有机化合物，在隔绝空气加热条件下，煤会分解为可燃气体、液体和固体三种产物，在不同温度下，产生的物质也有所不同。

1）干燥阶段：温度在120℃以前是干燥阶段，首先表面的吸附水分吸热而蒸发出来。

2）预热干馏阶段：120~200℃时，部分结晶水放出，吸附于煤上的CH_4与CO等气体析出，当达到250℃时开始有焦油及氨蒸气。

3）低温干馏阶段：当温升至350℃时，焦油蒸气显著增多，到了500~550℃时达到最大量。在此温度阶段内，CO、CO_2、H_2、CH_4及C_mH_n析出量逐步上升，此时产生的可燃气体称为半焦燃气，其发热量为25080~33440kJ/m³。

4）高温干馏阶段：温度由550℃升至1100℃时，气体产物中重碳氢化合物也会分解。燃气中H_2成分含量提高。温度达到1100℃时，产气量达到最大。此时的可燃气体称为焦炉煤气，其热值均为16720~18810kJ/m³。此阶段的固体残留物为焦炭，可用来炼钢。在没有天然气资源时可用焦炉气作为城市气源。

2. 固体燃料气化煤气

固体燃料气化是燃料热化学加工过程，是将煤气化成CO、CH_4及H_2等。当气化剂为空气时，生产空气发生炉燃气，主要生产反应为$CO_2 + C = 2CO + 172140kJ$，发热值为5400kJ/m³。气化剂采用水蒸气时，水蒸气遇炽热的碳时，会发生如下反应：$C + H_2O \rightarrow CO + H_2 - 118628.4kJ$，发热值为10500kJ/m³。由于这两种煤气发热值低，且毒性大，不可用作城市燃气气源，但可以用来加热焦炉和连续式直立碳化炉，以顶替出热值较高的焦炉煤气。

3. 油制气

根据制取方式不同，利用重油制取的城市燃气有重油蓄热热裂解气和重油蓄热催化裂解气。重油蓄热热裂解气以甲烷、乙烯和丙烯为主要组分，发热值为41900kJ/m³。重油蓄热催化裂解气中含氢较多，还含有甲烷和一氧化碳，发热值在17600~20900kJ/m³。生产重油的装置简单、投资省、占地少，建设速度快，管理人员少，启动和停炉灵活，既可作城市燃气的基本气源也可作城市燃气的调度气源。

5.1.3 液化石油气

液化石油气是开采和炼制石油过程中，作为副产品而获得的一部分碳氢化合物。其主要成分是丙烷、丙烯、丁烷和丁烯。这些碳氢化合物在常温常压下呈气态，当压力升高或温度降低时，转变为液态。从气态到液态，其体积缩小为原体积的1/250。气态液化石油气发热值为92100~121400kJ/m³。液态液化石油气发热值为45200~46100kJ/m³。在城市燃气事业中，液化石油气投资省，设备简单，供应方式灵活，建设速度快，是很好的城市气源。

5.1.4 沼气

各种有机物，如蛋白质、纤维素、脂肪、淀粉等，在隔绝空气的条件下发酵，并在微生物作用下产生的可燃气体叫做沼气。发酵的原料是取之不尽、用之不竭的粪便、垃圾、杂草和落叶等有机物，因此，沼气属于可再生能源。沼气中甲烷含量为60%，二氧化碳为35%。此外，还含有少量的氢、一氧化碳等气体。发热值约为20900kJ/m³。

5.2 城市燃气输配系统

城市燃气输配系统是负责将城市燃气从气源处输送到民用、商业和工业各个用户，保证用户安全可靠用气的系统。城市燃气输配系统是使城市千家万户安全可靠用上燃气的关键，是燃气工程核心部分之一。

现代化的城市燃气输配系统是复杂的综合设施，通常由下列部分构成：

（1）燃气管网 低压、中压以及高压等不同压力等级的燃气管网，城市的燃气输配管网担负着输气和配气功能。担负输气功能的管网是压力较高的，而配气管网压力较低。

（2）城市燃气门站 将从上游购进的燃气进行调压、除尘、计量等过程后输入城市管网系统。

（3）调压设施 各种不同压力级制的管网系统之间通过区域调压站或调压室联系。

（4）燃气储配站 城市燃气的用气是不均匀的，燃气储配站将用户用气量少时多余的燃气加以储存，而在用户用气量大时从储气设备里取出供给用户。

（5）监控与调度中心 城市燃气输配系统的管理中心。监控与调度系统随时监控城市燃气输配系统中主要设备和管网的运行情况并对监视过程中出现的情况进行及时反映处理。例如，在用气高峰出现时监控与调度中心发出指令从储气设备中取出燃气，在用气低谷时监控与调度中心发出指令把更多的燃气储于储气设备。

（6）维护管理中心 负责对管线和设备进行巡视、维护和维修。调压站等设备需要常规巡视，在系统中出现任何非正常情况时维护管理中心要马上采取措施抢修。

城市燃气输配系统设计应该保证合理、不间断、可靠地给用户供气，在发生故障时可关断某些管段而不影响系统工作。在运行管理上保证安全检修方便。采用系统方案应该有最大的社会经济效益。

5.2.1 输配管网的压力机制

1. 城市燃气管网的分类

我国城市燃气管网的分类方法之一，是根据燃气管道的输气压力来分类。

1）低压燃气管道：$p<0.01$ MPa。
2）中压 B 燃气管道：$0.01\text{MPa} \leqslant p \leqslant 0.2\text{MPa}$。
3）中压 A 燃气管道：$0.2\text{MPa} < p \leqslant 0.4\text{MPa}$。
4）次高压 B 燃气管道：$0.4\text{MPa} < p \leqslant 0.8\text{MPa}$。

5) 次高压 A 燃气管道：$0.8\text{MPa} < p \leqslant 1.6\text{MPa}$。

6) 高压 B 燃气管道：$1.6\text{MPa} < p \leqslant 2.5\text{MPa}$。

7) 高压 A 燃气管道：$2.5\text{MPa} < p \leqslant 4.0\text{MPa}$。

居民用户和小型商业用户一般直接由低压管道供气。中压 B 和中压 A 管道必须通过区域调压站或用户专用调压站才能给大型商业或工厂企业用户供气。不同级别管网通过调压站相连。一般由城市高压 B 或 A 燃气管道构成大城市输配管网系统的外环网。市区敷设次高压、中、低压管道。城市燃气系统中各级压力的干管，特别是中压以上的管道，应连成环网，初建时也可以是半环形或枝状，但应该逐步成环。

2. 城市燃气管网系统

城市燃气管网系统是城市输配系统的主要部分。根据所采用的管网压力机制不同可分为：

1) 一级系统：仅用低压管网来分配和供给燃气，一般只适用于小城镇的供气。如供气范围较大时，则输送单位体积燃气的管材用量将急剧增加。

2) 二级系统：由低压和中压两级管道组成。

3) 三级系统：包括低压、中压和次高压三级管网。

4) 多级系统：由低压和中压、次高压和高压管道组成。

图 5-1 所示是某大城市的燃气三级管网系统。

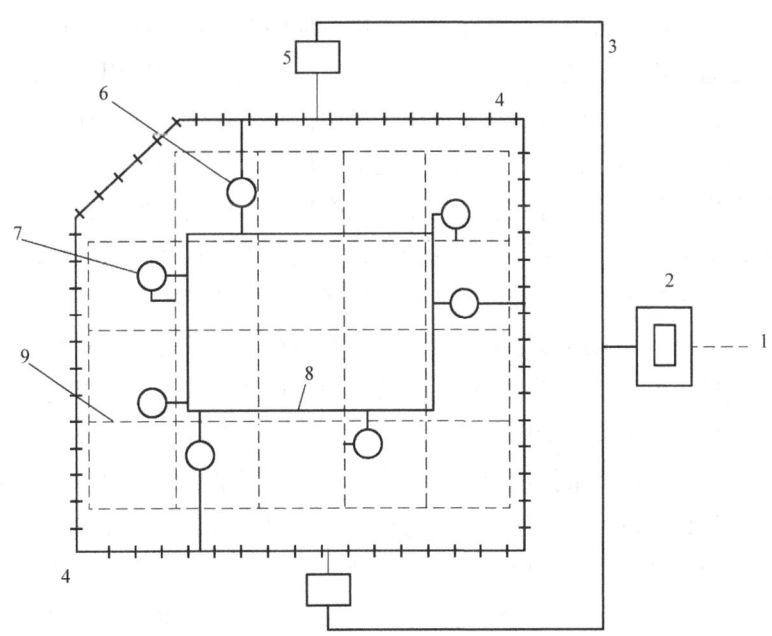

图 5-1　某大城市的燃气三级管网系统示意图

1—长输管线　2—燃气分配站　3—郊区高压管　4—高压管网
5—储气罐站　6—高中压调压站　7—中低压调压站　8—中压管网　9—低压管网

图 5-1 中的燃气管网系统，由低压、中压和高压管网组成，气源是来自长输管线的天然气（或者是高压的人工燃气），由建造在城市双侧的高压储气罐储气。郊区次高压管道形成半环，从城市两侧供给次高压气。次高压和中压管网成环。次高、中压以及中、低压管线间由调压器连接，中低压调压器数目很多，图 5-1 中没有显示。低压管线连接居民用户。工业用户和大型商业用户可通过调压器与中压管线相连。

城市燃气管网系统采用不同压力机制是必要的。首先，管网采用不同的压力机制是比较经济的。因为大部分燃气由较高压力的管道输送，管道的管径可选小一些，管道单位长度的压力损失可以选得大一些，节省了管材。其次，各类用户需要的燃气压力不同，居民和小型商业用户需要低压燃气，大型工业用户则需要中压和高压燃气。再者，市中心地区，人口密度较大，从安全运行和方便管理的观点看，也不宜敷设高压或中压 A 管道，只能敷设中压 B 和低压管道。随着科学技术的发展，有可能改进管道和燃气专用设备的质量，提高施工管理的质量和运行管理的水平，在新建城市燃气管网系统和改建旧有系统时，燃气管道可以采用较高压力，来降低管网的总造价和提高管道的输气能力。

3. 城市燃气负荷

设计城市燃气管网首先要确定的是城市燃气负荷。城市燃气供应对象一般有三种类型：居民、商业和工业。燃气是一种优质燃料，应力求经济合理地充分发挥其能效。由于我国气源尚不丰富，城市燃气一般优先供给居民生活，居民烧的小煤炉的热效率很低，只有15%～20%，采用燃气后，热效率可高达 55%～60%。燃气供应可大量节约燃料。对于大量的、分散的小用户，即居民生活用户及商业用户来讲，使用燃气有效地防止环境污染，节约劳动力及减轻城市交通运输量。城市燃气在气量分配时应兼顾工业和民用。工业企业有用气比较均匀的特点，所以工业企业用气量在城市用气量中占有一定比例，有利于平衡城市燃气使用的不均匀性，减少燃气储存容量，减轻高峰负荷，增加售气收费。

城市燃气需用量的计算，首先要确定用气量指标也称用气定额。影响居民生活用气指标的因素很多，如地区的气象条件，燃气价格，有无集中采暖和热水供应设备，居民每户平均人口数，住宅内用气设备的配置情况，公共生活服务网的成熟程度，居民生活水平和生活习惯等。居民生活用气定额通常是根据对各种典型用户用气进行调查和测定，并通过综合分析得到平均用气量作为用气指标。居民生活年用气量就是城市需要用气人口和居民用气定额之积。同理可得商业用气量指标和年用气量。对于新建燃气供应系统的城市，其用气量指标可以参照相似城市的用气指标确定。工业企业年用气量可以利用各种工业产品的用气定额及其年产量来计算。也可以将其他燃料的年用量，根据热平衡折合成燃气用量。各类用户的年用气量之和即为城市燃气年用气量。城市燃气年用气量还应计入未预见量，它包含管网燃气漏损量和发展过程中未预见的供气量。未预见量一般是年用气量的 5%。

城市燃气需用量是不均匀的，是随时间而波动的。用气不均匀性可以分为月不均匀性、日不均匀性和时不均匀性。影响居民生活及商业用气月不均匀性的主要因素是气候条件，故也称之为季节不均匀性。气温降低则用气量增多，在冬季，人们喜食热的食品，热水耗量大，故用气量增多。工业企业用气比较均匀，但夏季室外温度和水温较高，这类用户用气量也会适当降低。一年中各月的用气不均匀情况用月不均匀系数 K_1 表示。

$$K_1 = \frac{该月平均日用气量}{全年平均日用气量}$$

12 个月中平均日用气量最大的月称为计算月。将 12 个月中最大不均匀系数称为月高峰系数，用 K_m 表示。

影响日用气波动的因素有居民生活习惯，工业企业工作休息制度和室外气温变化等。用日不均匀系数 K_2 表示一个月（或一周中）日用气的变化情况。

$$K_2 = \frac{该月某日用气量}{该月平均日用气量}$$

计算月中日最大不均匀系数称为日高峰系数，用 K_d 表示。

城市中各类用户的小时用气工况均不相同，居民生活和商业用户的用气不均匀性最为显著。对于供暖用户，若为连续供暖，小时波动小；若为间歇式供暖，波动较大。工作日有早、午、晚三个用气高峰，早高峰最低。周末有午、晚两个高峰。通常用小时不均匀系数表示一日中小时用气量的变化情况，小时不均匀系数 K_3 可按下式计算

$$K_3 = \frac{该日某小时用气量}{该日平均小时用气量}$$

计算月中最大用气量日的小时不均匀系数的最大值称为小时高峰系数，用 K_h 表示。

城市燃气管网系统的管径及设备，均按计算月小时最大流量计算。只有掌握了可靠的小时用气波动的数据才能确定这个小时最大流量。一日中小时用气工况的变化图对燃气管网的运行，以及计算平衡时不均匀性所需储气容积都很重要。小时计算流量的确定，关系着燃气输配系统的经济性和可靠性。小时计算流量定得偏高，将会增加输配系统的金属用量和基建投资，定得偏低，又会影响用户的正常用气。城市燃气分配管道的计算流量

$$Q_h = \frac{Q_a}{365 \times 24} K_m K_d K_h$$

式中　Q_h——计算流量（m^3/h）；

　　　Q_a——年用气量（m^3/a）；

　　　K_m——月高峰系数；

　　　K_d——日高峰系数；

　　　K_h——小时高峰系数。

用气的高峰系数应该根据城市用气量的实际统计资料确定。需要很多人力物力去做实际调查。居民生活和商业用气的高峰系数，当缺乏用气量的实际统计资料时，可按下列范围选用：$K_m = 1.1 \sim 1.3$，$K_d = 1.01 \sim 1.2$，$K_h = 2.2 \sim 3.2$。

4. 低压燃气管网计算压力降

在燃气管网设计计算中，必须先确定调压站出口和最远端用户之间的允许压力降。

城市管网与用户的连接一般有两种方法，一种是直接连接，另一种是通过用户调压器。当城市管网与用户通过用户调压器连接时管网中的压力波动不影响用户处压力。绝大多数居民用户直接与低压管道相连，管网中流量变化和压力波动，影响燃具前的压力。燃气管道阻

力造成的压力降使燃气管道起点压力高，终点压力低，所以接在管道起点的燃具灶前压力高，接在管道终点的燃具灶前压力低。为满足燃具的燃烧稳定性和良好的运行工况，在设计燃气管网选取计算压力降时，应保证燃具前的压力在一定的范围内波动。

设燃具的额定工作压力为 p_n，最大允许压力为 p_{max}，最小允许压力为 p_{min}。

$$p_{max} = k_1 p_n$$
$$p_{min} = k_2 p_n$$

式中 k_1、k_2——最大压力系数和最小压力系数。

因为居民用户与低压管道直接相连，管道的最高压力不能大于燃具的最大允许压力 p_{max}，管道最低压力不能小于燃具的最小允许压力 p_{min}，则管道允许压力降为 $\Delta p = p_{max} - p_{min} = (k_1 - k_2) p_n$。

实践和研究工作表明，一般民用燃具灶前压力在 ±50% 的额定压力范围内波动时可以正常工作，故要求 $k_1 = 1.5$ 和 $k_2 = 0.5$。灶前压力由 $1.5 p_n$ 降至 $0.5 p_n$ 时，其热负荷将由 $1.2Q$ 降至 $0.7Q$。Q 为燃气的额定热负荷。考虑到高峰时不希望燃具热负荷过低，取 $k_2 = 0.75$。这时燃气的最低热负荷可达到 $0.86Q$。这样，可以确定低压管道允许压力降 Δp 为

$$\Delta p = (k_1 - k_2) p_n = (1.5 - 0.75) p_n$$

在最不利的情况下，即用气量最小的情况下，靠近调压站最近用户处有可能达到压力的最大值，但由调压站到此用户最小仍有约 150Pa 的阻力，这里包含煤气表阻力和干、支管阻力，故低压燃气管道（含市内和庭院管）总的管道允许压力降还可以加大 150Pa，即

$$\Delta p = 0.75 p_n + 150\text{Pa}$$

上述低压燃气管道（含市内和庭院管）总的管道允许压力降 Δp 即是设计燃气管网进行水力计算时所选的计算压力降。

可见，当设计制造出的燃具的 p_n 越大时，可以提高管道压力降，从而节约燃气管道消耗的金属材料。但是 p_n 也不能无限制地高，因为 p_n 过高造成管网压力过高，会使漏气的可能性增大，尤其在煤气表处。还有运行管理费用也会增加。

高、中压燃气管道的压力降主要决定于起点与终点压力。高、中压管道的起点压力取决于上一级管道连接的调压站或压气站。当终点供气对象为调压站时，终点压力应由调压站最低入口压力决定。当终点为工业用户时，则应由该用户要求的最低入口压力决定。

在管道计算压力降确定后，就可根据流体力学的水力计算公式进行水力计算，确定燃气管网的管径。

5.2.2 燃气储存及储配站

城市燃气的消耗量是不均匀的，是随时间变化的。但燃气气源的供应是均匀的，不随时间变化的。为了解决均匀供气和不均匀用气之间的矛盾，城市需要设置燃气储存设施，在用气低谷时储存燃气，在用气高峰时供给用户。常用的储气方法有：

1. 地下储气

地下储气是在用气淡季将燃气注入具有合适地质构造的地下空间，在用气高峰时将燃气取出供给用户。地下储气空间往往利用枯竭的油气田，含水多孔的地下结构，盐矿层或岩

穴。其中利用枯竭的油气田储气最为经济。地下储存燃气容量大，造价和运行费用省，单位储气量的投资少，可节省大量金属材料。地下储气是城市首选储气方式。一般用来解决季节不均匀用气和部分日不均匀用气的问题。难点在于在城市周围是否能找到经济的适合储气的地质构造。我国首座地下储气库储气量为 $1 \times 10^7 m^3$ 尚属小规模。西气东输工程开始建设大规模的地下储气库。在江苏金坛及刘庄建设地下储气库进行季节调峰。金坛储气库正在建设中，建设规模为有效储气 $17.4 \times 10^8 m^3$，是我国第一个利用盐穴进行储气的储气库。利用废弃的盐矿储藏天然气，既节约了投资，又可以稳定地质结构。同时也为油、气、电等能源的储备提供了成型的经验。刘庄储气库设计有效工作气量为 $2.55 \times 10^8 m^3$，已经开始启动建设。两座储气库建设规模为有效储气 $20 \times 10^8 m^3$。2020 年达到建设规模。气库建成后可满足长三角地区季节调峰和应急供气需求。

2. 天然气液态储存

天然气的主要成分甲烷，在 5.6kPa、温度 -161℃ 时即液化，液化后的天然气体积大大缩小，$1m^3$ 的天然气液化的体积只有 $1/600m^3$，可以储存在绝热储罐中。当用气高峰时，经气化后供出。

国际上液化天然气已经商品化。易于运输，适于国家之间的买卖。近年来全球 LNG 的生产和贸易日趋活跃，正在成为世界油气工业新的热点。为保证能源供应多元化和改善能源消费结构，一些能源消费大国越来越重视 LNG 的引进，国际大石油公司也纷纷将其新的利润增长点转向 LNG 业务，LNG 将成为石油之后下一个全球争夺的热门能源商品。如果能在中国大力发展 LNG，在很大程度上可弥补石油资源不足、保证能源供应的多元化、逐步提高我国环境质量，并且对我国的西气东输也能起到互补的重要作用。中国近年来，对 LNG 产业的发展越来越重视，我国正在规划和实施的沿海 LNG 项目有：广东、福建、浙江、上海、江苏、山东、辽宁。

3. 管道储气

高压燃气管束储气及长输干管末端储气，是平衡小时不均匀用气的有效方法。高压管束储气时将一组或几组钢管埋在地下，对管内燃气加压。利用长输干管储气是在夜间用气低峰时，燃气储存在管道中，这时管内压力增高，白天用气高峰时，将管道储存的燃气送出。

4. 储气罐储气

利用低压湿式储罐、低压干式储罐或高压储罐储存燃气来平衡日不均匀和小时不均匀用气是我国各城市最常见的调峰方式。储气罐储气与其他储气方式相比，金属材料耗量和投资都较大。但在没有其他储气方式的条件下，储气罐储气在所难免。人工燃气通常用低压储气罐进行储气，储气设施非常庞大。天然气用高压储罐储存。储气罐置于城市储配站内。

5.2.3　建筑物内燃气供应

建筑燃气供应系统的构成，随城市燃气系统的供气方式不同而有所变化，图 5-2 所示燃气系统，是城市燃气管网系统低压管道上某一用气建筑的室内燃气系统。该系统由用户引入管、干管、立管、用户支管、燃气计量表、用具连接管和燃气用具所组成。用户引入管与城市或庭院低压管道相接，在分支管处设阀门。

5.3 燃气燃烧与应用简介

燃气从气源出来经过输配系统分配到千家万户，需要在用户的燃具上燃烧来提供炊事、取暖或生产的热量。现代社会要高效率地利用所有燃料。为提高效率，空气和燃气混合比例要稳定和合适，这就要求燃料燃烧知识以及流体力学和热力学知识。

燃烧理论包括燃气的燃烧计算，燃气的燃烧反应动力学，燃气燃烧的气流混合过程，燃气燃烧的火焰传播。

用来实现燃烧过程的装置，称为燃烧器。燃气燃烧器是将燃气的化学能转化为热能的一种装置。按适用燃气种类分类，燃烧器分为人工燃气燃烧器、天然气燃烧器、液化石油气燃烧器、混合燃气燃烧器和通用燃烧器。按燃烧方法分为扩散式燃烧器、大气式燃烧器和无焰式燃烧器。

按扩散式燃烧原理设计，燃气进入燃烧器之前不预混空气，燃烧所需的氧气全部依靠扩散作用从周围大气中获得的燃烧器，称为扩散式燃烧器。按燃烧反应计算中燃气预先混合部分空气设计的燃烧器称为大气式燃烧器。按照燃烧反应计算，在燃烧前，空气和燃气全部预先混合送入燃烧喷嘴的燃烧器称为无焰式燃烧器。

根据空气供给方式的不同，扩散式燃烧器可分为自然通风和强制鼓风两类。自然通风式，依靠自然抽力或扩散供给空气，多民用。强制鼓风式，依靠鼓风机供给空气，多用于工业。

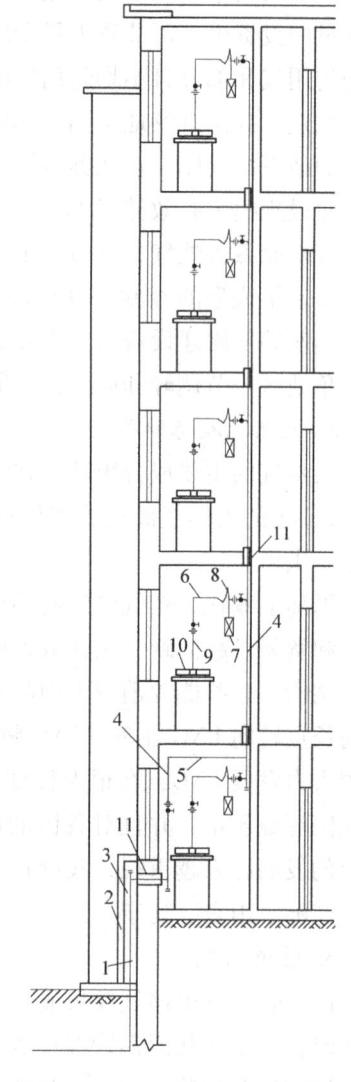

图 5-2 建筑物内燃气供应系统
1—用户引入管 2—砖台 3—保温层
4—立管 5—水平干管 6—用户支管
7—燃气计量表 8—旋塞及活接头
9—用具连接管 10—燃气用具 11—套管

大气式燃烧器比自然通风扩散式燃烧器火焰短、燃烧温度高，比无焰式燃烧器的热负荷调节范围宽，可以燃烧不同性质的燃气，燃烧效率比较高，燃烧比较安全，烟气中一氧化碳含量少，卫生条件较好；比强制鼓风扩散式燃烧器节省动力，调节方便，尤其因为采用引射器结构，具有自调性，即当燃烧器热负荷在一定范围内变动时，一次空气系数能维持常数。但大气式燃烧器热负荷不宜太大，热强度比无焰式燃烧器低，火焰稳定性不及扩散式燃烧器，且不适应正压炉膛。多孔大气式燃烧器应用非常广泛，在家庭及公共事业中的燃气用具如燃气灶、热水器、沸水器及食堂灶上用得最广泛。在小型锅炉及工业锅炉上也有应用。单火孔大气式燃烧器在中小型锅炉及某些工业锅炉上广泛应用。

无焰式燃烧器具有燃烧完全，火焰温度高，燃烧热强度高等特点。但它对火焰稳定性差，为了防止回火，使头部结构比较复杂，这就使得热负荷大的燃烧器体积庞大和笨重，噪声大。无焰式燃烧器主要应用在工业加热装置上。

习　　题

1. 城市燃气有几种？热值分别是多少？
2. 燃气管道有几种压力机制？压力分别在什么范围？
3. 对于一个城市，如何计算该城市的燃气用气量？
4. 民用灶具的最大允许压力和最小允许压力是多少？低压管道水力计算中，从调压站出口到最远端用户允许压力降是多少？
5. 为什么要储存燃气？燃气储存有几种方式？各有什么优缺点？
6. 常用燃烧器有几种？各有什么特点？

Chapter 5
Gas Engineering

Abstract: This chapter introduces different kinds of gas sources for city utility and their characteristics. This chapter briefly describes the configuration and pressure categories of city gas transmission and distribution system. Different kinds of gas burners are also summarized.

Key points: gas category, heat value of gas, gas density, pressure range of gas pipeline, gas load calculation, pressure of gas appliances, gas storage methods, gas appliances characteristics.

All combustible (or inflammable) gases are called fuel gas, or simply gas. Usually, combustible (or inflammable) gases include H_2, CO, CH_4, H_2S, etc.. Sometimes, fuel gas also includes some nonflammable gases, such as CO_2, N_2, rare gases, etc. Fuel gases, commonly used in city, are natural gas, coal gas, oil gas, liquefied petroleum gas and biogas. Gas engineering was originally the process of gasification of coal and supply coal gas to consumers for cooking, hot-water supplying, heating, air-conditioning and industrial process fuel. In 1812, England established the first manufactory to make coal gas. In 1865, the first coal gas manufactory of China was found in Shanghai. The production amount (or output) was small and coal gas was used for lighting purpose only. Gas engineering developed slowly afterwards. There were only 9 coal gas manufactories all over the country until 1949. Since 1950, the original coal gas industry was renovated and expended. Rapid growth of metallurgical industry promoted coal carbonization industry to a new level. As a result, city gas industry expended with coal carbonization gas as main source. At the same time, large amount of coal gasification gas manufactories were built to supply coal gasification gas to industrial consumers. With the development of petroleum and chemical engineering, oil gas and liquid petroleum gas was adapted as city gas sources in 1960's. Since 1980, gas engineering has grown rapidly. Gas projects have been constructed in many cities. The coal gas technology has been improved greatly. Different kinds of gas sources were available. With development of natural gas engineering, natural gas has substituted coal gas as the major gas source. Gas engineering in China has reached a new stage with unprecedented growth.

History of gas engineering in other countries follows similar pattern. At the beginning, coal gas dominated gas industry. Then, coal gas and oil gas co-dominated the market, followed by natural gas which is currently the major gas source for city supply.

The use of natural gas and, ultimately, an artificially produced substitute from coal and oil is a highly efficient use of primary resources, and all efforts are directed at continuing this trend.

Fuel gas is easy to ignite and combustion is easy to control with high combustion efficiency. There is no combustion residue and combustion produces less hazardous products. Fuel gas contains less carbon than coal and oil. Thus, fuel gas combustion emits less CO_2 than coal and oil do. Natural gas contains the least carbon among coal gas and liquid petroleum gas and is called green fuel.

The vigorous growth of gas engineering is a sign of civilized society and is the trend of history. First, modern society is different from primary life, cooking food on a faggot fire. The higher life standards require higher quality of energy. Gaseous fuel is warmly welcomed because it is convenient to use and clean. No doubt it will finally substitute the solid fuel which is inconvenient to use and pollutes environments. For industrial consumers, high quality products require high standard fuel. Traditional solid fuel may not be able to meet the requirements. Second, promotion of gas engineering is necessary to save energy and to avoid world energy crisis. Solid and liquid fuel combustion efficiencies are comparably low, while gaseous fuel combustion efficiency is high. China's energy resources are tight while energy utilization efficiency is low. At the same time, China is the second largest energy consuming country in the world. It consumes 11% of world energy totally consumed. Energy resources per person in China are 60%, 10% and 5% of the world average level for coal, petroleum and natural gas respectively. However, the utility efficiency of one ton coal is only 10.3% of Japan and 16.8% of Europe countries. Thus, it is necessary to reduce the usage of coal and increase the usage of gaseous fuel. The last, as global environment is getting worse, rapid development of gas engineering is the most important method to reduce pollution and to protect the atmosphere environment. China relies on coal heavily. Air pollution in China is severe mainly due to smoke from burning coal. Concentration of total suspended particles above city atmosphere exceeds required standards. Concentration of SO_2 in air is very high and is needed to be controlled. 90 percent of SO_2 particles and 70 percent of smoke and dust in atmosphere are because of coal burning. In recent years, Beijing took effective methods to control smoke pollution. Beijing is reconstructing smoke emissive coal burning boilers to cleaner natural gas burning boilers. Energy consumption structure in Beijing is improved with less coal and more natural gas. As a result, emission of contaminants is greatly reduced and air quality in Beijing is improved. Thus, it is important to increase the percentage of fuel gas (especially natural gas) consumption in China.

Development of city gas supply is an important part of China's twenty first century energy strategies. In 1990's, the project of transmission of natural gas from Shan-Gan-Ning (Shanxi Province, Gansu Province and Ningxia Province) to Beijing provided gas source to Beijing and Tianjin area. At the beginning of twenty first century, the project of transmission natural gas from western China to eastern China, the main artery of China's energy, is initiated. The total pipeline length of this project is 4200 kilometers, starting from Xinjiang and ending at Shanghai by going through 10 provinces, autonomous region and municipalities. This project has the longest pipeline, the biggest pipeline diameter, investment and transmission capacity with the most complex geographic construction conditions in China. The transmission capacity is 12 billion cubic meters natural gas. It will supply Central Plains, East China and the Yangtze River Delta. It will be connected with the second pipeline of natural gas transmission project from Shan-Gan-Ning to Beijing. In the coming decades, natural gas transmission pipeline in China will be connected to be a net system, linking Xinjiang, Shan-Gan-Ning, Qinghai, Chuanyu gas resources all together with Beijing, Tianjin, Tangshan area, Yangtze River Delta, Central Plains and Zhujiang Delta. Thus, China's natural gas transit system will posses multiple natural gas resources, complete network and big underground gas storage reservoirs as other countries' systems do. In China, people's knowledge of natural gas is rapidly increased. At the beginning of the above two major transmission projects' construction, end users were reluctant to commit to natural gas. As the construction is progressed, the demands of end users increased greatly, constantly exceeding the original quota. The desire for clean gaseous fuel is surprisingly big.

Natural gas engineering is still in its initial and rapid-growth stage. It is worth to mention that Liquid Natural Gas (LNG) plays an important role. China's economics keeps booming but China is short of energy resources to back up the economic growth. Coal takes major part of China's energy resource while petroleum and natural gas are just small part of it, far below world average level. As the price of petroleum is getting higher, importing LNG is a good way to solve China's energy crisis. Developing LNG industry can improve China's energy structure, safely supply energy to consumers, protect environment, and thus sustain the continuation of economic and society growth.

Gas engineering usually includes three parts: gas sources, gas transmission and distribution, and gas combustion and appliances.

5.1 Gas Sources

City gas sources are mostly natural gas, liquid petroleum gas, coal gas and biogas. Most cities in China use natural gas, liquid petroleum gas. Some medium and small sized cities use coal gas. Biogas is marsh gas, usually being used in small town and countryside.

5.1.1 Natural Gas

Natural gas falls into four categories: pure natural gas or gas field natural gas which is drilled from gas well; petroleum gas which accompanies petroleum drilled from oil well; condensed gas which contains light fraction of oil from gas condensate well; and mine drainage gas drilled from coal mine.

In prehistoric period, the climate in the earth was warm and wet. There were dense forests, all kinds of animals on land and fishes in water. Large amount of living things grew and died. Their remains heaped up at the low-lying land. After crustal movement, the sea land towered high as mountains and mountains became lakes. The remains of organisms were buried underground, underwent a complex process and changed into combustible mass under pressure and without oxygen. Among them, forests changed into solid fuel (coal). With the function of bacteria, organism remains changed to carbohydrate which is petroleum or natural gas depending on its status. Deposit containing solid fuel is coal bearing stratum. Sometimes combustible gas accompanies coal when coal is exploited. It is called mine drainage gas. Deposit containing liquid fuel is oil field. Combustible gas accompanying petroleum is called petroleum gas ($60 \sim 150$ m^3 petroleum gas can be collected with one ton of petroleum). Deposit containing gas fuel is natural gas field and the combustible gas from gas field is gas field gas or gas well gas. Condensed gas is rich natural gas deep in the earth. It is in its liquid status at 1500m underground. When it is tapped, liquid and gas phases are separated and the gas phase is called condensed gas.

Major component of pure natural gas (or simply natural gas) is methane. Natural gas also contains small amount of carbon dioxide, hydrogen sulphide and nitrogen, etc. Different gas field natural gas has different calorific value. But all natural gases' gross calorific values are above $35000kJ/Nm^3$. Petroleum gas contains 80% of methane. The rest are propane, butane and some rare gases. The calorific value of petroleum gas is above $40500kJ/m^3$. Besides methane, condensed gas contains 2%~5% pentane and hydrocarbon. Most part of mine drainage gas is methane. Its component varies depending on the way of gas production.

There are three steps to extract natural gas: well drilling, well completion, and well equipment installation. Separation equipment is installed at each well head to eliminate solid and liquid phase from natural gas. Natural gas is then measured and leaded to gas collecting pipelines. If concentrations of hydrogen sulphide, carbon dioxide, condensed oil and water in natural gas exceed standards for pipeline transmission, a gas purification factory is needed. Natural gas from gas collecting pipelines or gas purification factory is piped into long distance transmission starting station. After gas pressure regulation, dust removal and volume measurement, natural gas then enters long distance transmission pipeline. Compression stations, pipeline cleaning equipment, electrolytic protection station, valve rooms are installed on long distance transmission pipeline as needed. The number and pressure of compression stations should be determined by technical-economical calculations as they are relative to radius of long distance transmission pipelines and cost of gas compression. The end pressure of long distance transmission pipelines should match the pressure of gas storage equipments and city gas distribution pipe network. Gas gate station, also called gas distribution station, is the end point of long distance transmission and also gas source of city gas distribution system. In gate station, the volume of natural gas from long distance transmission pipeline is measured and the dusts are removed. Natural gas pressure is adjusted to that of city gas distribution system and odorant is added before the gas finally goes into the city gas distribution system.

5.1.2 Manufactured Fuel Gas

1. Dry Distillation of Solid Fuel and Coke Oven Gas

Solid fuel coal is a complex organic chemical compound. Heated without air, the coal can be decomposed into gas, liquid and solid phases. In different temperatures, the products are different.

1) Dry phase: When temperature is below 120℃, the absorbed water evaporates.

2) Preheat dry distillation phase: When temperature is between 120℃ and 200℃, part of crystal water evaporates. CH_4 and CO absorbed on coal start to separate out. When temperature reaches 250℃, coal tar vapor and ammonia appear.

3) Low-temperature dry distillation phase: When temperature raises to 350℃, coal tar vapor increases and it reaches its maximum when the temperature is 500~550℃. CO, CO_2, H_2, CH_4 and $C_m H_n$ are given out. The calorific value of combustible gas at this phase is 25080~33540kJ/Nm^3. The solid residue in this phase is half-coke.

4) High temperature dry distillation phase: The temperature continues to rise to 1100℃ from 550℃, coal tar vapor decomposes. Heavy hydrocarbon in gas phases decomposes too. H_2 concentration increases in gas phase. The gas produced amount reaches the maximum when temperature is 1100℃. The gas at this point is called coke oven gas. Calorific value of coke oven gas is 16720~18818kJ/Nm^3. The solid residue in this phase is coke which can be used for steelmaking. When there is no natural gas available, coke-oven gas can be used as city gas source.

2. Coal Gasification Gas

Solid fuel gasification is a thermochemistry process. Coal is gasified to CO, CH_4 and H_2. Generator gas with calorific value of 5400kJ/Nm^3 is produced when (agent) reactant is air. The main reaction is $CO_2 + C = 2CO + 172140kJ$. When the reactant is vapor, water gas with calorific value of 10500kJ/Nm^3 is produced. The reaction is $C + H_2O = CO + H_2 - 118628.4kJ$. Because the above two kinds of gases are poisoning and with low calorific values, they are not allowed to be used in cities. They can be used as industrial fuel for coke-oven gas furnaces.

3. Oil Gas

Oil gas is manufactured by thermal cracking of heavy oil and catalytic cracking of heavy oil. Oil gas from thermal cracking of heavy oil contains methane, ethylene and propylene. Calorific value is 41900kJ/Nm^3. Oil gas from catalytic cracking of heavy oil contains hydrogen, methane and CO. Its gross calorific value is 17600~20900kJ/Nm^3. The apparatus of producing oil gas from heavy oil is uncomplicated, cost-effective, space-saving, and easy to construct and operate. Oil gas is one kind of city gas sources.

5.1.3 Liquid Petroleum Gas

Liquid petroleum gas is a side product generated from refining process of crude oil. Its main components are propane, propylene, butane and butene. At normal temperature and normal pressure, those hydrocarbons are in gas phase. At higher pressure and lower temperature, these hydrocarbons are in liquid phase. The volume of gas phase is 250 times of volume of liquid phase of the same mass. Gas phase liquid petroleum gas' calorific value is $92100 \sim 121400 kJ/Nm^3$. Liquid phase liquid petroleum gas' calorific value is $45200 \sim 46100 kJ/Nm^3$. The cost of manufacturing liquid petroleum gas is small. Liquid petroleum gas supplying is simple. It is a good source of city gas.

5.1.4 Biogas

Air insulated organic substance, such as protein, cellulose, fat, starch, etc, will begin to ferment by the action of microorganism. The ferment process will give out combustible gas, biogas. The substances for fermentation are plenty and endless, such as garbage, riot weed, dead leaves and excrement and urine. Thus, biogas is a renewable source energy. Biogas contains 60% methane, 35% carbon dioxide and small amount of hydrogen and carbon oxide. Its calorific value is $20900 kJ/Nm^3$.

5.2 City Gas Distribution Systems

City gas distribution system is responsible to safely distribute gas from sources to residential, commercial and industrial consumers. City gas distribution system is the key part to supply gas to thousands of consumers in a city.

Modern city gas distribution system is a comprehensive and complex system. It usually includes the following:

(1) Gas network It is a pipe network consisting low-, medium-, secondary-high- and high-pressure gas pipelines. City distribution pipelines are responsible for city gas transmission and gas distribution. Higher pressure pipelines are responsible for gas transmission while lower pressure pipelines are for gas distribution.

(2) City gate station or city gas distribution station It receives gas transmitted from upstream. Gas volume is measured and gas pressure is regulated in gate station. Gas is then pumped to gas distribution system.

(3) Gas pressure regulating facilities Gas pressure regulator stations connect pipelines of different pressures.

(4) Gas storage station Demanding of gas in a city is not even. Gas storage station is a place to store gas when gas demanding is low and to supply gas when gas demanding is high.

(5) City gas dispatch and management center It is a management center of city gas distribution system, monitoring the operating situation of gas distribution pipelines and equipment. The center also gives out suitable orders to response to different situations of pipeline operation. For example, when the gas demand is in peak, the center will order the gas storage equipment to release more gas

into the pipelines. When the gas demand is low, the center will send out message to hold more gas in the gas storage equipment.

(6) Pipeline maintenance and repair center It is entrusted with the task of pipeline and equipment patrol, maintenance, and repair. Pipeline maintenance and repair center is responsible for daily check of gas pressure regulating stations in the system and repairs pipeline and equipment in time when there are emergencies.

City gas distribution system design should ensure reliable gas supply to users. The system should be able to continue to supply gas to consumers by shutting down part of the pipeline when there is an accident. The system should be easily maintained and safely operated. The system design plan should have the best social and economical benefits.

5.2.1 Pressures of Gas Distribution System

1. Municipal Gas Pipeline Categories

According to pressures, city distribution pipelines fall into the following categories:

1) Low-pressure pipelines: $p < 0.01\text{MPa}$.
2) Medium-pressure B pipelines: $0.01\text{MPa} \leqslant p \leqslant 0.2\text{MPa}$.
3) Medium-pressure A pipelines: $0.2\text{MPa} < p \leqslant 0.4\text{MPa}$.
4) Secondary high-pressure B pipelines: $0.4\text{MPa} < p \leqslant 0.8\text{MPa}$.
5) Secondary high-pressure A pipelines: $0.8\text{MPa} < p \leqslant 1.6\text{MPa}$.
6) High-pressure B pipelines: $1.6\text{MPa} < p \leqslant 2.5\text{MPa}$.
7) High-pressure A pipelines: $2.5\text{MPa} < p \leqslant 4.0\text{MPa}$.

Low-pressure gas pipelines are used to supply gas to residential and commercial consumers. Medium-pressure B and A pipelines are not allowed to connect to large commercial buildings or industrial consumers without using gas pressure regulator devices. Pipelines of different pressures are connected by gas pressure regulators. Main pipelines of different gas pressures should be formed as loops, especially medium-and above pressure pipelines. If it is not possible for the pipes to form loops at the first phase of the project, the pipelines should be connected to form loops gradually. High-pressure B pipelines are usually the outer loop and the main artery to supply gas to a city. High-pressure A pipelines are usually outside loops for large municipals.

2. Gas Network System

Gas network system, which is gas distributing pipeline network system, is the major part of city gas distribution system. According to pipeline pressures, gas network systems fall into the following categories:

1) System with one pressure level: The system has only one low-pressure pipeline and is usually selected to supply gas to a small town. This system would consume large amount of steel materials if it Wasselected to supply a bigger city.

2) System with two pressure levels: This system has low-and medium-pressure pipelines and is

selected to supply gas to a small- or medium-sized city.

3) System with three pressure levels: This system has low-, medium-and secondary high-pressure pipelines and is selected to supply gas to a medium- and big-sized city.

4) System with multi-pressure levels: This system posseses low pressure, medium pressure, secondary high-pressure, and even high pressure pipeline.

Fig. 5-1 shows a gas network system with three pressure levels for a big city.

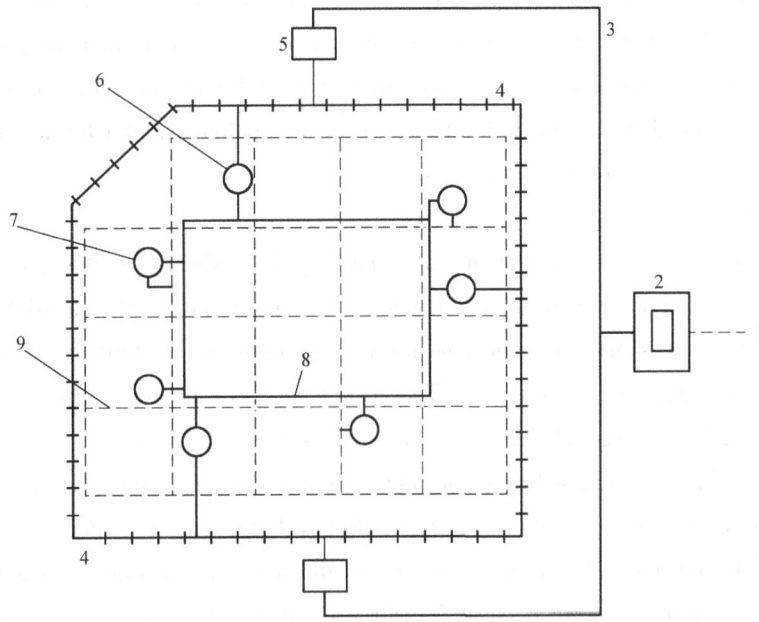

Fig. 5-1 Gas distribution system for certain city

1—Long distance pipeline 2—City gate station 3—Suburb secondary high-pressure pipeline
4—Secondary high-pressure network 5—Gas storage station
6—High pressure and medium-pressure regulator station 7—Medium-pressure and low-pressure regulator station
8—Medium-pressure pipelines 9—Low-pressure pipelines

The system shown in Fig. 5-1 consists of low-, medium- and secondary high-pressure pipelines. Gas source is natural gas from long distance transmission pipeline (or high-pressure manufactured gas). High pressure gas holders are located on both sides of the city holding peak shaving gas. The suburb high pressure pipelines are shaped as half circle to supply gas to the city. Secondary high-, medium-, and low-pressure pipeline are connected through gas pressure regulator devices. Because there are too many medium- and low-pressure regulators, they are not shown in the figure. Low-pressure pipeline is directly connected to residential consumers while industrial and big commercial customers are permitted to be connected to medium pressure pipelines through pressure regulating apparatus.

A gas network system with different pressure levels is a necessary for a city. First, it is economical for a city to choose a gas network system with different pressure levels. As most gas is transited by high-pressure pipeline, the unit pressure drop is selected to be bigger and diameters of pipeline are smaller than those for low-pressure pipelines. Thus steel materials are saved. Second, residential and small commercial customers need low-pressure pipelines while medium-pressure pipelines are needed for industrial consumers and large commercial customers. Third, for safety and operation reason, it is not appropriate to lay out high pressure or medium pressure A pipeline in the crowed downtown area. Only medium pressure B and low-pressure pipelines are allowed to be laid out in downtown area. With further development of technology, it is possible to increase pressure level in a newly built or renovated network system by improving the quality of pipeline, gas appliances, construction and operational management levels. The cost of pipeline will be further reduced and the pipeline capacity will be increased.

3. City Gas Load

To design a city distribution system, the first step is to determine the gas load of this city. There are three types of gas consumers: residential, commercial, and industrial. Gaseous fuel is the best quality fuel and should be made good use of. Gas resources in China are not rich. Residential consumers have the first priority to use gas. The coal stove for residential utility has low energy efficiency of 15% ~20%. Energy efficiency of gas utility is 55% ~60%. Thus, to supply gas to residential consumers has the biggest benefit of energy saving. For large amount, dispersed residential and commercial consumers, utilization of gas will effectively protect environment, reduce pollution, save labors and lessen traffic. However, when gas is allocated, residential, commercial and industrial demands should be balanced. Because industrial consumers use gas evenly, industrial consumers can be buffer to adjust the uneven gas load fluctuation, to reduce the storage volume needed and to shave peak. What's more, industrial consumers add profits to gas company.

Gas consumption norms should be determined in order to calculate city gas load. Factors affecting residential gas consumption norms include climate in the area, gas price, house heating method, with or without hot water supply, number of people living in the house and life style of that area, etc. Residential gas consumption norms are usually gained by investigation of large amount of different typical consumers and analysis of the data. The total gas demand of residential consumers is determined by multiple of the number of households and the norms of the cities. With the same method, the commercial gas consumption norms and total gas demand can be obtained. For a new city, the norms of similar city can be a reference. Industrial demand can be determined by heat balance calculation knowing the annually fuel consumption. City gas load is the total of different consumers' gas demand. An unanticipated amount of gas, usually 5% of the total city gas load, should be added to compensate leakage and to meet the demand of future new consumers.

Gas demands are uneven and fluctuating with time. The inconsistency can be expressed in monthly fluctuation, daily fluctuation and hourly fluctuation. The major factor affecting monthly fluctuation is weather. Monthly fluctuation is also called seasonal fluctuation. When the temperature is low, gas demands are high because more cooking, hot water and heating are needed. Industrial consumers consume gas in a steadier pattern but gas consumption in summer is also a little bit lower than that in winter. Uneven factor of monthly consumption K_1 is used to show monthly fluctuation of gas consumption.

$$K_1 = \frac{\text{average daily gas consumption of the month}}{\text{average daily gas consumption of the whole year}}$$

The largest K_1 among the 12 months is called maximum uneven factor of monthly consumption and the month with the largest K_1 is called design month.

Factors affecting daily fluctuation of gas assumption are temperatures, lifestyle of people, schedules of commercial and industrial consumers, etc. Uneven factor of daily consumption K_2 is used to show daily fluctuation of gas consumption.

$$K_2 = \frac{\text{daily gas consumption in a month}}{\text{average daily gas consumption in a month}}$$

The biggest K_2 in a month is called maximum uneven factor of daily consumption.

The hourly gas consumptions of different consumers in a city are different. Gas consumption hourly fluctuation of residential and commercial users is most enormous. Usually there are three gas demand peaks in a week day and two peaks in a weekend day. For continuous heating, gas consumption hourly fluctuation is not big. For intermittent heating, gas consumption hourly fluctuation is prominent. Maximum uneven factor of hourly consumption K_3 is used to show hourly fluctuation of gas consumption:

$$K_3 = \frac{\text{gas consumption in a certain hour of a certain day}}{\text{average hourly gas consumption the same day}}$$

The biggest K_3 is called peak hourly fluctuation coefficient.

The diameters of gas pipelines and capacities of equipments are determined by the gas flow rate of the peak hour in the peak day of design month, which is called hourly gas flow rate for hydraulic calculation. The hourly gas flow rate is obtained by analysis of reliable hourly gas consumption data. Hourly gas consumption data of a day is also very important for pipeline operation and determination of gas storage volume. The correctly determination of hourly gas flow rate is closely relative to economic efficiency and reliability of the pipeline system. If hourly gas flow rate is bigger than the correct value, cost of pipeline systems will be too high. If hourly gas flow rate is lower than the right value, the reliable gas supply to consumers will not be guaranteed. Hourly gas flow rate for pipeline hydraulic calculation is

$$Q_h = Q_a K_m K_d K_h / (365 \times 24)$$

Where Q_h—calculation hour flow rate for pipeline hydraulic calculation (Nm^3/h);

Q_a—annual gas load (Nm^3/a);

K_m—maximum uneven factor of monthly consumption;

K_d—maximum uneven factor of daily consumption;

K_h—maximum uneven factor of hourly consumption.

The above mentioned maximum factors are drawn from statistical analysis of practical gas consumption data. The data collection requires large amount of human labors. If there are not enough statistical data, the coefficients can be roughly selected as: $K_m = 1.1 \sim 1.3$, $K_d = 1.01 \sim 1.2$ and $K_h = 2.2 \sim 3.2$.

4. The Allowable Pressure Drop for Low-pressure Gas Pipelines

The allowable pressure drop due to friction between gas pressure regulator outlet and appliance is needed to determine for hydraulic calculation of gas network design.

There are two ways of connecting consumers' gas appliances to gas network, directly connection or connection through gas pressure regulator box. Gas appliance pressure is constant if it is connected with pipeline network through gas pressure regulator boxes. Most residential consumers' appliances are directly connected to gas network and thus the pressures of appliances fluctuate when the flow rate and pressure of gas in network change. Because of pipeline friction drag, the pressure of starting point of pipeline is higher than that of the ending point. Thus, the pressure of appliances connected to the starting points of the pipelines is higher than that connected to the ending points of pipelines. At design phase, allowable pressure drop for low-pressure pipeline should be chosen in a certain range to ensure steady gas combustion and excellent appliance operation.

p_n stands for rated pressure of a gas appliance. p_{max} stands for the maximum pressure of gas appliances and p_{min} stands for minimum pressure of gas appliances.

$$p_{max} = k_1 p_n$$
$$p_{min} = k_2 p_n$$

Where k_1, k_2—the maximum and minimum pressure coefficients.

Because residential appliances are directly connected to low-pressure pipeline, the highest pressure of pipelines may not exceed the maximum allowable pressure of gas appliances and the lowest pressure of pipelines may not lower than the minimum allowable pressure of gas appliances. Thus the pipeline allowable pressure drop is $\Delta p = p_{max} - p_{min} = (k_1 - k_2) p_n$.

Research and practice prove that residential gas appliances can operate at the pressure in the range of 50% rated pressure of the gas appliances which means $k_1 = 1.5$ and $k_2 = 0.5$. When pressure of gas appliance drops from $1.5 p_n$ to $0.5 p_n$, the gas appliance load will varies from $1.2Q$ to $0.7Q$. Q is gas appliance rated gas load. At peak hours, too low gas load is not desirable. If we choose $k_2 = 0.75$, gas load can reach $0.86Q$ which is acceptable. Thus, allowable pressure drop for low-pressure pipeline is

$$\Delta p = (k_1 - k_2) p_n = (1.5 - 0.75) p_n$$

At the most unfavorable situation, which is the lowest point of gas consumption fluctuation, the pressure of gas appliance nearest the gas regulator station reaches its maximum value. But there are at least 150Pa resistance from gas regulator device to this appliance. This resistance includes gas meter resistance, indoor main and branch pipeline resistances. Thus, allowable pressure drop for low-pressure pipeline is

$$\Delta p = 0.75 p_n + 150 \text{Pa}$$

Which is also the pressure drop chosen for hydraulic calculation for gas network design.

Increasing p_n of appliances can increase allowable pressure drop of pipelines. Thus, when design the network, pipeline diameter decreases and investment cost drops. On the other hand, increasing p_n increases the pressure of pipeline system and coherently increases the possibility of gas leakage. Higher p_n also demands higher quality standards of equipment and higher operation cost. Thus, there is an appropriate p_n value.

Medium- and high-pressure pipeline gas pressure drop for hydraulic calculation is the pressure difference between starting point and ending point of pipeline. The starting point can be gas regulating station or compression station. The ending point can be gas regulating station or industrial consumers.

When gas pressure drop limitation are determined, the pipeline diameters of gas network can be calculated using equations in fluid dynamics for hydraulic calculation.

5.2.2 Gas Storage and Gas Storage Station

Gas demand of a city is not constant and varies with time. But gas source supply is constant and does not change with time. To solve the confliction of constant supply and inconstant demand, city gas distribution system is equipped with gas storage station. Gas storage station stores gas during low demand and release gas at peak demand. The following are several commonly used storage methods.

1. Underground Storage

At low gas demand season, gas is pumped into underground space with proper geological structure. At high gas demand season, gas is withdrawn from the underground space. The proper geological structures are usually exhausted oil or gas fields, underground structure containing water and porosities, salty ore beds and caves. The most economical method is storage city gas in exhausted oil or gas fields. Underground storage reservoirs can store huge volume of gas with small investment and operation costs. This method saves thousands of tons of steal materials. It is usually used for seasonal peak-shaving and partial daily peak-shaving. It is an ideal storage method for a city. The difficult part is how to find an economical and suitable geological structure near the city to store gas. The capacity of the first underground storage reservoir in China is 10 million cubic meters. Large scale underground storage reservoirs have been under construction since the beginning of Western to Eastern Project. For example Jintan underground storage reservoir is being constructed in Jiangsu. Its capacity is planned to be 1.74 billion cubic meters. It is China's first underground storage reservoir utilizing exhausted salt mine. Utilization of exhausted sale mine to store natural gas not only saves cost but also stabilizes the geological structure. Capacity of Liuzhuang underground storage reservoir is planned to be 255 million cubic meters and the construction just started. Total effective storage volume of these two underground storage reservoirs is 2 billion cubic meters at the final construction phase in year 2020. By then, the above underground storage facilities will be able to do seasonal peak-shave and supply gas to consumers in emergency for the area of Yangtze River Delta.

2. Liquid Natural Gas Storage

Methane, major component of natural gas, will be liquefied at 5.7kPa and −161℃. The volume of liquid natural gas is much smaller, 1/600 volume of natural gas of the same mass. It can be stored in a heat insulated holders. Liquid natural gas will be gasified at gas demanding peak hours and be supplied to users.

Now liquefied natural gas (LNG) is an international commodity because it is easy to be transported and be traded between countries. Recently, global LNG production and trade are getting active. LNG is hot in oil industrial world. To ensure multiple energy sources and improve energy consumption structures, big energy consuming countries pay more attention to import of LNG. Big international oil companies consider LNG as their new profitable business. LNG will be the hottest global commodity. Importing LNG will compensate China's lacking of oil, enrich energy source varieties and improve environmental quality. LNG and West to East Project complement each other. Recently, China thinks highly of LNG. LNG projects along the coast under planning include: Guangdong, Fujian, Zhejiang, Shanghai, Jiangsu, Shandong and Liaoning.

3. Line-packing

To store gas by high pressure pipelines and by end section of long transmission pipelines are effective ways of hourly peak-shaving. Groups of high pressure pipelines are buried underground and gas inside is compressed to high pressure to be stored. End section of long transmission pipelines can store certain amount of gas during night time when gas demand is low and release gas at daytime when gas demand is high.

4. Store Gas with Gasholder

The most commonly used gas storage method in China is to store gas with low-pressure or high-pressure gasholders to balance daily and hourly gas demand fluctuations. Comparing with other storage methods, gasholder storage consumes more metal materials and costs more. But when other gas storage methods are not available, gasholder storage is the only way to store gas. Manufactured gases are usually stored in low-pressure gasholders which are huge facilities. Natural gas is stored in high-pressure gasholders. Gasholders are usually located in city gas storage and distribution stations.

5.2.3 Gas Supply System in Buildings

Gas supply system in buildings varies with city gas distribution system. Fig. 5-2 shows gas supply system in a building connected with low-pressure pipeline of city gas network. The system consists of service pipe, main, vertical pipe, gas meters, gas appliances and connecting pipe. Service pipes are connected with courtyard pipeline or low-pressure pipeline of city network.

5.3 Gas Combustion and Its Appliances

Gas coming from gas sources through pipelines provides heat for users by combustion on individual appliances. Modern society demands the highest possible efficiency in the utilization of all types of fuel. To achieve this, fuel and air must be mixed in the correct proportions under stable conditions implying a knowledge of the combustion characteristics of the fuel and the underlying aspects of fluid mechanics and thermodynamics.

Combustion theory combines combustion calculation, combustion reaction kinetics, fuel gas flow mixing process and flame spreading.

Burner is a device to complement combustion to convert gas from its primary fuel state into useful energy. Burner can be classified as manufactured gas burners, natural gas burners, liquid petroleum gas burners, mixed gas burners and universal burners. According to the mixing method of gas and air, burners can be classified into diffusion burner, aerated burner and flameless burner.

In a diffusion burner, air needed for combustion diffuses from atmosphere around the flame rather than being premixed with gas before entering the burner. Aerated burner is usually a perforated plate on which the partially premixed gas and air burns. Part of the air needed for combustion is entrained into the gas pipeline by a nozzle and venture throat and the gas-air mixture goes to the burner through the holes. In a flameless burner, gas and air needed by combustion are all premixed together before entering the burner.

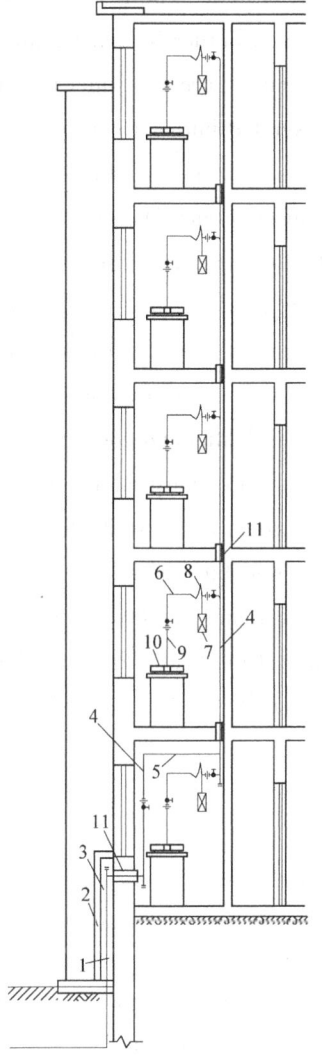

Fig. 5-2 Gas supply system in buildings
1—Service pipe 2—Brick platform 3—Insulation layer
4—Vertical pipe 5—Horizontal main 6—User branch
7—Gas meter 8—Cocks and movable joints
9—Connecting pipe 10—Gas appliance 11—Gasing pipe

Diffusion burners can be divided into two categories: natural-draught burners and forced draught burners. In natural-draught burners, air needed for combustion diffuses from the atmosphere naturally while in forced-draught burners gas and air are blown under pressure into a swirl chamber where the flame is established, with a fair amount of noise. Natural-draught burners are usually used for residential users while forced-draught burners are usually used for industrial users.

Flame of aerated burner is shorter than that of natural draught diffusion burner. Flame temperature of aerated burner is higher than that of natural draught diffusion burner. Heat output adjustable scope of aerated burner is wider than that of flameless burner. Aerated burner can burn different kind of gases. Aerated burner's combustion is safe and clean with minimal CO concentration in the flue products and combustion efficiency is high. Aerated burner saves electrical power comparing with forced-draught burner. Due to the structure of gas ejector, aerated burner is self-adjustable which means the primary air coefficient is constant even when heat output of burner varies to a certain degree. However, there is a heat output limit for aerated burner. Heating intensity is lower than that of flameless burner. The stability of flame is not as good as that of diffusion burner. Aerated burner is not able to work in positive pressure combustion chambers. Multi-orifice aerated burners are utilized widely by residential and commercial users, such as stoves and hot water heaters, and also in small sized boilers and industrial boilers. Single orifice aerated burners are often used in medium sized boilers and some industrial boilers.

Flameless burner burns gas completely with high flame temperature, strong heating strength. But flame stability is low. To avoid lift off and light back, burner structure is usually complex. Thus, if the load is big, the burner probably is huge and heavy with loud noises. This kind of burner is usually used in industrial.

Questions

1. How many kinds of gases are permitted to supply to city users? What are the heat values of the gases?
2. What's the pressure categories of city distribution pipeline system? What are the pressure ranges?
3. How to calculate the gas load for a city?
4. What's the maximum pressure and minimum pressure of residential gas appliances? For design and hydraulic calculation of low pressure pipeline, what's the allowable hydraulic pressure drop between the outlet of gas pressure regulator and the far end user?
5. Why do we need to store gas? How many gas storage methods do we usually use? What's their advantage and disadvantages respectively?
6. How many kinds of gas burners do we have? What's their features?

第 6 章
给 水 排 水

本章要点：本章分给水系统和排水系统两部分。给水系统中，给出了供水历史及给水工程中室内管道的背景及现状和分析了管网中泵及泵站的形式。排水系统中描述了废水的组成、收集及水处理。

知识点：明渠流的特点；废水的组成；泵和泵站的分类；水处理的目的。

6.1 供水历史

人类在史前时期就开始寻求洁净的水。人类最早的许多活动是不难推测的。一些人可能在地上挖沟，把水引到所需要的地方，后来，空心圆木可能作为最初的水管得到使用。

一定是在数千年后，我们更近代的祖先才学会建设城市，享受到管道供水进家和下水道泄水排污的便利。有关集中给水排水设施的最早考古记录可上溯至约五千年前的苏米里亚的尼波城。在尼波城的废墟中有一拱顶下水道，其楔形石块尖头向下，被砌成完美的拱形。水由井和蓄水池引入。完善的排水系统除去来自该城华丽的娱乐场所和居民区的废水。

最早关于水处理知识的记载现保留在梵文医学典籍和埃及壁刻中。约公元前 2000 年的梵文著作叙述了如何通过在铜器皿中煮沸，日光照晒，木炭过滤和在陶土器皿中冷却等方法来净化污浊的水。

人们已知最早的液体净化装置出现在公元前 15 世纪和公元前 13 世纪的埃及壁画中，一幅画描绘了如何用虹吸管吸水或者是吸取沉淀过的酒。另一幅画显示在当时埃及的厨房里使用油绳虹吸的方法。

公元 98 年，罗马水务长官塞克特斯·朱利叶斯·弗朗提纳斯作出了第一份有关供水和水处理的工程报告。他写了两本有关罗马供水的书。在这两本书中，他描述了位于一渡槽头的沉淀池。他的著作最先由著名的水利工程师克莱蒙斯·荷思切尔于 1899 年译成英文。

公元 8 世纪，阿拉伯炼丹术士詹伯写了一篇颇具专业水平的有关蒸馏的论文，其中涉及水和其他液体的各种蒸馏器具。

英国哲学家弗朗西斯.培根爵士写到过他用过滤、煮沸、蒸馏和絮凝澄清等方法净化水的试验。有关试验情况于 1627 年即他去世后一年发表。培根还指出澄清的水往往有益健康，令人"悦目"。

已知的第一个对砂滤池有插图的描述，由一位意大利的内科医生鲁克·安东尼奥·帕罗发表于 1685 年。他根据自己在奥土战争中的经历，写了一本关于军营中士兵保健的书。这很可能是有关公共卫生的最早的出版物。他描述并图示了砂滤池和沉淀法的使用。帕罗还指出他的过滤法与那些在威尼斯道吉宫和罗马卡蒂诺·萨切特宫筑井的人使用的方法原理是一样的。

最古老的在考古学上已知的水过滤的例子见于威尼斯及其占领的殖民地。蓄水池华丽的池口上载有日期，但人们尚不知过滤池建于何时。威尼斯这个建在诸岛上的城市，一千三百多年以来靠接蓄雨水作为该城市的主要淡水供应。人们建造蓄水池并把很多蓄水池和砂滤池相接。雨水自屋顶冲刷而下流至街道，在那儿被收集到有石格栅的集水池中，然后经砂床过滤至蓄水池。

关于威尼斯供水的一篇综述见于 1863 年的《实用力学期刊》。威尼斯陆地面积为 52002.1m^2，年平均降雨量为 0.8128m。几乎所有的这些降雨都被收集在 177 个公共的和 1900 个私人的蓄水池中。这些蓄水池日平均供水量约每人每天 19.09L。如此低的耗水量部分归于缺乏下水道以及人们惯于在废水池洗衣服和普遍饮酒。大约从 16 世纪开始，这些蓄水池一直是威尼斯的主要供水设备。

18 至 19 世纪在英、法、德、俄等国做了许多试验。亨利·达西于 1856 年在法国和英国取得了滤池的专利，除絮凝工艺外，在其他方面促进了美国快速砂滤池的问世。他似乎首先将力学原理应用于滤池设计。第一个供应全镇用水的滤池于 1804 年建于苏格兰的佩斯里，但水是用车送至用户的。到 1807 年，在苏格兰的格拉斯哥，滤后水由管道输往用户。

在美国，直到内战之后水处理问题才得一顾。解决水混浊的问题不像在欧洲那样迫切。第一批滤池属慢速砂滤型，和英国的设计相似。约在 1890 年，快速砂滤池在美国问世，并使用了絮凝剂以提高滤池的效率。这些滤池经稍许改进，不久便发展成目前使用的快速砂滤池。

6.2 给水工程

城市给水系统通常包括一个位于水源处的蓄水库，从蓄水库到城市附近的配水库的管道以及埋设在街道下面的将水送入住户、商店、工厂和机关的配水管。因此，给水工程的主要设备就是两座水库及其管道网。蓄水库的作用是储足一年或数年的用水量，以保证干旱期间全部高峰用水量。配水库的作用则是保证一天或一星期的用水量。由于有了蓄水库，给水水源可以小些，费用也少些；同样，由于有了配水库，管道和水泵都可以比没有配水库时小些，因而也便宜些。

美国某些城市的用水量按人口平均计在全世界是最高的。每人的用水量变化于 200～5000L/d 之间，平均每人约为 500L/d。但是不能认为气候较冷的国家最后也达到同样的用水水平，因为美国所需的最高用水量大多是由于夏季空调设备以及花园浇水方面所耗用的。

给水工程师必须研究所在地区的人均用水量（每人耗用的水量），并根据该地区里最先进的社区的用水量选定一个数值，所确定的人均用水量必须乘以今后大约 30 年或更长时间后的计划供水的估计人口数。由于供水和储水设施都不能像配水系统那样易于扩建，所以它们都必须设计得有足够的容量，以满足这一时期的需要。而配水系统则可随供水需求的增长及住宅的建设而扩建。

一旦计算出每年所需的供水量，并经包括消防部门在内的所有有关方面同意后，则确保能够真正永久地从所建议采用的集水处取得所需供水量就成为重要的问题。所谓集水处是将水泄入供水水源的区域。每年泄入水库的水量不可能超过该流域的降雨量，而且通常还要比之少得多。

给水水量通常可以从地表水（雨水）或地下水取水，或二者兼得。地表水和地下水均由雨水补给。地表水由地面径流补给。而泉水与井水则由进入地下的水，即渗透水补给，这两部分水量，加上蒸发水及树木和其他植物所吸收的水，组成总降雨量。即使城市给水包括该区域内的全部泉水及地表水，但由于水的蒸发和植物生长的需要，仍然不可能取得全部降雨量。

因此，把降雨量记录、径流量和渗透率，同河流流量记录及当地其他水文资料加以核对，是非常重要的。渗透水，即渗入地下变成地下水的雨水，能在地下作长距离的水平流动，可以流入或者流出集水区。如果每年的供水量超过每年的降雨量，地下水位一般将下降，其结果是不能获得所需要的供水量。这时必须寻找别的水源。

如果能将水储存在地下，就没有必要建造水库或储水池，而把水储存于地下往往是可能的。事实上，在伦敦地区，由于抽水的缘故，该地区白垩土层内的水位一个多世纪以来一直在不断下降。因此有人建议，今后不再使用一直沿用到现在的地面蓄水库蓄水，而改为向井内回灌净水以补充白垩土层内水量以达到蓄水的目的。这种地下储存的方法，目前正广泛地为许多国家的煤气工业所采用。在供气量多时，用压缩机通过井把煤气送入地下密封的砂层、石灰岩层或其他多孔岩层中储存，以供需气量大于供气量时之用。这种地下储气库往往比现有最大的储气罐大几百倍，已公认是一种实用价廉而安全可靠的储气方法。

6.3 室内管道工程——背景与现状

为保护人类健康，并为了提供给人们较舒适的生活方式而发展起来的最重要的系统之一就是室内管道系统，该系统就是用管道向用户输送饮用水，并将废物排入各种处理流程进行处理。在现代社会，我们必须认识到：室内管道系统对于社会犹如循环系统对于人体那样重要。为了避免传染病的爆发和化学污染，室内管道系统必须有效地进行工作。在住宅区内，良好的卫生设施要求室内管道系统应当没有交叉连接、倒流连接、配水出口淹没以及通风不良等现象，还应当向现代社会提供充足的优质饮用水。当今社会面临的最大困难之一在于：现存的较陈旧的管道系统可能逐渐损坏，并将给人们健康带来危害。同时，室内管道系统的维修方式也可能直接危害健康。

室内管道工程是指对饮水供应系统、生活用水或雨水排放系统及通风系统中的管道、装置、设备以及附件进行安装、维修、更换等作业。但它并不包括钻井、水软化设备的安装以及卫生用具、设备、器具和零件的制造或销售。室内管道系统是由充足的饮水供给系统、安全充足的排水系统、足够的器具及设备所组成。

长期以来，公共卫生人员对室内管道系统及公共饮用水配水系统中交叉连接、倒流连接和进水口淹没等问题一直很关注。这些交叉连接可能使饮用水受到非饮用水或污水的污染。虽然饮用水受污染的可能性似乎很小，但诸多问题确实存在。为了同这一污染问题作斗争，安装人员必须懂得水力学及其引起环境卫生公害的各种污染因素。他们还必须知道可采用哪些合格的装置和方法以防止倒流以及如何获得这些材料并适当地安装起来。

由于年代已久，许多地区的室内管道系统正趋于破损。与此相关的微生物的、化学的或物理的诸因素的巨大的潜在威胁未能给予足够的重视。

6.4 明渠流

明渠流是指渠道中流体部分界面暴露在大气压下的流体运动。这种渠道可以敞开在大气中，如天然河床、人工运河以及沟渠，也可以是封闭的。

等截面管道摩擦流动必须有压差来维持流动；横截面不变的明渠摩擦流动则是靠地球引力的影响，即明渠高度的变化来维持。与管流不同的是，明渠流的过水断面能够随着不同流动状况而改变，且受制于渠道的界限。例如，通过矩形断面明渠的流动，液体深度的变化会形成不同的矩形过水断面。

正如管流一样，明渠流的性质可能是层流，也可能是湍流。当液体是水的时候，最为常见的是湍流。在测定和控制河水流动以及确定灌渠设计要求时，对明渠进行分析是重要的。

首先，给出和明渠流有关的几个定义。当过水断面沿着流动方向不变时，这种流动称为均匀流；反之则称为非均匀流。因为在明渠均匀流中，液体的深度是不变的，液体的表面与渠底是平行的。当液体的深度变化时，就会形成明渠非均匀流（也称为变速流）。当渠道断面的形状或渠底的形状改变时，就会产生这一种流动。如果下游方向的深度增大，流速就会减慢，而形成滞流；如果下游方向的深度减小，速度则增加，就会形成加速流。

在任何一个足够长的坡度及断面保持不变的渠道里，都会形成均匀流动。下面给出一个形成均匀流的例子。图 6-1 所示为某一坡度有变化的灌渠。由于渠流坡度有变化，沿流动方向的重力分量大于阻滞流动的渠壁的切力，故流动就会产生加速，随着流速增大，切力也相应增大，达到某一速度时，切力与重力分量相等。在这种平衡条件下，速度和液体的深度保持不变，流动则变成明渠均匀流。

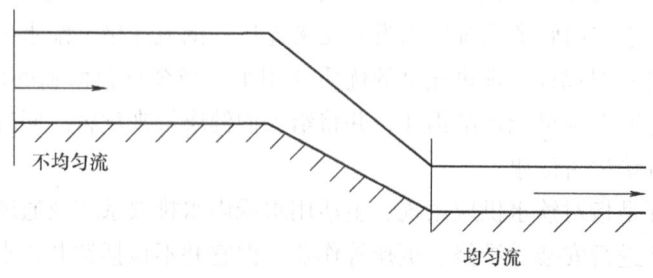

图 6-1 明渠流

从图 6-1 可以看出，渠底坡度的变化会形成明渠非均匀流。当一种障碍物，如溢洪道，建在能形成均匀流的倾斜渠道上时，就会形成渐变流。障碍物后水面所形成的轮廓被称为回水曲线。

6.5 泵和泵站

在供水系统中，泵和泵送机械有以下的服务目标：从水源（地表水或地下水）提水，或者通过高扬程泵把水迅速送到居民区，或者用低扬程泵将水打入净水厂；将水从低压供水区增压至高压供水区、单独的消防水源和高层建筑物上层；使水进出水处理厂，在此过程中，反冲过滤池使水由沉淀池和其他处理构筑物流出，抽排沉淀固体和向运行设备供水（特别是压力水）。

如今大多数给水和废水的输送都是由离心泵或轴流泵来完成的。水穿过叶轮时的流向确定了泵的类型：在开式或闭式叶轮泵中表现为辐流，该泵具有螺旋形或涡轮式外壳，水通过单吸或双吸进入叶轮；在轴流泵中表现为轴向流；在开式叶轮混流泵中表现为混流。轴流泵不是离心泵。这两种泵都可称为旋转动力泵。

开式叶轮泵的效率不如闭式叶轮泵，但其可令相当大的漂浮物通过而不致被堵塞。因此，它们在提升废水和污泥时是大有用场的。单级泵仅有一个叶轮；而多级泵则有两个或两个以上的叶轮，且每一级叶轮都将水打入下一级叶轮中。多级叶轮井泵可本身带有潜于水下的电动机或位于泵站地面上的原动机的轴驱动。

除离心泵和轴流泵外，水和废水系统可包括：活塞泵，其大小从手压罐形泵到20世纪装有蒸汽驱动装置的大型泵机不等；装有两个或两个以上转子的旋转泵（其形状从网式瓣轮到齿轮变化，多被用作小型灭火泵）；水锤泵，利用大量低压水形成的冲击来驱动少量的水（为冲击水的1/2~1/6），使其通过输水管到达较高高程，这一过程同水锤引起的压力波及其操作程序一致；射流泵，或称喷射器，用于井中和脱水操作中，引带高速空气射流或水射流通过喷嘴进入管道狭窄部分；气升泵，其内由朝上的空气管释放的气泡通过喷射管提升井水或排水坑的水；往复式喷射器，被置于压力容器内，水（特别是废水）在容器内积蓄，而当浮球阀被上升水推开并使压缩空气进入容器内时，水就会从容器中通过一喷射管喷出。

抽水机组的选择要和系统水头及泵的特性相一致。系统水头是泵的静水头和动水头之和。因此，它随着所需流量及贮水量、吸水水位的变化而变化。泵的特性取决于泵的大小、转速和设计。

6.6 废水收集

在古老城市，造排水沟的唯一目的不过是将雨水排出城外。这些沟最终被加上盖板，成为我们今天所说的雨水管道。

随着供水事业的发展和室内卫生间使用的增多，对被称为生活污水的家庭污水的排放的需求呼声日高。污水排放可由两种途径中的一种来完成：①生活污水排放进雨水管道，于是雨水管道既排放污水又排放雨水，被称为合流排水管道。②敷设新的地下管道系统用以排放污水，这些管道称为生活污水管道。

新建城市和老城中较近时期（1900年后）兴建部分几乎都分别建有生活污水管道和雨水管道。

除了生活污水，下水道还需输送工业废水、渗透水和入流水。

工业废水量通常可以用水记录确定。其流量也可在仅为专门工业服务的检查井内用小型流量计测得。一般使用巴氏槽，流速与水流深度成正比。工业用水流量，全天变化幅度很大，必须进行连续记录。

流入生活污水管道的地下水为渗透水。污水管常敷设于地下水位以下，而管道的裂隙会使水渗入。对新的、敷设质量高的污水管道来说，其渗透量最小，可达 $500m^3/(km \cdot d)$。既然有额外的水必定要通过污水管和废水处理厂，渗透水当然是不利的。因此，尽可能减少渗透量是有意义的；这就必须管理、维修好污水管道，并使下水道附属建筑物避开大树，因为树根会扎入污水管，使之严重损坏。

生活污水管的第三个进水来源称为入流水，即生活污水管无意收集的雨水。一般入流水来源于低洼地带的多孔检查井盖板处，由此雨水流进了检查井。污水管紧靠小河和排水管渠；二者的高程高于污水管的检查井，或检查井有破裂处，这也是入流水的主要来源。一般，旱季流量和雨季流量之比在 1:1.2~1:4 之间。

生活污水流量在不同季节、一周内的每一天和一天内的每一小时都在改变。设计污水管时，三个重要的流量为平均流量、高峰（及最大）流量和极小流量。最大流量和最小流量之比的平均值为总流量的一个函数。这是由于一个较高的日平均排水量就意味着有一个较大的社区，其极值水量的变化幅度要平稳一些。

从住宅区和工厂企业收集废水的污水管道，几乎总是采用明渠或重力流管道。在一些地方用压力污水管，但其维修费用高，且用武之地仅限于严格限制用水或重力流管道无法有效敷设的情况。

建筑物连接管道通常用直径为 0.1524m 的陶土管或塑料管，与一般敷设于街道下面的污水支管相连接。污水支管的口径要大到足以输送可能出现的最大高峰流量而不至超载（充满）；支管通常由陶土、石棉、水泥、混凝土制成，或用铸铁管。污水支管将废水顺次排放到俗称为"截留器"的污水截留管里。这些截留管集水面积很大，最后将废水排放到污水处理厂。

用于收集和截流的污水管在敷设时，须有足够大的坡度以便在枯水期保持足够的流速；但当流量处于最大值时，不要大到造成过高的流速。此外，污水管必须要有检查井，一般井距为 120~180m，以便于清通和检修。每当污水管改变坡度、大小或方向时，也需设检查井。

在有些情况下，不能使用重力流管道或使用重力流管道不划算，则污水须用水泵排放。

6.7 废水的组成

表6-1中的数据显示了在初步沉淀前后生活污水的近似组成。生化需氧量和悬浮固体

（非过滤残渣）是确定生活污水特性的两种最重要的指标。质量浓度为 240mg/L 的悬浮固体相等于 454.25dm³ 的生活污水中含 0.109kg 的悬浮固体，而 200mg/L 的 BOD 相当于 454.25dm³ 的生活污水中含 0.0907kg 的 BOD。在初步沉淀中，悬浮固体和生化需氧量分别减少约 50% 和 35%；大约 70% 的悬浮固体是挥发性的，挥发性固体指 550℃ 时烧失的悬浮固体。

表 6-1　普通生活污水的近似组成　　　　　　　　　　　（单位：mg/L）

组成＼质量浓度	沉淀前	沉淀后	经生化处理
全部固体	800	680	530
全部挥发性固体	440	340	220
悬浮固体	240	120	30
挥发性悬浮固体	180	100	20
BOD	200	130	30
氨氮中含氮	15	15	24
总氮中含氮	35	30	26
溶解磷中含磷	7	7	7
总磷中含磷	10	9	8

全部固体（蒸发残渣）就包括有机物和溶解盐；后者的含量在相当程度上取决于城市废水的硬度。在生活污水中氮的含量直接和有机物（BOD）的含量有关。总氮的 40% 左右为溶解氨。如果原废水在集水污水管中被长时间滞留，占较大百分比的氨氮会由废水中的蛋白质和尿素的脱氨基作用生成。每升废水中含 10mg 的磷大约等于人均每年 1.36kg 磷的排出量。其中约 2lb（1lb = 0.45kg）来自合成洗涤剂中的磷酸盐助洗剂。

在经生物处理过的废水中氮和磷的过剩表明：生活污水中，营养物的含量超过了生物的需求。生物处理需要的生化需氧量、氮和磷（BOD/N/P）的质量比约为 100:5:1。处理所需的这三者的准确比例取决于处理工艺和废水中氮、磷化合物的生物有效性。100:6:1.5 这一最小比值一般和未经沉淀的生活污水的处理相关，而 100:3:0.7 这一比值适合于氮和磷呈溶解状态的废水。表 6-1 所列普通生活污水在沉淀前后此比例分别为 100:17:5 和 100:19:6，两者皆超过 100:6:1.5 这一最小比例。对缺乏营养物的工业废水的生物处理而言，可溶性磷靠添加 H_3PO_4 获得；而可溶性氮靠添加 NH_4NO_3 获得。

废水中的生物可降解的有机物质一般可分为三类：碳水化合物、蛋白质和脂肪。碳水化合物为碳的水合物，其通式为 $C_nH_{2n}O_n$ 或 $C_n(H_2O)_n$。

形式简单的蛋白质为由肽键连接的氨基酸组成的长链分子。这样的蛋白质在活性物质的结构（如肌肉组织）和动力学（如酶）两方面都是重要的。二十一种普通氨基酸，当在长肽键上被连接在一起时，就形成大部分自然界中见到的简单蛋白质。由于蛋白质包含所有的基本营养素，作为细菌基质的蛋白质混合物是绝好的生长媒介。另一方面，由于纯碳水化合物不包含合成所必需的氮和磷，所以它们不宜作为一种生长媒介。

类脂物，连同碳水化合物与蛋白质一起，形成大部分活细胞的有机物。它是生化物质的多相聚集，而这些物质又具有在不同程度上溶于有机溶剂（如乙醚、乙醇、已烷和丙酮），同时仅微溶于水的共有特性。类脂物可按它们共同的化学和物理特性分为脂肪、油和蜡。简单脂肪，当被水解作用分解时，将产生脂肪酸。

实际上，并非所有的可生物降解的有机物都可以被分成这三种简单的类别。许多天然化合物，如脂蛋白和核蛋白都有碳水化合物、蛋白质和脂肪组合结构。

废水中，约20%～40%的有机物可认为是非生物可降解有机物。有些有机化合物，尽管特殊细菌可使它们分解，在这个意义上是生物可降解的，但由于废水处理过程中时间的限制而必被环境卫生工程师认定是部分生物可降解的。例如，木质素，一种在木材纤维中和纤维素有联系的聚合非碳水材料，在实际应用上，是非生物可降解的。纤维素本身易被生活污水细菌的全体种群排斥。饱和碳氢化合物，因其物理特性及对细菌作用的排斥性，所以是处理中的一大难题。

6.8 水处理

市政给水处理的目的是向人们提供化学指标和细菌指标合格的生活饮用水。为了生活饮用，处理过的水感官性状必须合格，即浊度、色度适当，无异味。工业用水的水质要求往往比生活用水更严格。因此，工业用水可能要求附加处理。例如，锅炉用水必须除盐以防产生水垢。

通常，市政供水水源为深水井、浅水井、河流、天然湖泊和水库。井水一般水温低，水质清澈、均匀，易处理为城市用水。处理中须去除溶解气体和不需要的矿物质。最简单的处理为消毒和加氟。深井水要加氯以提供余氯保护，防止在配水系统中被污染。至于靠地表水来补充的浅水井，加氯既是对地下水消毒又可提供余氯保护。加入氟化物是为了减少龋齿发病率。硬度过大的水一般靠沉析软化。如有必要，将石灰和纯碱与原水混合即可去除可沉降的析出物。在终滤前，用二氧化碳来稳定水。曝气通常是对大多数地下水体进行处理的第一步，以去除其中的溶解气体和增加溶解氧。

地表水水源主要让人担忧的是污染和富营养化。其水质取决于流域内的农业耕作、市政和工业排水管道的布局，诸如水坝之类的河流开发，季节变化以及气候条件。长时期的暴雨冲走耕地和林区的泥沙和有机物；而枯水流则会导致下水道排放的废水污染物含量大大提高。冬夏之间，河水温度变化显著。湖泊和水库的水质主要取决于季节。城市水质控制实际应从河流流域的管理开始，以便保护原水水源。严重污染的水体处理起来既困难，成本又高。尽管一些地区能勘测到地下水，或者在泵送能及的范围内以污染较轻的地表水源来替代，然而本国人口的大多数是从附近的地表水水源取水的。给水厂的运作任务则是将原水处理成家用合格的安全饮用产品。

地表水的一级处理是用混凝、沉淀和过滤等方法对水进行化学澄清。比起河水来，湖泊和水库全年水质更均匀且要求的处理级别也低些。自然净化可使混浊度、大肠菌数、色度下降并能消除水质日间的差异。另一方面，在夏秋两季，藻类的繁殖可能提高混浊度和产生难以去除的味道和气味。加氯通常是水处理的最初和最后的工序，它对原水消毒并使处理后的水保持余氯。过量的预加氯和活性炭吸附被用来去除产生味道和气味的化合物。要根据水的特性和处理费用来选择用于混凝的特定的化学药品。河水作为原水，总是需用具有极大操作伸缩性的最齐全的处理设施去应付原水质的逐日变化。在化学处理之前，预备工序常为预沉淀以减少泥沙和可沉淀的有机物。许多河水处理厂有二级化学混凝和沉淀以便于进一步的处理和灵活的处理。其处理单元可能是连续操作，或是分级处理，即一级进行软化，另一级进行混凝。多达十几种的化学药品可在不同的运行条件下使用，以提供令人满意的成品水。

来自水处理过程中的两种主要废物为污泥和冲洗废水：前者来自沉淀池，由化学混凝和软化反应所产生；后者来自反冲洗滤池。这些排放物的成分变化很大，含有从原水中提取的浓缩物质和在水处理过程中添加的化学药品。这些废料源源不断地产生，但却间歇地被排放。

习 题

1. 分析明渠流的特点。
2. 列出生活废水的近似组成。

Chapter 6
Water Supply

Abstract: This chapter introduces the principal characters of water supply system and sewerage system respectively. The preceding section describes the developing process of water supply system, meanwhile, gives the present common types of pipe systems and pump stations. Another section discusses the component parts of sewage water. How to collect and disposal waste water is also introduced in this chapter.

Key points: open channel flow, composition of wastewater, pump and pump station, water processing

6.1 History of Water Supply

Man's search for pure water began in prehistoric times. Much of their earliest activity is subject to speculation. Some individuals might have led water where they wanted it through trenches dug in the earth. Later, a hollow log was perhaps used as the first water pipe.

Thousands of years must have passed before our more recent ancestors learned to build cities and enjoy the convenience of water piped to home and drains for water-carried wastes. Our earliest archeological records of central water supply and wastewater disposal dated back about 5000 years, in Nippur of Sumeria. In the ruins of Nippur, there was an arched drain with the stones set in full "voussoir" position, each stone being a wedge tapering downward into place. Water was drawn from wells and cisterns. An extensive system of drainage conveyed the wastes from the palaces and residential districts of the city.

The earliest recorded knowledge of water treatment is in the Sanskrit medical lore and Egyptian Wall inscriptions. Sanskrit writings dating about 2000 B.C. tell how to purify foul water by boiling in copper vessel, exposing to sunlight through charcoal, and cooling in an earthen vessel.

The earliest known apparatus for clarifying liquids was pictured in Egyptian walls in the fifteenth and thirteenth centuries B.C. The first picture represents the siphoning of either water or settled wine. A second picture shows the use of wick siphons in an Egyptian kitchen.

The first engineering report on water supply and treatment was made in A.D. 98 by Sextus Julius Frontinus, water commissioner of Rome. He produced two books on the water supply of Rome. In these he described a settling reservoir at the head of one of the aqueducts. His writings were first translated into English by the noted hydraulic engineer Clemens Herschel in 1899.

In the eighth century A. D. an Arabian alchemist, Geber, wrote a rather specialized treatise in distillation that included various stills for water and other liquids.

The English philosopher Sir Francis Bacon wrote down his experiments in the purification of water by filtration, boiling, distillation and clarification by coagulation. This was published in 1627, one year after his death. Bacon also noted that clarifying water tended to improve health and increase the "pleasure of the eye".

The first known illustrated description of sand filters was published in 1685 by Luc Antonio Porzio, an Italian physician. He wrote a book in conserving the health of soldiers in camps, based on his experience in the Austro-Turkish War. This was probably the earliest published work on mass sanitation. He described and illustrated the use of sand filters and sedimentation. Porzio also stated that his filtration was the same as "by those who built the wells in the Palace of the Doges in Venice and in the palace of Cardinal Sachett, at Rome".

The oldest known archeological examples of water filtration are in Venice and the colonies she occupied. The ornate heads on the cisterns bear dates, but it is not known when the filters were placed. Venice, built on a series of islands, depended on catching and storing rainwater for its principal freshwater supply for over 1300 years. Cisterns were built and many were connected with sand filters. The rainwater ran off from the house tops to the streets, where it was collected in stone-grated catch basins and were filtered through sand into cisterns.

A comprehensive article on the water supply of Venice appeared in the *Practical Mechanics Journal* in 1863. The land area of Venice was 52002.1m^2 and the average yearly rainfall was 0.8128m. Nearly all of this rainfall was collected in 177 public and 1900 private cisterns. These cisterns provided a daily average supply of about 19.09L per capita per day. This low consumption was due in part to the absence of sewers, the practice of washing clothes in the lagoon, and the universal drinking of wine. These cisterns continued to be the principal water supply of Venice until about the sixteenth century.

Many experiments were conducted in the eighteenth and nineteenth centuries in England, France, Germany, and Russia. Henry Darcy patented filters in France and England in 1856 and anticipated all aspects of the American rapid sand filter except coagulation. He appears to be the first to apply the laws of hydraulics to filter design. The first filter to supply water to a whole town was completed at Paisley, Scotland, in 1804, but this water was carted to consumers. In Glasgow, Scotland in 1807 filtered water was piped to consumers.

In the United States little attention was given to water treatment until after the Civil War. Turbidity was not as urgent a problem as in Europe. The first filters were of the slow sand type, similar to British design. About 1890 rapid sand filters were developed in the United States and coagulants were introduced to increase their efficiency. These filters soon evolved to our present rapid sand filters with slight modification.

6.2 Water-supply Engineering

A water supply for a town usually includes a storage reservoir at the source of the supply, a pipeline from the storage reservoir to the distribution reservoir near the town, and finally the distribution pipes buried in the streets, taking the water to the houses, shops, factories and offices. The main equipment is thus the two reservoirs and the pipeline between them. The function of the storage reservoir is to keep enough water over one or several years to provide for all high demands in dry periods, and the distribution reservoir has the same function for the day or the week. The storage reservoir by its existence allows the supply sources to be smaller and less expensive. And the distribution reservoir similarly allows the pipeline and pumps to be smaller and cheaper than they would be if it did not exist.

In the United States, some of whose cities have the largest water use in the world per person, the average use per person varies from 200 to 5000 liters per day, averaging some 500 liters/day/person. But it can not be assumed that colder countries will eventually reach the same level of use, because much of the highest US demand comes from the water spent in summer on air conditioning equipment and the watering of gardens.

Water engineers must therefore study the water use per person (consumption per head) in their own country and choose a figure based on the most advanced community there. The chosen consumption per head must be multiplied by the estimated population at the date for which the supply is being planned, some thirty years ahead or more. The supply and storage equipment must be designed to be large enough for this period since neither of them is so easily extended as the distribution system. This can be extended as the need arises and as the houses are built.

Once the volume of the required yearly supply has been calculated and agreed with all concerned, including the fire department, it is important to make sure that it really is permanently obtainable from the catchment area proposed. The catchment area is the area which drains towards the supply, and the yearly amount of water drawn off to the storage reservoir cannot be more than the rainfall on the catchment area and should usually be very much smaller.

A water supply may be obtained from surface water (rain) or from underground water or both. Both are refilled by the rainfall, the surface water by the runoff, and the springs or wells by the water which enters the ground, the infiltration water. These two quantities, plus the evaporation water and the water used by the trees and plants, make up the total rainfall. Even if the community water supply includes all the springs as well as the surface water in the area, it still does not obtain all the rainfall because of evaporation and the needs of plant life.

It is therefore important to check the rainfall records and the runoff and infiltration values with the records of the stream, flows and other water information. Infiltration water, the rainfall which enters the ground and becomes ground water, can travel for long horizontal distances, and it may pass into or out of the catchment area. If the yearly water supply exceeds the yearly rainfall, the ground water level will generally fall and eventually it will become impossible to obtain the required supply. Another source will have to be found.

It is not essential to build storage or impounding reservoir if the water can be stored in the ground, and this may often be possible. In face in the London area, where the water level in the chalk has been steadily falling for more than a century because of pumping, it has been suggested that further storage shall be not by the surface reservoirs which have been used until now, but by recharging the chalk with purified water through wells changed for the purpose. This practice of underground storage is being widely used by the gas industry in many countries. Gas is sent underground by compressors through wells into a sealed underground sand, limestone, or other porous formation at a time when the gas supply is large, to be stored until the demand is larger than the supply. These underground containers for gas are often hundreds of times as large as the largest gas tank in existence and have been found to be a cheap, practical, and safe way of storing gas.

6.3 Plumbing—Background and Status

One of most important systems developed for the health of man and providing man with a better way of life has been the system of plumbing, which is the piping of potable water to its ultimate use and the draining away of waste materials to a variety of treatment processes. It is essential in our modern society to recognize that plumbing is to society what the circulatory system is to man. It is a system which must function efficiently to avoid outbreaks of epidemics and to avoid chemical pollution. Good health practices require that plumbing in a community be free of cross-connections, back flow connections, submerged inlets and poor venting. It also must transport a good quality of potable water in adequate quantities in order to serve our modern society. One of the great difficulties that we face as a society is that older existing plumbing may deteriorate and may create health hazards; also, repair of plumbing may be carried out in such a way that they will create direct health hazards.

Plumbing is the practice, materials, and fixtures used in installing, maintaining, and altering of pipes, appliances, and appurtenances, utilized for potable water supply, sanitary or storm drainage and venting systems. Plumbing does not include the drilling of water wells, installing water softening equipment, or sale of the manufacture or plumbing fixtures, appliances, equipment or hardware. Plumbing systems consist of an adequate potable water supply system, a safe adequate drainage system and ample fixture and equipment.

Public health personnel have long been concerned with cross-connections, backflow connections and submerged inlet in plumbing systems and public drinking water supply distribution system. These cross-connections make the contamination of potable water with non-potable water or contaminated water possible. Although the probability of contamination of drinking water seems to be remote, a multitude of problems definitely exist. In order to combat this problem, installers must understand the hydraulic and pollution factors which can cause environmental health hazards. They must also know what types of standard backflow prevention devices and methods are utilized and how to obtain the materials and install them properly.

It can be assumed that plumbing systems in many areas are rapidly deteriorating because of the age of the structures. As a result of this change, many individuals fail to pay adequate attention to the enormous potential hazard of disease and injury due to microbiological, chemical or physical agents.

6.4 Open Channel Flow

Open channel flow is the term applied to fluid motion in which a liquid in a conduit has part of its boundary exposed to atmospheric pressure. The conduit may be completely open to the atmosphere, as in natural river beds or artificial canals and channels, or it may be closed.

In the case of flow with friction through a constant-area pipe, a pressure difference has to exist to sustain the flow. In the case of flow with friction in a channel of constant cross section, the effect of gravity—that is, changes in elevation in the channel—sustains the flow through the channel. As contrasted with pipe flow, the cross-sectional area of the flow can change with different flow condition, subject to the confines of the channel. For example, for flow through a rectangular cross section, a change in the depth of the liquid results in different rectangular cross section.

Just as in pipe flow, the flow may be laminar or turbulent in character, with turbulent flow constituting the most frequent type when the liquid is water. The analysis of open channel flows is important in situations relating to the determination and control of river flow and in establishing design requirements for irrigation canals.

Before proceeding, a few definitions associated with open channel flow will be given. When the cross section of the flow does not vary along the direction of the flow, the flow is called uniform. Otherwise it is called non-uniform flow. Thus in uniform open channel flow, the liquid depth is constant and the surface of the liquid is parallel to the channel bottom. When the depth of the liquid varies, we have non-uniform open channel flow (also called varied flow). This type of flow occurs when the shape of the channel crosses section changes or when the shape of the channel bottom changes. If the depth increases in the downstream direction, the velocity of the flow slows down and we have retarded flow; while for depth decreasing in the downstream direction, we obtain velocity increases and have accelerated flow.

Uniform flow is achieved in any channel that is sufficiently long and that has a constant channel slope and cross section. An example of how uniform flow is established will now be given. An irrigation canal has a change in slope, as shown in Fig. 6-1. Due to the change in the slope of the channel flow, the flow experiences acceleration because the component of the gravity force along the flow is greater than the shear force along the channel wall retarding the flow. As the flow accelerates, the shear force will increase as a result of the increased velocity until a value of the velocity is reached when the shear force equals the gravity component. At this condition of equilibrium, the velocity and liquid depth remain constant and the flow becomes uniform open channel flow.

Non-uniform flow caused by a change in the slope of the channel floor is illustrated in Fig. 6-1. When a barrier, such as spillway, is placed in the path of uniform flow along a sloping channel, we obtain another example of gradually varied flow. The resulting profile of the water surface behind the barrier is called the backwater curve.

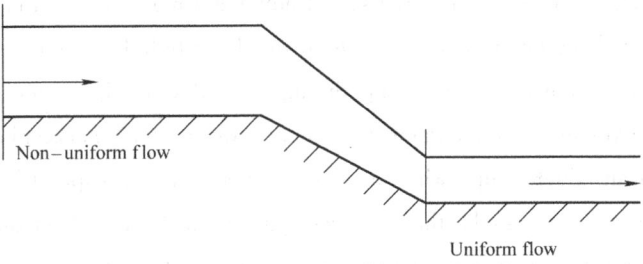

Fig. 6-1　Establishment of uniform channel flow

6.5　Pumps and Pumping Stations

Pumps and pumping machinery serve the following purposes in water systems: lifting water from its source (surface or ground), either immediately to the community through high-lift installations, or by low-lift to purification works; boosting water from low-service to high-service areas, to separate fire supplies, and to the upper floors of many-storied building and transporting water through treatment works, back washing filters, draining component settling tanks, and other treatment units, withdrawing deposited solids and supplying water (especially pressure water) to operating equipment.

Today most water and wastewater pumping is done by either centrifugal pumps or propeller pumps. How the water is directed through the impeller determines the type of pump. There is radial flow in open- or closed-impeller pumps, with volute or turbine casings, and single or double suction through the eye of the impeller pumps, axial flow in propeller pumps, and diagonal flow in mixed-flow, open-impeller pumps. Propeller pumps are not centrifugal pumps. Both can be referred to as rotodynamic pumps.

Open-impeller pumps are less efficient than closed-impeller pumps, but they can pass relatively large debris without being clogged. Accordingly, they are useful in pumping wastewaters and sludges. Single-stage pumps have but one impeller, and multistage pumps have two or more, each feeding into the next higher stage. Multistage turbine well pumps may have their motors submerged, or they may be driven by a shaft from the prime mover situated on the floor of the pumping station.

In addition to centrifugal and propeller pumps, water and wastewater systems may include displacement pumps, ranging in size from hand-operated pitcher pumps to the huge pumping engines of the twentieth century built as steam-driven units; rotary pumps equipped with two or more rotors (varying in shape from meshing lobes to gears and often used as small fire pumps); hydraulic rams utilizing the impulse of large masses of low-pressure water to drive much smaller masses of water (one half to one sixth of the driving water) through the delivery pipe to higher elevations, in synchronism with the pressure waves and sequences induced by water hammer; jet pumps or jet ejectors, used in wells and dewatering operations, introducing a high-speed jet of air or water through a nozzle into a constricted section of pipe; air lifts in which air bubbles, released from upward-directed air pipe, lift water from a well or sump through an eductor pipe; and displacement ejectors housed in a pressure vessel in which water (especially wastewater) accumulates and from which it is displaced through an eductor pipe when a float-operated valve is tripped by the rising water and admits compressed air to the vessel, the water will pass from the vessel jet pipe and jet.

Pumping units are chosen in accordance with system heads and pump characteristics. The system head is the sum of the static and dynamic heads against the pump. As such, it varies with required flows and with changes in storage and suction levels. Pump characteristics depend on pump size, speed, and design.

6.6 Collection of Wastewater

In old cities, drainage ditches were constructed for the sole purpose of moving storm water out of the cities. Eventually, these ditches were covered over and became what we now know as storm sewers.

As water supplies developed and the use of the indoor water closet increased, the need for transporting domestic wastewaters, called sanitary wastes, became obvious. This was accomplished in one of two ways: ①discharge of the sanitary wastes into the storm sewers, which then carried both sanitary wastes and storm water, and were known as combined sewers, and ②construction of a new system of underground pipes for removing the wastewater, which became known as sanitary sewers.

Newer cities, and more recently built (post-1900) parts of older cities almost all have separate sewers for sanitary wastes and storm water.

In addition to sewage, sewers also must carry industrial wastes, infiltration and inflow.

The quantity of industrial wastes can usually be established by water use records. Alternatively, the flows can be measured in manholes which serve only a specific industry, using a small flow meter in a manhole. Typically, a Parshall flume is used, and the flow rate is calculated as a direct proportion of the flow depth. Industrial flows often vary considerably throughout the day and continuous recording is mandatory.

Infiltration is the flow of groundwater into sanitary sewers. Sewers are often placed under the groundwater table and any cracks in the pipes will allow water to seep in. Infiltration is the least for new, well-constructed sewers, and can go as high as $500m^3/(km \cdot d)$. This flow is of course detrimental since the extra volume of water must go through the sewers and the wastewater treatment plant. It thus makes sense to reduce this as much as possible by maintaining and repairing sewers, thus makes sense to reduce this as much as possible by maintaining and repairing sewers, and keeping sewerage easements clear of large trees which could send roots into the sewers and cause severe damage.

The third source of flow in sanitary sewers is called inflow, and represents storm water which is collected unintentionally by the sanitary sewers. A common source of inflow is a perforated manhole cover placed in a depression, so that storm water flows into the manhole. Sewers laid next to creeks and drainageways which rise up higher than the manhole elevation, or where the manhole is broken, are also a major source. Lastly, illegal connections to sanitary sewers, such as roofdrains, can substantially increase the wet weather flow over the dry weather flow. Commonly, the ratio of dry weather to wet weather flow is between 1:1.2 and 1:4.

Domestic wastewater flows vary with season, day of the week and the hour of the day. The three flows closely concerned when designing sewers are the average flow, the peak or maximum flow, and the extreme minimum. The ratio of average to both the maximum and minimum flows is a function of the total flow, since a higher average daily discharge implies a larger community in which the extremes are evened out.

Sewers that collect wastewater from residences and industrial establishments almost always operate as open channels, or gravity flow conduits. Pressure sewers are used in a few places, but these are expensive to maintain and are useful only when there are severe restrictions on water use, or the terrain is such that gravity flow conduits cannot be efficiently constructed.

Building connections are usually made with clay or plastic pipe, 0.1524m in diameter, to the collecting sewers which commonly run under the street. Collecting sewers are sized to carry the maximum anticipated peak flows without surcharging (filling up) and are commonly made of clay, asbestos, cement, concrete or cast iron pipe. They discharge in turn into intercepting sewers, known colloquially as interceptors, which collect large areas and discharge finally into the wastewater treatment plant.

Collecting and intercepting sewers must be placed at a sufficient grade to allow for adequate velocity during low flow, but not so great as to promote excessively high velocities when the flows are at their maximum. In addition, sewers must have manholes, commonly every 120 ~ 180m to facilitate cleaning and repair. Manholes are also necessary whenever the sewer changes grade (slope), size or direction.

In some cases it becomes either impossible or uneconomical to use gravity flow, and the wastewater must be pumped.

6.7 Composition of Wastewater

The data in Table 6-1 represents the approximate composition of domestic wastewater before and after primary sedimentation. BOD and suspended solids (nonfiltrable residue) are the two most important parameters used to define the characteristics of a domestic wastewater. A suspended-solids mass concentration of 240mg/L is equivalent to 0.109kg of suspended solids in 454.25dm^3, and 200 mg/L of BOD in equivalent to 0.0907kg of BOD in 454.25dm^3. Reduction of suspended solids and BOD in primary sedimentation is approximately 50% and 35%, respectively. Approximately 70% of the suspended solids are volatile, defined as those lost upon ignition at 550℃.

Total solids (residue on evaporation) include organic matter and dissolved salts; the concentration of the latter is dependent to a considerable extent on the hardness of the municipal water. The concentration of nitrogen in domestic waste is directly related to the concentration of organic matter (BOD). Approximately 40% of the total nitrogen is in solution as ammonia. If raw wastewater has been retained for a long time in collector sewers, a greater percentage of ammonia nitrogen results from deamination of the proteins and urea in wastewater. Ten milligrams per liter of phosphorus is approximately equivalent to 1.36kg phosphorus contribution per capita per year. About 2 lb (1 lb = 0.45kg) of this is from phosphate builders used in synthetic detergents.

The surplus of nitrogen and phosphorus in biologically treated wastewater reveals that domestic wastewater contains nutrients in excess of biological needs. The approximate BOD/nitrogen/phosphorus (BOD/N/P) weight ratio required for biological treatment is 100/5/1. The exact BOD/N/P ratio needed for treatment depends on the process and the biological availability of the nitrogen and phosphorus compounds in the wastewater. A minimum of 100/6/1.5 is commonly related to treatment of unsettled sanitary wastewater, while 100/3/0.7 is generally adequate for wastewater where the nitrogen and phosphorus are in soluble form. The average domestic wastewater listed in Table 6-1 has a ratio of 100/17/5 before sedimentation and 100/19/6 after sedimentation, both of which are in excess of the minimum 100/6/1.5. for biological treatment of industrial wastewaters deficient in nutrients, soluble phosphorus can be supplied by adding H_3PO_4 and soluble nitrogen by adding NH_4NO_3.

Table 6-1 Approximate composition of an average domestic wastewater (mg/L)

composition \ mass concentration	Before Sedimentation	After Sedimentation	Biologically Treated
Total solids	800	680	530
Total volatile	440	340	220
Suspended solids	240	120	30

(续)

composition / mass concentration	Before Sedimentation	After Sedimentation	Biologically Treated
Volatile suspended solids	180	100	20
BOD	200	130	30
Ammonia nitrogen as N	15	15	24
Total nitrogen as N	35	30	26
Soluble phosphorus as P	7	7	7
Total phosphorus as P	10	9	8

Biodegradable organic matter in wastewater is generally classified into three categories: carbohydrates, proteins, and fats. Carbohydrates are hydrates of carbon with the empirical formula $C_n H_{2n} O_n$ or $C_n (H_2 O)_n$.

Proteins in simple form are long-chain molecules composed of amino acids connected by peptide bonds and are important in both the structural (e. g., muscle tissue) and dynamic aspects (e. g., enzymes) of living matter. Twenty-one common amino acids when linked together in long peptide chains form a majority of simple proteins found in nature. A mixture of proteins as a bacterial substrate is an excellent growth medium, since proteins contain all the essential nutrients. On the other hand, pure carbohydrates are unsuitable as a growth medium since they do not contain the nitrogen and phosphorus essential for synthesis.

Lipids, together with carbohydrates and proteins, form the bulk of organic matter of living cells. The term refers to a heterogeneous collection of biochemical substances having the mutual property of being soluble to varying degrees in organic solvents (e. g., ether, ethanol, hexane, and acetone) while being only sparingly soluble in water. Lipids may be grouped according to their shared chemical and physical properties as fats, oils, and waxes. A simple fat when broken down by hydrolytic action yields fatty acids.

Actually not all biodegradable organic matter can be classed into these three simple groupings. Many natural compounds have structures that are combinations of carbohydrates, proteins, and fats, such as lipoproteins and nucleoproteins.

Approximately 20% ~40% of the organic matter in wastewater appears to be non-biodegradable. Several organic compounds, although biodegradable in the sense that specific bacteria can break them down, must be considered by sanitary engineers as partially biodegradable because of time limitations in waste treatment processes. For example, lignin, a polymeric noncarbohydrate material associated with cellulose in wood fiber, is for practical purposes nonbiodegradable. Cellulose itself is not readily available to the general population of domestic wastewater bacteria. Saturated hydrocarbons are a problem in treatment because of their physical properties and resistance to bacterial action.

6.8 Water Processing

The objective of municipal water treatment is to provide a potable supply—one that is chemically and bacteriologically safe for human consumption. For domestic uses, treated water must be aesthetically acceptable—free from apparent turbidity, color, and objectionable taste. Quality requirements for industrial uses are frequently more stringent than domestic supplies. Thus additional treatment may be required by the industry. For an example, boiler feed water must be demineralized to prevent scale deposits.

Common water sources for municipal supplies are deep wells, shallow wells, rivers, natural lakes, and reservoirs. Well supplies normally yield cool, uncontaminated water of uniform quality that is easily processed for municipal use. Processing may be required to remove dissolved gases and undesirable minerals. The simplest treatment is disinfection and fluoridation. Deep well supplies are chlorinated to provide residual protection against potential contamination in the water distribution system. In the case of shallow wells recharged by surface waters, chlorine both disinfects the groundwater and provides residual protection. Fluoride is added to reduce the incidence of dental caries. Excessive hardness is commonly removed by precipitation softening. Lime and, if necessary, soda ash are mixed with raw water, and settleable precipitate is removed. Carbon dioxide is applied to stabilize the water prior to final filtration. Aeration is a common first step in treatment of most groundwater to strip out dissolved gases and add oxygen.

Pollution and eutrophication are major concerns in surface water supplies. Water quality depends on agricultural practices in the watershed, location of municipal and industrial outfall sewers, river development such as dams, season of the year, and climatic conditions. Periods of high rainfall flush silt and organic matter from cultivated fields and forest land, while drought flows may result in higher concentrations of waste-water pollutants from sewer discharges. River temperature may vary significantly between summer and winter. The quality of water in a lake or reservoir depends considerably on season of the year. Municipal water quality control actually starts with management of the river basin to protect the raw water supply. Highly polluted waters are both difficult and costly to treat. Although some communities are able to locate groundwater supplies, of alternate less polluted surface sources within feasible pumping distance, the majority of the nation's population draw from nearby surface supplies. The challenge in waterworks operation is to process this water to a safe, potable product acceptable for domestic use.

The primary process in surface water treatment is chemical clarification by coagulation, sedimentation, and filtration. Lake and reservoir water has a more uniform year-round quality and requires a lesser degree of treatment than river water. Natural purification results in reduction of turbidity, coliform bacteria, color, and elimination of day-to-day variations. On the other hand, growths of algae may cause increased turbidity and may produce difficult-to-remove tastes and odors during the summer and fall. Chlorination is commonly the first and last steps in treatment, providing disinfection of the raw water and establishing a chlorine residual in the treated water. Excess prechlorination and activated carbon are used to remove taste- and odor-producing compounds. The specific chemicals used in coagulation depend on the character of the water and economic considerations. River supplies normally require the most extensive treatment facilities with greatest operational flexibility to handle the day-to-day variations in raw water quality. The preliminary step is often presedimentation to reduce silt and settleable organic matter prior to chemical treatment. Many river water treatment plants have two stages of chemical coagulation and sedimentation to provide greater depth and flexibility of treatment. The units may be operated in series, or by split treatment with softening in one stage and coagulation in the other. As many as a dozen different chemicals may be used under varying operating conditions to provide a satisfactory finished water.

The two primary sources of waste from water treatment processes are sludge from the settling tank, resulting from chemical coagulation or softening reactions, and wash water from backwashing filters. These discharges are highly variable in composition, containing concentrated materials removed from the raw water and chemicals added in the treatment process. The wastes are produced continuously, but are discharged intermittently.

Questions

1. Please analyses the characteristics of open channel flow.
2. Please approximately list components of domestic wastewater.

第7章 电力系统和设计

本章要点：本章介绍了建筑内电力系统的种类和特性，配电系统的组成，电力系统的压力机制和常见设备的种类和特性，并简单介绍了电力系统的设计。

知识点：配电系统的选择，电压差和电压分布，接地，短路和分断能力，常见电力设备，建筑电荷载计算，电力系统设计步骤。

7.1 配电系统

建筑配电系统多种多样。某个特定建筑的电力系统取决于其建筑的大小以及主要负荷特征，例如设备的额定功率、电压、相位。频率是电力系统的另一个重要特征。但是一个城市或地区通常使用一个频率指标，例如在中国频率指标是50Hz，而在美国频率指标是60Hz，在欧洲国家是50Hz。除了特殊情况之外都应该使用这一频率指标。

一般大型建筑包含多种形式的负荷，如单相的照明电气和三相电动机。尽管这种多重系统建设费用较高而且难以维护，但在同一建筑内设置多种配电系统仍比较常见，因此，在设计时应该研究其成本效益从而进行比较选择。一般来说，在同一建筑内存在一个以上配电系统时，常由一个满足建筑物的主要负荷的主系统，以及一个或多个由主系统分出来的满足次要负荷的子系统组成。

例如一建筑有300kV·A的单相负荷和20kV·A的三相负荷，则应该选择一个既可以满足单相负荷要求又有处理三相负荷的二级系统或子系统的多重配电系统。

建筑电力系统可以分为三个电压等级。

1) 超低压系统电压小于等于50V。这一等级通常用于控制、信号、通信系统。

2) 低压系统电压一般低于600V。除了非常大容量的设备，如一个735499W的电动机，这一等级通常用于提供照明和动力设备用电。

3) 中压系统电压一般在600~100000V。这一等级通常用于配电变压器降压，从而满足建筑配电系统和设备用电。

在建筑配电系统中，380V的低压系统比较常见。中高压系统仅用于建筑面积为数十万平方米的高层建筑或者工业厂房。

7.1.1 小于100kV·A的负荷系统

住宅和小型建筑负荷一般小于100kV·A，单相，电压为120V或240V，因此，应选择

120～240V 的单相三线制的系统。

7.1.2 负荷大于 100kV·A 的系统

当负荷大于 100kV·A 时一般使用三相电源。但是对于单元住宅或小型商业中心，尽管其负荷远远大于 100kV·A，也可以完全使用单相电源。考虑到供电设备经济性和较小电缆尺寸的要求，一般随着载荷的增大应该使用更高的电压等级。

7.2 电压差和电压分布

7.2.1 公共电压

大多数公用电力系统将其发电厂和变电站之间的供电电压自动调节成额定电压的 1%。但是当公用电力系统负荷过大时供电电压会降低。在法定范围内，5% 的波动是比较常见的。

特殊情况下，当公共电网超载过大时电力公司会将配电额定电压降低 5%～10%。建筑内的二级电压以及用电负荷也将以同样的比例相应降低。但是当电压降低过大时，建筑设备会受到不利的影响，例如电动机过热、能效降低、敏感电器或电子仪器出现故障或跳闸等。

7.2.2 电压差

电压差是电力系统分别在无负荷和满负荷状态下最高压和最低压之间的压差。电压差包括通过变压器、配电设备、馈线和支线的电压降。

7.2.3 电压分布

公共电压波动和电压降的累积影响可能使建筑配电系统在负荷较低时，如夜晚或周末时段，用电设备电压过高，或者在满负荷状态下出现欠压。严重的过电压和欠压会缩短用电设备的寿命甚至烧毁设备。以白炽灯为例，低于其额定电压 5% 的压降会使光通量（流明）降低 20% 左右。因此，在建筑配电系统中降低电压差非常重要。

7.3 接地

7.3.1 接地系统

电力系统有意或偶然与地面连接被称为接地。一般来说，所有的建筑用电系统都在与地面电压最低的地方接地。这样做的原因如下：

1) 接地是对意外连接高压电源的系统和电器进行过压保护。高压电源如配电系统的一级电压侧，其电压可能高达几百万伏。

2）当建筑和其电力系统被雷电击中时，电流可能损坏电器的绝缘导线而击中地面。如果系统适当接地，电流就会绕过馈线和电器直接被引向地面。

3）接地保护人员免遭电击。如果系统和电器都接地而设备电路意外短路，电路保护装置（熔断器或断路器）会跳闸或切断线路。如果系统没有接地，设备线路任何的意外接地都可能使碰巧摸到该设备的人触电。

4）接地系统比不接地系统更加经济。电路的接地端不用开关。因此，一个单相电路只需要一个单级开关，而不接地的单相系统则必须有一个双极开关。

7.3.2 不接地系统

虽然接地是一般建筑电力系统的首选，但它有一个较大的缺点：只要其不接地端意外接地，该系统就会轻易跳闸或中断供电。这对于有类似医院手术室的照明电力这种关键负荷的系统来说尤其是一个问题。因此，手术室的供电系统是不接地的。但是不接地系统应该同主系统分开，单设变压器和一个高敏感度的地面探测系统以识别任何意外接地。该检测系统可使电力系统继续运行，直到故障（意外接地）排除。

7.3.3 接地方法

通常的做法是使用地下水管道为接地电极，因为水管埋地广泛和稳固。然而经验表明，电力系统的这种接地方式可能会造成对水管的腐蚀。因此，在管道上安装绝缘接头或使用塑料管道材料来防止腐蚀。另一个不太有效但尚可接受的方法是把库珀棒或金属板放入地面作为接地电极。一个更加可靠但比较昂贵的方法是在建筑地下设置一个接地网或在建筑周围设置接地环路成为一个接地系统。接地有两个必要条件。

1）系统接地。整个配电系统应该在系统上不带电的或电压最低的点接地。不接地线路与地面或与接地线（通常是不带电的）之间的电压是对地的电压。

2）设备接地。所有类似电动机外架或电器外壳的导电外壳都应该由一个单独的导体接地。尽管金属线槽可以代替地面，但最好使用设备接地导体。

7.3.4 极化

由于建筑室内电力系统是接地的，因此，所有用电器的外壳如电灯插座的外壳、电气工具的金属外壳或洗衣机的钢外壳等都应该接地，以保障使用者的安全，可以使用带有接地极的电源插座来满足这一要求，插座的不接地端比接地端小，因此不会插错。

7.3.5 接地故障断路器

为了保证安全，一些为游泳池、厨房、加油站、盥洗室、洗衣店或露天设备提供电力的电容和电路应该设计接地故障断路器，如果感应到不接地端和接地端之间电路的电流不平衡时会自动跳闸或断路。这种不平衡表明电路的不接地端可能有电流泄露，因此，需要设置接地故障断路器（GFCI）。

7.4 短路和分断能力

7.4.1 短路

为了防止由于电阻产生的热量（I^2R）损失而导致的电线过热，电路只能通过有限的电流。所限制的电流主要取决于其所连接负荷的电阻。根据欧姆定律，当负荷电阻被短接，电路会流过特别大的电流，这就是短路。电路电阻很小时，短路电流会是正常电流的 10～30 倍。在这种超高电流下，多数电器和线路都会被因此引起的过度高温所损坏。此外，这还很有可能引起火灾。

7.4.2 短路计算

为了避免短路引起的过热和磁力，系统内所有的电路和电器都必须有大于或等于系统本身的计算短路能力的分断能力。电力系统短路能力的计算非常复杂。保守来说，它可高达系统正常满负荷电流的 20～30 倍。

7.4.3 分断能力

为了保护系统和电器不被短路引起的高温、电弧和火所损坏，所有配电线和电缆必须有熔断器和断路器等保护设备。所有安装有用电设备的电力系统也必须具有一个大于计算短路电流的分断能力（IC）。

7.5 电力设备

从电厂发电、变电、配电设备和负载端保护装置，电力系统包括不同等级的电力设施。

7.5.1 配电柜和配电盘

配电柜是由配电系统中开关以及电路保护装置集合组装的。配电柜是一个小系统的配电中心，或一个大型系统配电中心的一部分。

配电盘是配电系统中最后的开关以及电路保护装置的集合组装。根据所连接负荷的不同，配电盘可分成照明配电盘、动力配电盘、热力配电盘、专用配电盘或组合配电盘。尽管配电柜总被认为是距离供电系统末端最近的配电设备，但配电柜和配电盘没有明显的区别。

7.5.2 变压器

变压器是一种输电设备，其主要功能是将系统电压从一个级别转到另一个级别。变压器根据磁感应原理运行：初级和次级线圈共同缠在一个钢硅芯上。入口端是初级，出口端是次级。若电压从初级到次级是升高的,就称为升压变压器;若电压下降,就称为降压变压器。电压随着电磁感应从初级转到次级。所产生的电压与初级和次级线圈的匝数成正比。

7.5.3 开关

开关是电路中闭合、断开或改变电路连接的装置。

轻型开关通常是单刀单掷开关。当电源需要在不同位置转换时,就需要三路和四路的开关。一般来说,第一个和最后一个开关必须是三路开关,中间的开关必须是四路开关。

7.5.4 保护装置

电路中的馈线、配电设备、支线和用电器等必须加以保护,不能使其承受各种原因引起的超过其额定值的电压或电流。这种超过额定值的情况可能由很多原因导致,例如设备超载或内部、外部的电力故障会引起过电流,初级、次级线路之间短路或雷击会引起过电压,由电源的变换会引起三相系统极性反相。

最常见的防止由过载引起的损坏的方法是在馈线、支线或电器等关键的地方安装保护装置。这些装置分为三大类:继电器、断路器和熔断器。建筑配电系统和用电器一般使用断路器和熔断器。

1. 断路器

断路器与熔断器等其他保护装置相比,优势在于:
1)系统跳闸时可迅速复位。
2)结构紧凑。
3)适于远程控制,可与其他设备实现电气联锁。
4)可作为断开开关(但不应用作运行开关)。

2. 熔断器

熔断器也是电气保护装置,当感应到异常电流时熔断器会使熔体熔化从而断开电路。这是一种自毁装置。

单元件熔断器的运行原理非常简单。熔体由铅锡锑共晶合金制成,这种合金有单一的熔点温度而且在达到熔点之前不会软化。熔体元件有"瓶颈段(狭窄部分)",当电流过高时会因过热而熔断。

3. 保护装置的应用

由于生产技术不断进步,200A 的单极和双极的小型低压断路器在经济性上已经与相应的熔断开关相当。因此,断路器普遍应用于照明和插座板。但是对于载流容量大的负载,尤其是有 40000A 或更高短路电流的系统来说,熔断开关无疑更加经济。短路电流超过 50000A 的系统常将熔断器和断路器联合使用。

7.6 电气系统设计及配线

电气系统设计是楼宇设计中的一个主要组成部分。所有设备如空调、水泵、风扇,以及电梯等都是由电力作为动力源。甚至燃气燃油设备，如锅炉、加热器都需要电力。电力系统的选择通常受楼宇设备的影响。例如如果一个楼宇的各房间使用独立的家用空调，那么配电系统基本为单相220V系统；如果楼宇的各房间使用中央空调制冷系统，那么配电系统应为380V的三相四线制系统。

7.6.1 电气系统设计步骤

电气系统设计有五项基本步骤：
1）建筑需求分析。
2）电力负荷计算。
3）电力系统选择。
4）与结构设计以及其他设计相协调。
5）绘制电气设计图及编写说明书。

实际上这些步骤是随着工程进度不断反复的。建筑照明、机器设备等楼宇设备的荷载决定了建筑所需电功率，以及电力系统的选择。然而，在这些步骤完成之前，需要提前知道设备种类，建筑工程师需要知道电气设备间的大小及位置，结构工程师需要了解主要设备的重量，暖通工程师需要知道系统选型以便对暖通设备成本进行评估。因此，要根据经验或者统计数据做合理的假设。这些假设在设计过程中不断被修正，最后定下来。

7.6.2 建筑需求分析

建筑电气系统设计的第一步是分析建筑计划中的建筑需求。影响电气系统的主要因素包括：

1）所有者因素。比如建筑物类型，使用者的数量，当前及将要被安装或预留的电气设备的数量。

2）成本因素。该建筑是否有严格的预算限制，是普通中等水平还是高水平的建筑物等。

3）建筑因素。建筑物尺寸、楼层数量、层高、电梯等。

4）建筑环境。建筑是否供暖、是否有空调、是否采用中央空调等。

5）照明标准。照明水平以及光源的主要形式。

6）其他机械系统。冷热水、污水、消防系统等对电力的需求。

7）建筑设备。电梯、计算机等。

8）辅助系统。如建筑管理系统、时钟、火灾警报、通信、广播和电视天线、计算机网络等。

9）未来需求。与建筑系统其他的组成不同，电力负荷是逐年增加的。一栋建筑能够持续使用近百年，而随着技术的进步，电力系统则每二十到三十年需要升级一次。设计者必须对未来荷载以及大致的荷载增长做出明确的判断。一般来说，在主干线以及一个或多个支路中，最小留出25%的冗余。

7.6.3 计算建筑电荷载

建筑电力负荷可根据不同的种类进行分析。

1. 照明

照明设计通常是建筑师、室内设计师、照明设计师以及电气工程师合作的结果。多数建筑中，照明负荷占电力总负荷中很大一部分。一般来说，固定照明设备的电压为 220V，单相制。光源技术的持续发展使得电能转化为光能的效率大大增加，由此减少了建筑照明对电能的需求。

2. 机械设备

机械设备对电力的需求随着建筑、气候条件机械系统类型及其运行策略的不同而不同。为了进行电力规划，电力的初步数据由机械设计工程师提供，并随着设计过程逐步校正。

机械系统包括暖通空调、泵、消防系统。冷却器、锅炉、泵、风扇这些设备通常需要较大电力，设计为三相 380V 更为经济。然而，住宅用电气设备通常为 120V 或 220V 单相。

3. 楼宇设备

楼宇设备包括提升机、家用设备、娱乐设备，以及各种操作设备。这类设备对电力的需求随着其容量和特性大不相同。建筑设备的电力需求通常由建筑师、用户或者不同的专业顾问共同提供。

近年来随着楼宇通信系统的不断增加，对电力的需求急剧增大。例如办公楼内即插即用电力的需求加倍的增大。对于当今各种类型的建筑包括住宅的数据处理以及通信设备的需求，几年前还能被接受的标准现在不够了。

4. 附属系统

通常，附属系统不需要很大的电力，因此，通常设计采用 220V，单相。根据不同的建筑功能——住宅、商业或工业，可能需要一个或多个以下的系统：

1) 建筑管理系统。
2) 安保系统。
3) 时钟系统。
4) 火灾报警系统。
5) 通信系统。
6) 收音机和电视天线系统。
7) 公共广播系统。
8) 数据和网络系统。
9) 专业系统。

电力规划中，多数建筑的附属系统通常需要一个或两个 20~30A，单相电流便足够了。

5. 方便电源

方便电源是为家用电器、个人计算机、办公设备、实验室设备、服务设备、便携灯，以及音频视频设备所准备的电源。随着家庭、办公室以及学校电气设备的增加，对于电源插座的需求迅速增加。

典型的办公室和家用电器的总负荷已经超过了照明需求，成为建筑电力系统负荷的主要部分。因此，方便电源电路的设计必须经过仔细分析，充分考虑选择合适的容量及位置。

6. 连接负荷及需求负荷

永久的有线电力设备为固定的负荷。即插即用的电力设备是方便负荷。所有电气设备铭牌上都有额定电流（A）、额定功率（W 或 kW），或者视在功率（V·A 或 kV·A）。这些参数可以用来计算系统或整个建筑物的总负荷。

(1) 设计负荷 电力系统的连接负荷是连接到该系统所有电力负荷的代数和。它没有考虑这些负荷什么时间怎样使用。

(2) 实际负荷 电力系统的实际负荷表明所有负荷中可同时使用的净负荷。当所有的设计负荷在同一时刻使用时，则实际负荷就等于连接负荷。实际上，在多数建筑中，实际负荷总是低于设计负荷。

7.6.4 系统选择与典型设备等级

实际设计时，在可选择的系统中，设计者必须衡量多种其他因素来做最后的选择。

这些因素包括投资成本，维护费用，系统可靠性、安全性，空间可用性，以及对其他需要电力的建筑系统的影响。通常，一些机械设备的相数和电压是标准的。在这种情况下，必须选择与设备标准相一致的电力系统。

在负荷分析的基础上，需要选择电力系统以满足负荷特征。例如如果建筑负荷基本为 220V 单相，那么系统应选择 220V 单相，或者 220/380V 三相四线制。三相四线制的优势是比较经济，它用一个普通的中性线来承担三个单相的负荷。然而，随着感应负荷的增加，例如办公室的计算机，三次谐波会使中性线过热。这种情况下，建议每个电路需要一个单独的中性线。

一个较大建筑的电力系统应是单相与三相相结合，由一个或多个高压系统提供的低压系统。

对于较小的建筑，通常单一电力系统就可满足。然而某些情况下，更愿意将较大的电力负荷与照明和电气负荷相分离，这样来减小由于大负荷的开关导致的系统电压起伏。电气设计工程师必须尽早地选择系统，并且告知建筑及机械工程师，才能使他们的设备选型相匹配。总体来说，初步设计期间，以下设备对系统选择有较大的影响。

(1) 电梯 根据其速度和容量不同，电梯的功率通常范围是 15 ~ 200hp（1 hp = 745.7W）。它们通常装备有三相电动机，其电压与建筑电力系统电压一致。

(2) 餐饮设备 30kW 左右的餐饮设备可以是单相或三相的，高容量设备通常是三相的。任何情况下，设备电压必须与建筑系统相一致。例如如果建筑电力系统电压是 208V，设备额定电压为 240V，那么设备输出量很可能减小 15%，除非安装变压器。当系统电压高于设备电压时，相反的情况会发生。

(3) 机械设备 大功率的机械设备基本需要三相电，诸如风扇、盘管以及单体类的小功率设备，可能是单相或三相的。初设阶段，对于这样设备的选择需要机械工程师和电力工程师的配合。

（4）家用电器　尽管有其他选择，但多数家用电器都是220V单相系统。如果一个较大住宅或公寓建筑选择380V三相四线制系统，那么或者有专门设计的电器，或者需要本地变压来使系统电压与设备电压一致。

7.6.5　电气系统设计与其他设计相协调

1. 建筑系统的衔接

建筑系统需要复杂的接口。例如一个由100个房间组成的高层建筑，采用集中制冷或供热系统，由380V三相三线主电力系统为中央设备供电，另外220/380V三相四线系统给照明和电器负荷供电。另一方面，如果每个单元有各自的电表给所有连接负荷，包括个人独立供热制冷设备，那么电力系统可能由几个小的120/240V系统组成，每个小单元用一个小系统，即使整个建筑很大。通常，机械系统的选择影响电力系统的选择。

2. 空间设计

空间设计不是很复杂，但是对于建筑设计过程至关重要。一旦电力或机械位置在建筑中确定，就很难再改变其大小和位置，否则将会影响其他的规则或系统。

（1）无障碍　所有设备在检查、保养维修时必须易接近。

（2）安全性　电气设备是危险的。可能接近的每一侧都要有足够的空间距离。

（3）普通通道空间　为了减小由通道需求引起的建筑有用空间的损失，往往采用中间为通道，通道两边用于安装电气设备的设计。作为通道，走廊经常被用来安装壁挂式配电盘或者仪表板。

（4）电气设备与结构单元的整体化　结构地板配电是地板配电的一种流行方法，适用于办公室，特别是有开敞外景设计的办公室。尽管地下配电的初投资比其他系统的大，但是统计表明其具有经济性，投资回报期较短。

习　题

1. 虽然电力设备不像其他机械设备一样占据很大的空间，但是电力系统设计和电力设备安装却与建筑设计元素关联更紧密。为什么？
2. 电力系统设计的几个基本步骤是什么？它们是否遵循一个逻辑顺序？
3. 为什么未来电负荷在系统设计中很重要？一般工程上如何取值？
4. 三相电力系统比单相电力系统优越在哪儿？
5. 如果一件新的电气设备要安装在一个电压和相数与之不同的建筑内，应该怎么办？
6. 如果一个标有50Hz的设备接在一个60Hz的系统上，应该怎么办？
7. 在居民或商业建筑里支路电流中最小的电线规格是多少？
8. 一个电流标示为30A的支路可以连接多大额定电流的移动电气设备？
9. 三相电流的电线应该安装在同一个管道中还是不同管道中？

Chapter 7
Power System and Electrical Design

Abstract: This chapter introduces different kinds of power distribution systems used for buildings and their characteristics. This chapter describes the configuration and pressure categories of power distribution systems. Different kinds of electrical equipments and their features are also summarized. This chapter also briefs the design of power distribution systems.

Key points: selection of power distribution system, voltage spread and profile, grounding, short-circuit and interruption capacity, common power equipment, determine electrical load, electrical design procedure.

7.1 Power Distribution Systems

There are numerous power distribution systems used for buildings. The systems that are most appropriate for a specific building depend on the size of the building and the characteristics of the predominant loads, such as power rating of the equipment, voltages, and phases. Frequency is another important characteristic of a power system. However, a country or region normally uses a standard frequency, such as 60 hertz (Hz) in the United States and 50 Hz in China and European countries. The standard frequency should be used except in unusual applications.

Most large buildings contain loads with diversified characteristics, such as single-phase lighting and appliance and three-phase motors. Thus it is quite common to have more than one power distribution system in the same building, although multiple systems are costly and difficult to maintain. Cost-benefit studies should be made to compare options. As a rule, if more than one system is necessary, the main system should be selected to satisfy the predominant loads with one or more subsystems which are converted from the main system for the minor loads.

For example, if a building contains 300 kV · A of single phase load and 20 kV · A of three-phase load, then the electrical power distribution system selected should be most appropriate for the single-phase load with a second system or a subsystem to handle the three-phase load.

Electrical power systems used in buildings may be divided into three voltage classes:

1) Extra-low voltage systems (50 volts and below). This class is normally used for control, signal, and communication systems.

2) Low-voltage systems (nominally below 600 volts). This class is normally used to supply

lighting and power equipment, except extremely large equipment such as a single 735499W motor.

3) Medium-voltage systems (600 to 100,000 volts). This class is normally used to supply distribution transformers with step-down voltages to build distribution systems and equipment loads.

For power distribution system within buildings, low-voltage systems up to 380 volts are most common. Medium- and high-voltage systems are used only in large buildings with several million square feet in floor area or in industrial plants.

7.1.1 Loads Less Than 100kV · A

Residential and small buildings typically have a demand load less than 100 kV · A. Loads are normally rated for 120 or 240 volts, single phase. Thus, a 120 to 240-volt, single phase three-wire system is most appropriate.

7.1.2 Loads Greater Than 100kV · A

Loads greater than 100 kV · A are usually served by three-phase systems. An exception is multiunit apartment or small shopping centers, where it is entirely appropriate to use a single-phase system, even if the total load far exceeds 100 kV · A. As the load increases, systems at higher voltages are favored, owing to economy of equipment and reduction of wire size.

7.2 Voltage Spread and Profile

7.2.1 Voltage of the Utility

Most utility power systems regulate their supply voltage automatically at the generating plant and at the distribution substation to within 1 percent of the nominal voltage. However, when a utility power system is overloaded, its supply voltage may drop. A 5 percent fluctuation is quite common and is within the legal limit of utility regulations.

Under unusual circumstances, when a utility network is extremely overloaded, the utility company may resort to lowering its distribution voltage by 5 to 10 percent of its normal voltage. This will correspondingly lower the secondary voltage in the building by a similar percentage and more or less reduce the building demand load by the same magnitude. However, when the voltage drops excessively, the building equipment may suffer detrimental effects, such as overheated motor, lowered energy efficiency, or the malfunction or tripping of sensitive electrical or electronic instruments.

7.2.2 Voltage Spread

Voltage spread is the difference between the maximum and minimum voltages of the system under no-load and full-load conditions, respectively. Voltage spread accounts for the voltage drop through the transformers, distribution equipment, feeders, and branch circuits.

7.2.3 Voltage Profile

The cumulative effect of utility voltage fluctuations and the voltage drop within the building distribution system may subject the load equipment to an overvoltage when the system is lightly loaded, such as night or on weekends, and an undervoltage at full-load conditions. Excessive overvoltage or undervoltage may shorten the life of or even burn out the load equipment. In the case of incandescent lamps, a 5 percent voltage drop below their rated voltage will reduce the light output (lumens) by nearly 20 percent. For this reason, it is imperative to minimize the voltage spread within the building distribution system.

7.3 Grounding

7.3.1 Grounding System

When an electrical system is connected to the earth, either intentionally or accidentally, it is said to be grounded. In general, all building electrical systems are intentionally grounded at the point where the voltage to ground is the lowest. There are several reasons for grounding:

1) Grounding protects the system and equipment from overvoltage due to accidental contact with high voltage sources, such as the primary voltage side of the distribution system, which may exceed several hundred thousand volts.

2) When lightning strikes a building and its electrical system, the electrical wiring and insulation on equipment may break down, and lightning current will flash over to seek the ground. If the system is properly grounded, the lighting current will follow a direct path to the ground, by passing the feeders and equipment.

3) Grounding protects people from heavy electrical shock. If the system and equipment are grounded and the electrical circuit is accidentally shorted to the equipment, the circuit protection device (fuses or circuit breakers) should trip and cut off the circuit. If the system is not grounded, then any accidental grounding of the wire through the equipment may pass through a person who happens to be touching the equipment.

4) A grounded system is more economical than an ungrounded one. The grounded side of a circuit must not be switched. Thus on a single-phase circuit, only a single-pole switch is required, whereas a double-pole switch must be used on an ungrounded single-phase system.

7.3.2 Ungrounded Systems

While grounding is preferred for general building systems, it does have one major disadvantage: A grounded system can easily be tripped, or put out of service, whenever its ungrounded side accidentally touches ground. This is a problem especially with critical loads, such as lighting and power for hospital surgical rooms. For this reason, the electrical power supply to the surgical room is ungrounded. However, ungrounded power systems should be isolated from the main system through individual isolation transformers and equipped with a sensitive ground detection system to recognize any accidental grounding. The detection system allows the power system to continue operation until the fault (accidental grounding) is corrected.

7.3.3 Grounding Methods

A common practice is to use an underground water main as the grounding electrode, because the water main is extensively and solidly buried in the ground. However, experience indicates that grounding an electrical system in this manner may cause corrosion of water main. Because of this problem, water utilities discourage such grounding by installing nonconductive couplings at the main or by using plastic piping materials. A less effective but still acceptable alternative is to use cooper rods or plates driven into the ground as the grounding electrode. A more reliable, but costlier method is to install a grounding grid under the building or a grounding loop around the building as a system ground. There are two grounding requirements.

1) System grounding. The entire distribution system should be grounded at the neutral, or lowest-voltage, point of the system. The voltage between an ungrounded line and the ground (earth) or the grounded line (usually neutral) is the voltage to ground.

2) Equipment grounding. All electrically conductive enclosures, such as the frame of a motor or the enclosure of an electrical appliance, should be grounded by a separate color-coded (green) conductor. Although metal raceways can be used as the ground, an equipment-grounding conductor is preferred.

7.3.4 Polarization

Since one side of all building interior distribution systems is grounded, the enclosure of any electrical equipment, such as the shell of a lamp socket, the metal case of any electrical tool, or the steel enclosure of a clothes-washing machine should be connected to the grounded side of the electrical circuit to safeguard the person who operates the equipment. This requirement is satisfied by the installation of polarized receptacles with equipment-grounding terminals. The ungrounded side of the receptacle is smaller than the grounded sides; thus, it can receive only the smaller blade from the equipment plug.

7.3.5 Ground Fault Circuit Interrupter

For added safety, certain receptacles and circuits that supply loads for swimming pools, kitchens, garages, bathrooms, laundries, or outdoor equipment should be of the type that can trip or cut out the circuit if an imbalance of current flow is sensed between the grounded and ungrounded sides of the circuit. Such an imbalance indicates that current is leaking through the ungrounded side of the circuit; thus, the situation should be corrected by a ground fault circuit interrupter (GFCI).

7.4 Short-circuit and Interruption Capacity

7.4.1 Short Circuit

The electrical circuit is designed to allow only a limited amount of current to flow through; this is done to prevent overheating of the wires due to I^2R loss. The limitation on the current is largely due to the resistance or impedance of the load to which it is connected. If the resistance or impedance of the load is bypassed, or shorted, then, according to Ohm's law, an abnormally high current will flow through the circuit. This is called short circuit. Depending on the remaining resistance or impedance of the circuit, the short-circuit current could be 10 to 30 times as high as the normal current. At this abnormally high level, most equipment and wiring will be ruined by the excessive amount of heat generated. Furthermore, there will most likely be fire of combustible components within or in the vicinity.

7.4.2 Short-circuit Calculations

To avoid damage from excessive heat and the magnetic force created by a short circuit, all electrical circuits and equipment connected to the system must have an interrupting rating, or, interrupting capacity, equal to or greater than the calculated short-circuit capacity of the system. The calculation of the short-circuit capacity of a power system is very involved and complex. Conservatively, it can be as high as 20 to 30 times the normal full-load current of the system.

7.4.3 Interrupting Capacity

To prevent the system and equipment from being destroyed by heat, arcing, and fire caused by a short circuit, all distribution wires and cables must be protected by devices such as fuses and circuit breakers. All equipment or devices installed on the power system must also carry an interrupting capacity (IC) greater than the calculated short-circuit current.

7.5 Power Equipment

There are various levels of equipment in an electrical power system, starting with the power service, transformers, and distribution equipment and ending with the load-end protection devices.

7.5.1 Switchboards and Panel Boards

A switchboard is an assembly of switches and circuit protection devices from which power is distributed. The switchboard serves as the main distribution center of a small system or as a portion of the distribution center of a large system.

A panel board is an assembly of switches and circuit protection devices as the final serving point of the power distribution system. Depending on the load to which it connected, a panel board may be identified as a lighting, power, heating, specialty, or combination panel board. There is no clear demarcation between a switchboard and a panel board, although a switchboard is always referred to as the distribution equipment closest to the supply end of the system.

7.5.2 Transformers

Transformers are power transmission equipment primarily intended to convert a system's voltage from one level to another level. All transformers operate on the principle of magnetic induction: Primary and secondary coils are wound on a common silicon steel core. The incoming side is the primary, the outgoing side the secondary. If the voltage is increased from primary to secondary, the transformer is a step-up transformer; if the voltage is decreased, the transformer is a step-down transformer. With magnetic induction, voltage is induced from the primary to the secondary. The resulting voltage is directly proportional to the ratio of the primary-to-secondary winding turns.

7.5.3 Switches

A switch is a device for making, breaking, or changing the connections in an electrical circuit.

Light switches are normally single-pole, single-throw switches. When lights need to be switched from more than one location, three-way and four-way switches are used. As a rule, the first and last switches must be three-way switches, and the in-between must be four-way switches.

7.5.4 Protective Devices

Electrical circuits that include feeders, distribution equipment, branch circuits, and the load equipment must be protected from exceeding their ratedcapacity, which may occur as a result of many circumstances. Some examples are: Overcurrent, due to mechanical overload or internal or external electrical faults; Overvoltage, due to short circuiting between primary and secondary wiring or due to a lighting strike; Reverse in polarity of a 3-phase system, due to a change of power service.

The most common method used to prevent the damage caused by overloading conditions is the installation of protective devices at strategic locations, e.g., feeder, in a branch circuit, or at the equipment. These devices are divided into three general types: relays, circuit breakers, and fuses. For building systems and equipment, circuit breakers and fuses are usually used.

1. Circuit Breakers

The advantages of circuit breakers over other types of protection devices, namely fuses, are:

1) Easily resetted when the system is tripped.

2) More compact.

3) Adaptable for remote control and electrical interlock with other equipment.

4) Can serve as disconnect switches (although they should not be used as an operating switch).

2. Fuses

A fuse is an electrical protective device that melts upon sensing an abnormal current and opens the circuit in which it is installed. It is a self-destructive device.

The operating principle of a single-element fuse is very simple. The fusible link is made of a lead-tin-antimony eutectic alloy that has a single-temperature melting point without softening prior to reaching its melting point. The fusible element is precisely made, having bottlenecks (narrow sections) that melt upon overheating due to a higher current flow.

3. Application of Protective Devices

Through improved mass production technology, small low-voltage circuit breakers for single- and double-pole breakers up to 200A are now as economical as the corresponding fused switches. Thus, circuit breakers are universally used for lighting and receptacle panels. However, for large-ampacity loads, especially systems with 40000 amperes or higher of available short-circuit current, fused switches are definitely more economical. A combination of fuses and circuit breakers is often used for systems having an available short circuit in excess of 50000 amperes.

7.6 Electrical System Design

Electrical system design is an integral part of the building design process. All building equipment, such as air conditioners, pumps, fans, as well as elevators and appliances, is electrically powered. Even gas or oil-fired equipment, such as boilers and heaters, requires electrical power. The selection of an electrical power system is often influenced by building equipment. For example, if the building apartment uses individual room air conditioners, the electrical distribution system will probably be a 220V, single-phase system, where as if each apartment is served by a central chiller and air-handling system, the electrical distribution system will be a 380V, three-phase, four-wire system.

7.6.1 Electrical Design Procedure

Generally, there are five basic steps in electrical system design:

1) Analyze building needs.

2) Determine electrical load.

3) Select electrical systems.

4) Coordinate with the structure design and other design decisions.

5) Prepare electrical plans and specifications.

In practice some of these steps may be temporarily bypassed in order to keep pace with the project's progress. For example, the power needs for a building are determined by its lighting, mechanical, and building equipment loads, from which the electrical power system is selected. However, before these steps can be completely finished, the utility company may wish to know the types of services in advance; the architect would like to know the sizes and locations of the electrical equipment rooms; the structural engineer would like to know the weight of all major equipment; and the HVAC engineer would like to know any system options for evaluating the cost of HVAC equipment. Therefore, reasonable assumptions must be made based on experience or statistical data. The assumptions will have to be assessed, modified and finalized at each phase of the design process.

7.6.2 Analysis of Building Needs

The first step in electrical system design is to identify the needs of the building established by the architectural program. Following are the major factors affecting electrical systems:

1) Occupation factors. Type of building occupancy, number of occupants, present and future electrical appliances to be installed or anticipated in the building, etc.

2) Cost factors. Whether the building has an austere budget; the building is of average equality, or is a high-image building, etc.

3) Architectural factors. Size of the building, number of floors, floor-to-floor height, building footprints, elevations, etc.

4) Building environments. Whether the building is heated, whether it is air-conditioned, whether the systems are central of unitary, etc.

5) Illumination criteria. Lighting level and the predominant type of light sources to be used.

6) Other mechanical systems. Need for electricity for cold water, hot water, sewage disposal, fire protection systems, etc.

7) Building equipment. Vertical transportation systems, computers, etc.

8) Auxiliary systems. Systems such as building management, time clock, fire alarm, telecommunication, radio and TV antenna, network, etc.

9) Future needs. More than any other components of the building systems, electrical power load in buildings has been known to grow consistently year after year. While the structure may last hundreds of years, the electrical power system may need to be upgraded every 20 to 30 years, owing to advances in technology. The designer must make an independent judgment or consult with the architect or building management for specific future loads as well as for general growth. In general, a

minimum of 25 percent spare capacity should be provided at the power main and at one or more power distribution centers.

7.6.3 Determination of Electrical Loads

Electrical loads for buildings can be analyzed according to a number of different categories.

1. Lighting

Lighting design is usually the coordinated effort of the architect, interior designer, lighting designer and the electrical engineer. Lighting accounts for one of the largest electrical loads in most buildings. In general, lighting fixtures are designed for 220V, single-phase power. A continuous improvement in light source technology has increased the efficiency of converting electrical energy to lighting energy, which in turn has reduced the need for electrical power for lighting in buildings.

2. Mechanical Equipment

Electrical power required for mechanical equipment varies widely with the building, type of climate, type of mechanical systems, and intended method of operation of these systems. For planning purposes, preliminary data on power are obtained from the design mechanical engineers and are updated periodically as the design progresses.

The mechanical system includes the HVAC, plumbing, and fire protection systems. Equipment, such as chillers, boilers, pumps and fans, usually requires a large power capacity and is more economically designed for higher voltages, such as 380V, three phase power. However, residential equipment is normally designed for 220V, single-phase power.

3. Building Equipment

Building equipment includes vertical transportation equipment, and household, recreational, and miscellaneous operational equipment. The power requirement for this type of equipment varies widely in capacity and operating characteristics. The electrical power required for building equipment is usually gathered by the architect, the user, or various specialty consultants.

With the escalation of communication systems in buildings, the demand for electrical power has increased dramatically in recent years. For example, the demand for convenience power (plug-in types of equipment) in an office building has increased several folds. What were acceptable standards a few years ago are now inadequate for use with data-processing and communication equipment in all types of buildings, including residences.

4. Auxiliary Systems

Normally, auxiliary systems do not require a large power capacity, thus, they are usually designed for 220V, single-phase power. Depending on the type of occupancy—residential, commercial, or industrial—each building may require one or more of the following systems:

1) Building management systems.

2) Security systems.

3) Time clock systems.

4) Fire alarm systems.

5) Telecommunication systems.

6) Radio and TV antenna systems.

7) Public address systems.

8) Data and networking systems.

9) Specialty systems.

For power-planning purpose, usually one or two 20~30 A, single-phase circuits are sufficient for each auxiliary system in most buildings.

5. Convenience Power

Convenience power is power provided for plug-in equipment such as household appliances, personal computers, office equipment, laboratory instruments, service equipment, portable lights, and audio and video equipment. With the proliferation of electrical appliances in homes, offices, and schools, the demand for on floor power for plug-in equipment has increased steeply.

The total appliance load for typical offices and homes has already exceeded that required for lighting and becomes a dominant load of the building electrical systems. The design of convenience power circuits must, therefore, be carefully analyzed with regard to capacity and appropriate location.

6. Connected and Demand loads

Permanently wired electrical equipment is a fixed load. Plug-in electrical equipment is a convenience load. All electrical equipment has a nameplate current rating in amperes (A), or working power in W or kW, or in apparent power in V · A or kV · A. Any of these power ratings may be used to calculate the total loads of the systems or the entire buildings.

(1) Connected Load The connected load of an electrical power system is the algebraic sum of all electrical loads connected to the systems. It does not take into account how and when these loads are being used.

(2) Demand Load The demand load of an electrical power system indicates the net load that would probably be used at the same time for each load group. When all connected loads are used at the same time, the demand load is equal to the connected load. However, in most buildings, the demand load is always lower than the connected load.

7.6.4　System Selection and Typical Equipment Ratings

In actual design applications, the designer must also weigh the various other factors in alternative systems before making the final selection.

These factors include cost of investment, cost of maintenance, system reliability, serviceability, space availability, and the impact on the other building systems which require electrical power. Often, the phase and voltages of some mechanical equipment are standardized without options. In such cases, the power system must be so selected as to be compatible with the equipment standard.

On the basis load analysis, electrical power systems are selected to complement the load characteristics. For example, if the loads in the building are predominantly 220V, single-phase, then the systems should be either a 220/380V, single-phase, three-wire or a 380V, three-phase, four-wire system. One of the advantages of a three-phase, four-wire system is its inherent economy. It allows one common neutral wire to serve up to three single-phase loads. However, with the increased use of inductive loads, such as computers in offices, there is a tendency to overheat the common neutral wire owing to the third harmonics. In such a case, an individual neutral wire for each circuit is recommended.

The electrical power system for a large building could be a combination of single-phase and three-phase, low-voltage systems supplied by one or more high-voltage systems.

Naturally, for smaller building, a single power system will suffice. However, in some applications, it is desirable to separate the large power load from the lighting and appliance loads to minimize voltage fluctuation of the system due to the on-off nature of the larger load. The design electrical engineer must select the system early and inform the architect and the mechanical engineers of any options, so that equipment selected by them will match properly. In general, the following equipment greatly affects the selection of the system during the preliminary design period.

(1) Elevators   Elevators usually range from 15 to 200 hp (1hp = 745.7W), depending on their speed and load capacity. They are usually equipped with three-phase motors whose voltage is compatible with that of the building power system.

(2) Food Service Equipment   Food service equipment of 30 kW or less could be either single-phase or three-phase; equipment of higher capacity is usually three-phase. In all cases, the equipment voltage must match that of the building system. For example, if the building power system is 208V and the equipment is rated for 240V, then the equipment output will probably be reduced by 15 percent in capacity unless a local transformer is installed. The reverse is true when the system voltage is higher than the equipment voltage.

(3) Mechanical Equipment   While large pieces of mechanical equipment are always designed for three-phase power, smaller equipment, such as fans, coils, and unitary equipment, may be made for either single-phase or three-phase power. The selection of such equipment must be a joint decision of the mechanical and electrical engineers during the preliminary design phase.

(4) Household Appliances   Although there are other options, most household appliances are made for a 220V, single-phase system. If a 380V, three-phase, four-wire system is selected for a large residence or an apartment building, then either specially designed appliances must be used or local load-size transformers must be installed at the equipment to boost the system voltage to match that of the equipment.

7.6.5 Electrical System Design Coordination with Other Design Decisions

1. Interfacing of Building Systems

Building systems require complex interfacing. For example, in a high-rise building consisting of 100 apartments served by a central cooling and heating system, the main electrical power system should be a 380V, three-phase, three-wire system for the central equipment and a 220/380V, three-phase, four-wire system for lighting and appliance loads. On the other hand, if each apartment has its own electrical meter for all connected loads—including individual unitary heating and cooling units—then the electrical power system would probably be multiple of small 120/240V systems, one for each apartment—even though the building is large. Usually, the selection of the mechanical systems affects the selection of the electrical system.

2. Space Planning

Space planning is not an exact science, yet it is vital to the building design process. Once the electrical or mechanical space is allocated within the building, it is difficult to change its size or location, as doing so will undoubtedly affect the work in progress of many other disciplines or systems.

(1) Accessibility All equipment and devices must be accessible for inspection, service, and replacement.

(2) Safety Electrical equipment is hazardous. Sufficient clearance must be provided on all sides that require access.

(3) Common Access Spaces To minimize the loss of useful building space due to access requirements, double-loaded, center-aisle design is preferred. As passageways, corridors are frequently utilized for wall-mounted switchboards and panel boards.

(4) Integration of Electrical and Structural Elements The electrification of structural floors is a popular method for distributing on-floor power. It is most applicable for offices, especially offices with an open landscape design. Although the initial cost of installation of underfloor distribution systems is greater than that of other systems, statistics have proved their overall economy, with short payback period.

Questions

1. Although electrical equipment does not require as much space as most mechanical equipment, the design of electrical systems and the layout of electrical components demand even closer interfacing with the architectural elements in space. Why?

2. What are the basic steps in electrical design? Must they be followed in a logical order?

3. Why is the system capacity for future loads important? What is the general practice?

4. Name the advantages of a three-phrase system over a one-phase system?

5. If a piece of new equipment that will be installed in a building has a different voltage rating or phase connections, what would you do?

6. What would you do if equipment rated for 50 Hz is connected to a 60Hz system?

7. What is the minimum size wire for branch circuits in residential buildings and for institutional buildings?

8. If a branch circuit is rated for 30A, what is the maximum rating of portable equipment that can be connected to this circuit?

9. Should all three phases of a circuit be installed in the same conduit or in different conduits?

第 8 章
建筑照明

本章要点：本章介绍了光学物理方面的基本知识，照明设备的基本参数和照明系统的组成，以及建筑光环境的设计方法。

知识点：亮度，光通量，发光强度，照明控制方法，光源基本因素，照明设计过程，建筑照明要求，照明系统的选择。

照明是利用自然或人工产生的光源，为工作和生活提供一个理想的视觉环境。本章涉及光的特性、人的视觉及适用于建筑环境的照明基本知识。

8.1 光照与照明

8.1.1 光照与视觉

人眼结构是这样的：当光线进入眼角膜和晶状体后，光能便集中在视网膜上，并通过视觉神经细胞传送到大脑，随后大脑把信息传回眼睛，形成光学影像。双眼的影像将信息整合成三维图像。

人类是按照色彩对比和亮度对比两种方式识别事物的。我们可以轻易看到蓝色背景下的红色物体，但在相同红色背景下却不容易看到，即必须要有足够的色差，我们的眼睛才能看清物体。同样，我们可以看到白纸上的黑色字体，但在灰色纸张上却不容易看到，甚至在黑色纸张上就完全看不到。因此，必须要有亮度对比，我们的眼睛才能看清物体。

1. 亮度和亮度对比

简单来说，亮度是指我们的眼睛感知到的源自于物体的光量。光可以是物体自身发出的（如太阳或光源），也可以是由物体反射的（如桌面或书中的纸张），还可以是通过物体透射传播的（如彩色玻璃窗或灯罩）。亮度对比可以有多种表示，通常使用式（8-1）。

$$C = |L_t - L_b|/L_b \tag{8-1}$$

式中 C——对比度；

L_t——目标亮度（cd/m^2）；

L_b——背景亮度（cd/m^2）。

当 L_t 比 L_b 暗时，使用绝对值 $|L_t - L_b|$，且 C 总是小于 1。

2. 视觉舒适

尽管高亮度对比可以改进视觉敏感度，但长时间在过高的对比度下看东西会导致视疲劳。

将黑色文字打印在浅色纸上,这样通常情况下效果会更好,如棕黄色、乳白色或淡蓝色。显然,当把黑色文字打印在深色纸张上,如深红色、蓝色或其他颜色,会降低视觉敏感度。

3. 眩光

当光源或物体的亮度过高时,会干扰视觉,这就是眩光。导致视觉生理不适的眩光,称为不适眩光。确实影响视觉能力的眩光,称为失能眩光。直接发自于光源的眩光,称为直接眩光。被物体的表面反射的眩光,称为反射或间接眩光。可将光源设置偏离视线以避免直接眩光。如果可行的话,可选用无眩光材料或低反射率的材料以削弱间接眩光。

8.1.2 光学物理

1. 光度单位

基本的光度量见表8-1。

表8-1 基本光度量

物 理 量	符 号	单位及缩写
能量(光能)	Q	流明·小时(lm·h)
功率(光通量)	F	流明(lm)
强度(标准烛光)	I	坎德拉(cd)
照明(照度)	E	勒克斯(lx)
亮度(照度)	L	坎德拉/平方米(cd/m²)

2. 光能

光能可以由其他形式的能量转化,如热能、电能和化学能。由于电能转化过程的效率最高,因此最常使用。在照明系统设计中,光能通常不计算在其中,因为光能会迅速转化为热能并且不易储存。

3. 光通量和发光强度

光通量是能源消耗速率。在照明系统中,光通量是光源在单位时间内向外辐射的能量。光通量的单位为流明(lm)。如果电能转化为光能,不计能量损失,那么1W辐射能可转化为683lm的单一波长的绿光。如果转换成白光,转换率仅约为200lm/W。

流明是发光强度为1坎德拉(cd)的点光源,在单位立体角(1球面度)内发出的光通量。坎德拉是发光强度的单位。通俗来讲,1cd大约是点亮一支蜡烛的光强度,这是一个形象但不科学的比喻,因为蜡烛的大小和材料可以是任意的。根据定义,1cd即1流明/球面度。一个球体有4π(12.57)球面度。因此,1根蜡烛相当于12.57lm。

4. 照度

照度是单位面积的光通量,其数量类似于热力学中单位面积的Btu/h(1 Btu = 1055.06J)或电力学中的单位面积的瓦特数。在工程术语中,虽然光强度取代了照度,但在实践中,照度仍然有着广泛的应用。国际标准中,照度单位用勒克斯(lux 或 lx)表示。根据定义,照度可表示为

$$E = \frac{光通量}{面积} = \frac{F}{A} \tag{8-2}$$

式中　　E——照度（lux）；

　　　　F——光通量（lm）；

　　　　A——面积（m^2）。

图 8-1a 中描绘了照度和光通量之间的关系，即光通量从点光源中辐射出。图 8-1b 描绘了光强度（坎德拉，cd）、光通量（流明，lm）和照度（勒克斯，lux）之间的关系。

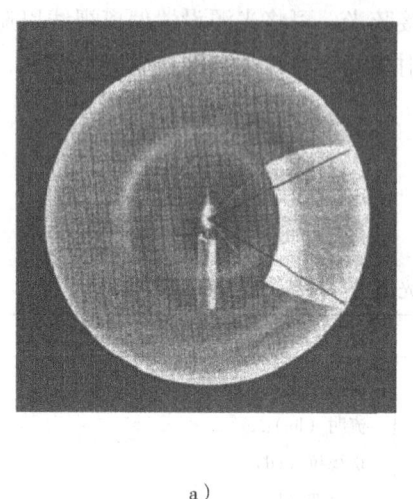
a）

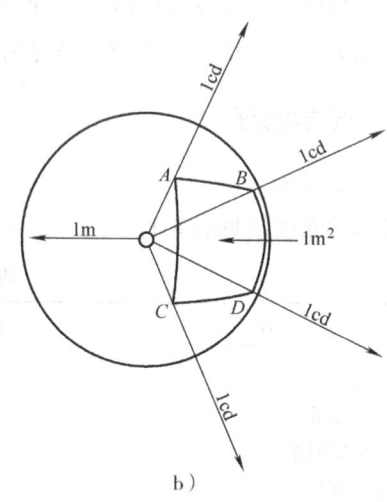
b）

图 8-1　照度和光通量之间的关系
a）位于透明球体中心的蜡烛光源　b）光源与照度

图 8-1a 表示位于透明球体中心的蜡烛光源。8-1b 表示在半径为 1m 处，球面上任意一点的照度均为 1 lx（lm/m^2）。区域 $ABCD$ 向内对应的立体角为 1sr。因此，光通量密度为 1lm/sr，即相当于起初设定的 1cd 发光强度。球体总面积为 12.57m^2，且每平方米面积上的光通量为 1lm，因此，该光源总共提供 12.57lm 的光通量。

自然界和建筑物中的照度水平见表 8-2。

表 8-2　自然界和建筑物中的照度

位　　置		最低水平/fc
星光		0.0002
月光		0.02
路灯		1.5 – 10.0
日光	阴影（户外）	100 ~ 1000
	直射阳光	5000 ~ 10000
过道空间（走廊等）		5 ~ 10
办公室照明		50 ~ 70
教室（幼儿园至大学）		20 ~ 70
绘图室		70 ~ 150
体育器材室（学校至专业器材室）		30 ~ 300

注：1fc = 10.764lx。

5. 发光强度

在给定方向下的光通量定义为单位立体角下的光通量，或垂直于该方向的表面上的光通量除以球面度上的立体角（$I = d\Phi/d\omega$）。这一定义严格适用于点光源。然而在实际中，光大多发生于一个较大的光源，如白炽灯照明灯具，其尺寸相对于其测量照明范围可忽略不计，则该定义也适用。

（1）倒平方定律　倒平方定律规定，被照面上一点的照度 E 与点光源发光强度 I 和光源与被照面的垂直距离 d 有关系。如果光线直射入被照面，定律可表示为

$$E = \frac{I}{d^2} \tag{8-3}$$

式中，距离 d 单位为 m；照度 E 单位为 lux；发光强度 I 单位为 cd。

此定律可直接用于照明系统的设计计算，前提是光源与被照面之间的直线距离至少是光源最大尺寸的 5 倍。

（2）余弦定律　朗伯余弦定律规定，在任意被照面上，任意表面上的照度随入射角的余弦的变化而变化。角度 θ 是被照面的法线与光线的夹角。倒平方定律和余弦定律可统一成以下形式

$$E = \frac{I}{d^2}\cos\theta \tag{8-4}$$

倒平方定律说明了光源和受光面之间距离增大时，同样大小的光通量投射到更大的面积上。朗伯余弦定律表明，光通量如不是投射到正对的表面上，则可以分布到更大的面积上。

6. 光亮度与视亮度

光亮度即从物体表面反射或透过的光通量，等于受光面的亮度乘以表面反射因子或透射因子。我们的眼睛感受到的亮度既和可测的光亮度有关，又和我们眼睛的适应性有关。假如我们的眼睛已适应较低亮度的环境，如在电影院，即使很小的光点也会显得很明亮。同理，在白天，一个非常亮的汽车前照灯也会不那么明亮。因此，光亮度与视亮度不能混为一谈，虽然很多时候二者之间会互换使用。一个物体或表面的视亮度会随周围环境光线减弱而显得更明亮。为了减小不适的视明亮感，设计者应避免将光源放在直视的视线中并且降低与周围光源的亮度差。

光亮度是有方向性的，根据不同的视角及受光面特性，光亮度可表示为流明（lm）/球面度（sr）或坎德拉（cd）/面积（m^2）。光亮度可表示为

$$1 \text{亮度} = 1 cd/m^2 \tag{8-5}$$

表 8-3 给出了典型自然和人工光源的估计光亮度值。

表 8-3　各种光源的估计光亮度值

光　源	典型亮度值/（cd/m^2）
太阳（从地球上看）	1540000000
月亮（从地球上看）	8000
阳光下的雪	31000
多云的天空	2000

（续）

光　　源	典型亮度值/（cd/m²）
烛光	10000
白炽灯（60W）	30000
荧光灯（40W）	17000

8.1.3　照明控制

照明空间内的光源太明亮或来自错误的方向，都会造成视觉不适或利用率低下。或由于错误的灯光颜色会导致较低的色彩识别率。因此，出于以上原因，必须严格控制照明系统。

光在干净、无杂质的空气中将无弯曲、无损失地传播，直到传播到另一种介质上，会发生反射、吸收、透射、折射、散射或光偏振等。利用这些在不同材料上的不同特性可创造出良好的照明环境。

（1）反射　光线可以在介质表面发生反射。如果表面是光滑的，如镜面，反射光遵从反射定律：反射角等于入射角。即使是透明材料也会有光在其表面发生反射现象。

（2）散射　如果介质表面是不光滑的，反射光将发生漫反射，其方向可能是定向的，也可能是完全没有方向的散射，遵循"余弦分布"。

（3）透射　当介质是透明的（光洁的玻璃）、打磨的（蚀刻玻璃）或完全漫射的（白玻璃），光线可以某种方式穿过。

（4）吸收　当光线射向不透明介质、透明或半透明的介质时，会被部分吸收，损失部分能量。吸收的那部分光的能量与透射光及反射光的能量是总量守恒的。

（5）折射　在两种不同材料的介质界面，光线方向会发生改变。例如空气和玻璃，光的传播方向会发生改变，这种现象称为折射。折射是控制光最有效的手段，常为照明设计师所用。斯涅尔（Snell）折射定律是指

$$n_1 \sin i = n_2 \sin r \tag{8-6}$$

式中　n_1——光传播时第一个介质的折射率；

i——入射光线与介质接触面法线的夹角；

n_2——光线发生折射后第二个介质的折射率；

r——折射光线与介质接触面法线的夹角。

（6）偏振　光线都是以在相互正交的平面上振动的波的形式高速传播着。偏振即光线只在一个平面中振动，这种偏振的材料称为偏振片。当光线同时穿过光轴相互成90°的两个偏振片时，光线将被完全偏振。一个比较常用的偏振技术就是偏振太阳镜，这是公认最有效减少太阳眩光的方法。如果将两个偏振太阳镜呈直角放置，阳光几乎是百分之百地被过滤。因此，多层次的偏光镜片多用于照明系统的控制中。

光线控制的6种方法可随意组合，用于照明系统的设计。

8.2 照明设备及照明系统

产生光的方法有很多,比如太阳能(日光)、燃烧、化学反应或电能的转化。所有的这些光源,太阳光是最丰富的,也是免费的。然而,夜晚没有太阳光,同时一天中太阳光的变化也是很大的,有时阳光很明亮很刺眼,暴露在下面较长时间会感觉很热。尽管如此,如果适当控制,如采用太阳镜或空调,太阳光将是所有光源中最经济的。

在建筑中,电气照明已成为夜间使用的唯一光源,并且在白天补充太阳光的不足。通常情况下,即使有足够的日光也要使用电气照明。例如正在进行演讲的教室或会议室,或在很多体育赛事中,低角度入射的太阳光会导致眩光,使运动员和观众视线不清晰。燃烧型光源,如煤气灯,只限于装饰使用。

照明设备的基本组成即是光源,通常叫做灯。提供照明的一盏灯或多盏灯称为照明装置。虽然在学术界遭到反对,"照明装置"更易于被公众和设计及建造业的专业人士接受。因此,照明装置和灯这两种说法可在本部分交换使用。

灯具是为特定的灯设计的,通常不适合于其他类型。其中一个原因是灯具的结构不同,另一个原因是灯会产生大量的热量,从而影响材料、通风以及灯泡及其周围表面的清洁。因此,灯具和灯泡要匹配,并要控制在规定的功率内。

灯具是室内设计的重要组成因素,因为它们往往处于显眼的位置。除了照明功能,其他性能(如尺寸、质地、形状和颜色)也必须同时考虑。要创建一个成功的照明设计,建筑师、室内设计师、照明工程师必须同时了解各种光源及各照明装置的性能。本节将介绍灯泡、灯具及照明系统基本知识。

照明设计师有责任通过使用高效的光源和设备,尽量减小能源消耗,同时创造一种美观的环境,以提高生产力。例如在美国,照明消耗约占所有电力能源消耗的25%。而消耗掉的每千瓦时电,都有相应数量的污染物释放到了大气中。

8.2.1 电光源

电光源被称为灯。虽然成千上万的灯有不同的用途,但根据其工作原理可大致分为四类。

白炽灯将电能转化成热能使灯丝发光(红光或白光)。这个过程与黑体放热非常相似。

荧光灯含有汞蒸气。适当的施加电压,电弧会产生对立电极,产生紫外线。紫外线激发灯泡里面的荧光粉涂层,即可发出可见光。

高强放电(HID)灯在外罩灯泡的电弧管内产生高强度光。电弧管内金属气体可以是汞、钠或其他复合金属蒸气。外罩灯泡可以不涂或涂有荧光粉。HID 灯可分为汞蒸气灯、金属卤素灯和高压钠灯。

其他各种各样不同原理的灯泡,虽然在建筑物中的应用很有限,但未来技术和生产力的突破有望给建筑学和环境设计提供新的方向。一些有前景的技术类型如下:

1)短弧灯,如氙气灯系列,采用小型电弧管发光,最接近一个真实的高亮度点光源,主要应用于搜索灯、投影机等光学仪器上。

2) 低压钠灯（LPSs）是一种波长范围在 589~589.6nm 之间黄色光的单色灯。其转化效率高达 180lm/W，但其颜色阻碍了其应用范围。主要应用在高速公路和仓储场中。

3) 电致发光灯通过交流电激发荧光粉发光，因此，可制作成任何形状、大小和形式。电致发光灯能通过混合荧光粉来产生不同的颜色。虽然这些灯效率极高，约 200 lm/W，但其使用仅限于标志和装饰。

4) 无极灯是通过激发电磁或微波能量，而无须使用电极的一种气体灯。这种灯通过使用专门设计的装置或使用"光管"，在未来建筑照明应用中有很光明的前景。

8.2.2 选择光源及设备要考虑的因素

在众多灯泡中做出选择需要考虑很多因素。

1. 光输出

光输出，用流明表示，定义如下：

1) 初始流明：当灯为新的时，以其额定功率输出，通常在使用 100h 后测定。

2) 平均流明（average lumen）：初始流明与灯达额定寿命时流明数的平均值。

3) 期望流明（mean lumen）：在灯达寿命值的 40% 时输出的流明。

4) 光束流明：最开始使用时灯中间光束的流明数，通常规定排除光照强度不到最大光强度 10% 的光束。

2. 强度

光强度定义为灯或灯具在各角度的坎德拉（cd）数。这些数据通常由灯具制造商的光强分布曲线图提供。

3. 发光效率

发光效率，或者说效率，即单位电能（瓦）的光通量数，即流明/瓦（lm/W）。理论上讲，1W 的电可转化为 683 lm 的单色绿光，或约 200 lm 的可视频谱波长的白光。以此为参照，10~25 lm/W 的灯远未达到理想值。灯的实际效率应考虑其配件的损耗，即灯效率，单位为流明/瓦，仅指灯；或称净灯效率，对于放电发光的灯具（荧光和 HID 等）则同时包括了灯和配件。

4. 灯具效率

灯具效率即灯具输出的总照度与所有灯输入照度的比值，以百分比表示。灯具效率是一个比较发光强度分布特性类似的灯具的理想量度，但无法度量光线是否合理地使用。假如想照亮墙壁上的一幅画，一个无任何遮挡的 100% 功率的灯泡，如果不加以方向性的控制，则其效率只有 60%。

5. 额定灯泡寿命

灯具的额定寿命是指其中 50% 的灯泡保持照明的时间。额定寿命遵循根据大量数据统计出来的寿命曲线。图 8-2 给出了白炽灯的寿命曲线。

例：如果一盏白炽灯的寿命是 750h，建筑中安装的灯具在 500h 后依然正常工作的灯具百分比为多少？

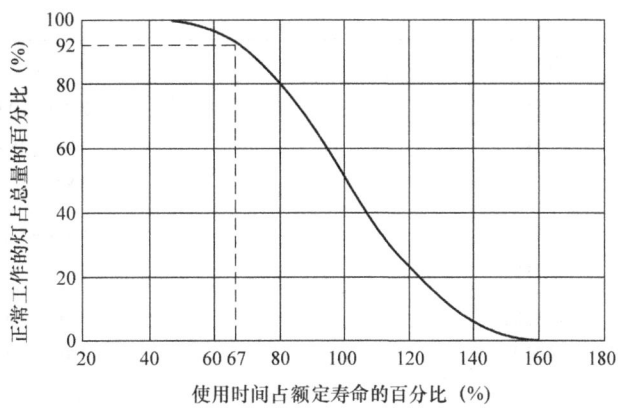

图 8-2　白炽灯的寿命曲线

解：灯具使用的时间是 2/3，或 67% 的额定寿命。如图 8-2 所示，92% 的灯依然正常工作。

6. 照度折损

灯具输出功率随时间下降。光的损失被称为照度折损，可能高达灯具初始输出功率的 20%~30%。这一点必须在照明设计时考虑到。不同灯具的典型照度折损特性见表 8-4。

表 8-4　不同灯具的典型照度折损特性

灯 类 型		估计光输出（%）	
		50% 寿命时	100% 寿命时
白炽灯	通用型	90	82
	钨卤素灯	97	92
荧光灯	轻负载（低亮度）	92	90
	中负载（标准）	85	82
	高负载（高输出）	75	65
高强放电	汞（H）	77	60
	金属卤素（MH）	70	65
	高压钠（HPS）	90	70

7. 色温

色温是灯泡显示的色彩，用温度（开尔文，K）表示。表 8-5 列出了一些典型灯泡的色温特性。

表 8-5　典型灯泡的色温特性

光　源		色温范围/K
白炽灯	60W	2500~2700
	100W	2700~2900
	500W	2900~3100
	钨卤素灯	3000~3200

(续)

光源		色温范围/K
荧光灯	暖白	2900~3000
	冷白	4000~4500
	日光	6000~6500
汞	纯粹的	5500~5800
	改进的	4400~4500
金属卤素	纯粹的	3700~3800
	改进的	3200~4000
高压钠	正常	2000~2100
	色彩改进的	3000~4000
低压钠		1700~1800
照相泛光灯		3200
照相闪光灯		5500

8. 显色指数

显色指数（CRI）是与同色温光源的参考或基准光源下物体外观颜色的比较。一个色温在3000K的白炽灯被CIE视为理想基准光源，定义为 $CRI=100$，并用以比较所有其他色温低于5000K的灯泡。$CRI=100$ 并不意味着这种特殊的白炽灯能表示所有其他物体或材料的真实颜色。之所以选择这种灯，是因为其有平滑的光谱频率分布（SPD），没有极端的能量窄带出现。

9. 偏色指数

偏色指数（CPI）表示光源在最优基础上所显示的颜色质量，如红色肉类、绿色蔬菜、蓝天和肤色等。

10. 闪烁和频闪效应

理论上讲，60Hz的电流通过灯时光以每秒120次波动，这就是所谓的闪烁。由于白炽灯灯丝的滞留特性和放电灯的荧光粉涂层，闪烁通常不明显，除非是HID灯。当HID灯照亮一个快速移动的物体时，物体看起来会是静止或是以较低的谐波频率运动，这就是所谓的频闪效应。可以使用超前－滞后镇流器和三相电路来消除或减少此现象。

当电力系统的频率低于60Hz时，闪烁及频闪效应将会被放大。相反，在较大的频率下，闪烁就不那么明显了。

11. 亮度

从物理上讲，高光强小光源，如白炽灯，非常适合用于照明控制，但对于人们的视觉舒适度来讲却太过明亮。光源的位置及用途要仔细选择，不舒适的眩光可以通过相应的手段减小，具体的方法在前面章节有所讨论。

12. 强度控制

光照强度可通过多级开关或调光来控制。白炽灯的明暗可以使用自耦变压器或固态调光器来调节。荧光灯和 HID 灯可以通过特别的镇流器和电路来调节，但成本较高。

13. 配件

在选择光源前应考虑的配件主要有光源的镇流器、启动器和调光器等。

8.2.3 光源的比较

下面介绍选择光源时需考虑的几点要素：

（1）效率　白炽灯，包括钨卤素类，是效率最低的光源，荧光灯或 HID 灯的效率是其 3~5 倍。

（2）光谱功率分布　没有光源能够产生整个可见光谱的光线。即使是 7500K 的日光，也是蓝光较多，红光较少。白炽灯多产生橙色和红色部分的光谱，荧光灯多产生蓝色和绿色的光谱。低压钠灯只能产生一个非常狭窄的黄色的光谱而缺乏所有其他的颜色。

（3）显色　这是在照明设计中非常重要的一方面。许多新的光源具有良好的显色品质和高发光效率。高压钠灯在照明系统中的显色指数 CRI 为 80，颜色相比于显色指数 CRI 为 100 的白炽灯来讲并不逊色。类似结论也适用于金属卤素灯。

（4）色温　白色光源所显示的色彩，无论是暖色的（黄、红）或冷色的（蓝、绿），都可表示为黑体沿普朗克轨迹在 CIE 色度图上的温度。

（5）额定寿命　不同灯具的寿命差别很大，一般情况下，荧光灯和 HID 灯的寿命是普通白炽灯的 10~20 倍。这就意味着在荧光灯或 HID 灯的平均寿命周期内，使用白炽灯可能要更换 20 次。

（6）经营成本　荧光灯和 HID 灯在消耗能源和维护费用上比白炽灯要节约很多。在很多室内空间，包括高度装饰的商业空间中，白炽灯只适用于特殊照明用途，而非日常空间照明。

8.2.4 灯具

灯具，通常被称为照明装置，是一个包含了一个或多个灯泡、结构支撑、附件、电线及控制体的完整照明单元。灯具可按其结构、物理特性和光度等标准来划分，最重要的有：

（1）光源　灯具内的灯为白炽灯、卤素灯、荧光灯、金属卤化物灯、高压钠灯、低气压钠灯等。

（2）功率　用于单个或者多个灯，无论其最大尺寸为多少等。

（3）供电　供电电压为 110V、220V，还是 380V，无论交流电还是直流电。

（4）用途　灯具用于室外、室内、水下、地下、航空、电影院、道路标志等。

（5）施工　灯具是否防水、防风、防尘、防爆、耐腐蚀等。

（6）安装方法　灯具安装在天花板、预埋、悬挂、支架、墙壁、地板或柱装等。

（7）控制媒介　棱柱镜头、散射板、百叶窗、具体截断角度、散射板、反射特性等。

（8）镇流器　镇流器的类型和数量、镇流因子（BF）、镇流效率因子（BEF）等。

（9）特殊性能　是否有电磁屏蔽性能、内置应急灯或内置电池等。

（10）光线分布　室内灯具的类型被 IES 分为六类，被 CIE 分为五类。分类标准是在水平面以上、以下光通量的分布百分比及其特性。六类是指：

1）直接式，大约有 90% 以上的光通量是向下的。

2）半直接式，60%～90% 的光通量直接向下，其余向上。

3）散射式，40%～60% 的光通量是直接向上或向下的，光在各方向的分布基本平均。

4）直接-间接式，40%～60% 的光通量直接上下方向照射，水平照射基本没有。CIE 协会将直接-间接式也算作散射式。从设计者角度来讲，这两类应区别开来，因为从墙亮度、眩光和利用系数等属性上看，它们产生完全不同的空间效果。

5）半间接式，60%～90% 的光通量是向上的。

6）间接式，90%～100% 的光通量是向上的。

8.2.5　照明系统的比较

对于每一个照明系统，有成千上万种灯具可供购买；对于每个灯具，灯的种类、尺寸和棱镜、百叶、挡板等控制媒介上也有多种方式。因此，只阐述其中几种组合方式是毫无意义的。但是对照明系统可作如下概括：

1）直接系统是使用直接分布式灯具的照明系统，这是在水平方向最有效的照明系统。然而，此系统容易产生直接和反射眩光。有很多方法来克服眩光，例如使用大型低亮度天花板。

2）半直接系统有部分向上的组件，将会削弱天花板与灯具的亮度对比并改善空间亮度关系。

3）散射式系统中灯具的光通量大致上均匀地分布在各个方向。这种系统通常要的是一种浅阴影的建模效果，但会产生直接眩光。该装置通常吊装，如果和天花板距离太近，这种系统将会和半直接系统效果类似。

4）直接间接系统类似于一般的散射系统，只是光通量在水平面 10°～30°以下是被减弱或屏蔽的。这一特性将大大减少直接眩光，尤其是在视频显示屏中。

5）在间接系统中，更多的光通量是向水平面以上的，这会降低直接眩光。反过来，太高的天花板亮度可能会使人感到不适。除非有足够的屋顶高度并且灯具安装高度在制造商建议使用的范围内，否则最好不要安装这种系统。间接系统是理想的视频展示空间。如果整体照度水平不足以满足阅读等需要，系统可能需要辅以局部照明。

在上面任何系统中，墙面的颜色和反射是非常重要的。对于不同的照明系统墙面的颜色和反射影响是截然不同的。

8.3　建筑光环境设计

人类对光有着本能的生理需求和心理依赖，在物质极大丰富、产品日新月异的今天，人们有条件追求更高质量的光，不仅要求照明，更希望针对不同的场合对光线进行精确的控制。与此同时，人们对于光还有着越来越高的装饰和艺术感的需求。

8.3.1 天然光和人工光

现阶段人工环境中的主要自然光源主要有三种——昼光（通过云层或局部多云的天空漫反射的光）、日光（晴朗或局部多云的天空下直射的太阳光束）、反射光（通过自然或人工表面发射的光）。根据不同的光源种类，采用相应的措施对建筑物进行合理的自然采光就显得尤为重要，对应不同的建筑类型选择适宜的自然光采光形式（侧面采光、顶部采光、中庭采光）是建筑自然采光设计阶段的重要环节。办公室、家居室等小型民用、公用房间宜采用侧面采光形式。侧面采光不仅能使室内人员透过采光玻璃直接看到外部自然界和人，又不受高度限制。但是会使室内人员在局部位置产生眩晕感，对于产生眩光的可能性，可以采用局部隔挡加以控制调节。对人员流动较少的仓库、车间等建筑，可以采用眩光率较低（尤其在低太阳高度角时）的顶部采光即顶棚天窗进行采光。对于商场、办公楼等大型建筑应采用中庭采光，它不仅能满足人对外界的视觉欣赏要求且产生眩光的概率又极低，对高度又没有任何的限制且可以获得极佳的光线穿透深度。但是并不是所有建筑都能满足设计中庭的需要，并且如设置中庭则其在全晴天日光照射下顶层与底层有较大的温度差，这就使得空调设计可能需要进行负荷设计改良。由此使得中庭采光局限于部分建筑群体。虽然自然光具有很多优点，但它的应用却受到时间、地点、外部气候条件等的限制。往往在某时某地不能满足人员对建筑光环境的需要，而利用人工光即人工照明就可以大大弥补这一不足。建筑内不仅在自然光较弱的夜间需要利用人工照明，在某种特定环境下也需要 24h 的人工光供给。根据人工光的用途范围可以把其分为两大主要方面：工作照明（功能性照明）及装饰照明（艺术性照明），分别着眼于满足人们生理上的实际需要及心理上的观赏需要。在进行人工照明设计时，需要综合考虑光源、灯具、安装功率、照明质量及相应的供电线路和设备。由于光源的革新、装饰材料的发展，人工照明已不只是满足室内一般照明、工作照明的需要，而进一步向环境照明、艺术照明发展。它在商业、居住、大型公共建筑的室内环境中，已成为不可或缺的室内设计要素。

建筑光环境设计中要综合考虑自然光与人工光的搭配运用。在设计人工照明时又要考虑光源与灯具等的配合方式，同时亦要照顾建筑室内人员的情绪波动等。在进行光环境设计时，应充分考虑光环境给人带来的心理上的效果。明亮的环境使人感到开敞；一个均匀的高照度的白光会给人以透明的感觉；当一个高照度区域位于大空间之中，变化亮度的不均匀照明，包括极端的闪烁、移动或闪光照明，以及用刺激色所形成的周边环境，都给人以兴奋感，并使人乐于交谈；无刺激性因素的环境会使人感到单调；而处于黑暗的环境时，人就会产生不安全感和恐怖感。

8.3.2 室内光环境对室内空间设计的作用

1）室内光环境的正确运用可以强化室内空间的界面关系，改变界面对室内环境空间的限定程度和范围。

2) 室内光环境可以强化室内整体环境氛围，有效体现室内环境的整体格调、意境。针对不同的空间场合，体现不同的空间情趣与风格。

3) 室内光环境可以强化室内空间的序列层次，增强空间环境的方向性，突出室内环境的视觉中心。

4) 室内光环境可以丰富空间内容。改善空间的比例关系，限定空间领域。

5) 室内灯光造型本身具有一定的空间艺术性。

8.3.3 创造符合室内装饰要求的光环境的有效途径

1) 注重自然光环境的引入与应用，诺曼·福斯特说过："自然光总是在不停地变，它可以使建筑富有特征，在空间和光影的相互作用下，我们可以创造戏剧性。"尽管人工照明占据了越来越重要的地位，自然光仍然是光环境设计中最具表现力的因素之一。其作为空间构图因素烘托了环境氛围，表现空间意境。人们渴求阳光、自然的心理正逐渐增强。利用好自然光是室内室外空间环境有机相融的有效手段。

2) 选择符合整体空间环境效果的灯具和光源，灯具和光源的选择要从形成空间环境整体构成要素出发，既具有个性特征又要成为室内装饰的构成元素。

3) 采用新设备设施，智能化控制。在照明技术快速发展的当今社会，智能化是发展的趋势。采用新的方式方法有助于方便快捷地达到所需的光环境效果，并有利于节能和管理控制。

8.3.4 照明设计过程

照明设计过程可以分为5个阶段，最后一个阶段实际上是设计阶段的一个延伸，涵盖了施工前后的活动。

1) 规划和概念形成（PC）。
2) 示意性设计或初步设计（SD）。
3) 深入设计（DD）。
4) 施工文件（CD）。
5) 建设期内的服务内容——招标谈判（BN），施工管理（CA），后期评审。

这些阶段之间总会出现重叠。在一些简单的工程中，几个阶段可能结合在一起。《照明手册》对于设计中需要考虑的问题有完整的描述。

将照明作为一个设计元素集成到项目的整体设计中是非常重要的。每个阶段的照明设计均不同程度地受到其他专业设计的影响。事实上，某些照明方案是通过与项目的其他设计团队的直接合作演化而来的。与项目中的各位设计专家保持沟通对合作成功和整体设计来说至关重要。

事实上，在每个项目中，照明设计工程必须严格按照既定时间表执行。工作开始之前，设计专家必须安排好每个阶段的时间，留出充足的时间以满足项目的特定需求。否则可能会出现超出时限、协调不力、预算超支等情况。

8.3.5 设计考虑因素

1. 设计表现

照明设计是一种营造视觉效果的规划，它的目的是满足视觉需求或是与照明设计相关联的系统需求。明确特定空间内的视觉表现类型是良好设计的基础。设计师应从用户或项目决策者那里获取所需信息。同时，调查用户现有设施通常也非常有效。任务一经明确，符合用户需求和预期的视觉表现标准就可以确定了。

2. 亮度选择

针对不同的应用类型，如办公室、教育设施、组织机构、工业园区以及居民区，相应的亮度比率都能在美国照明工程学会（IES）《照明手册》中找到。一般来说，要求更好的能见度和视觉灵敏度的工作和紧靠的背景间需要高亮度对比。而事实上低亮度却更有利于视觉上的舒适。良好的照明设计是在相互冲突的要求间找到平衡，达成一个适当的解决方案。

3. 视觉舒适

要达到视觉舒适则不能在视野范围内受到长时间过亮的光照刺激。一种衡量视觉舒适性的指标是在日光或内部照明系统的照明环境下的视觉舒适性概率（VCP）。当 $VCP \geqslant 70$ 时，可以看做达到了视觉舒适。反射眩光会导致能见度的降低。设计低反射眩光照明系统的时候可以使用等效球面照明（ESI）方法，设计时需要用到特定的电脑软件。一般而言，通过使用合适的墙面材料以及控制光通量方向的方法可以使反射眩光最小化。

4. 建筑照明需求

很多情况下，照明提升了建筑的形式及细节。项目的前期设计阶段，照明专家就应尝试确定何种建筑属性需要强化照明。当整体照明设计改变时，建筑照明需求也应同时考虑，演化出更加统一的解决方案。间接的天花板照明，凹壁照明以强调垂直表面，隐蔽处的柱顶辅助照明都是普遍的例子。

在很多情况下，一个灯具可以成为建筑照明装饰品。反映特定主题或装饰性的吊灯和烛台往往成为内部空间建筑照明的焦点。

5. 灯光增强空间印象

研究和实践都已表明照明在人们形成印象的过程中起明显的作用。尽管照明的首要任务是对视觉需要的支持，它加深或减弱用户体验的作用也不能忽视。

以下几个例子说明了照明的布局、强度和颜色是如何增强用户对于空间的印象的。

1) 提供均匀的墙体照明，营造空间的宽敞感。

2) 提供不均匀照明，使用相对较低的光照强度，强调光线的边缘设置，营造放松的环境。

3) 提供高亮、均匀的照明，营造视觉清晰的印象。

为了增强预想的印象，对这些因素的特意关注将帮助照明设计师决定如何以及在何处布置照明。这种影响主观印象的照明设计方案会增强用户对空间的体验。

6. 色彩

为了更好地理解色彩、色度、色彩渲染以及色彩的使用，照明设计师可参照美国照明工程学会（IES）《照明手册》的第五章。人们常常误用色度、渲染等术语。简单地说，色度指的是光源的颜色形式，比如色温；色彩渲染指的是光源使表面和对象表现出如人们预期那样的色温的能力。这两个因素对于确定照明设计中的光源有重要意义。

7. 系统整合

照明只是建筑设计众多系统中的一个。对于一个成功的建筑环境来说，结构、供热通风与空气调节、消防、给水排水以及配电同样很重要。设计师必须仔细考虑照明对其他系统可能产生的影响，反之亦然。天花板吊顶内灯具和其他系统经常会有冲突。消防喷淋头间距可能会从根本上改变照明设施的预定安装计划。照明方案的巨大能量消耗可能迫使设计师选择更大的空调机组，这样会显著增加初投资。在一个涉及多专业的项目中，这些只是经常出现的问题中的几个。

尽管建筑系统内的一些冲突不可避免，整个设计团队成员之间的密切合作将会带来更好的效果。定期的设计会议及协作会议能够确保重要信息的及时共享。深入地考虑和理解其他团队的需求是良好协作的关键。

8. 能源

照明系统的能源消耗始终是设计的根本考量因素。鉴于大多数电能都是由化石燃料燃烧生成，照明系统需要供给的燃料越多，产生的污染物就越多。随着照明能耗逐步升高，建筑的业主和住户需要支付更多的费用以维持系统运行。更高的功率需求往往也会影响空调的初期成本和长期运行费用。

与能源相关的国家、地区和地方法律在过去十年里发生了引人注目的增长，并将在可以预见的未来继续保持增长。照明设计师必须熟知影响建筑设计的相关法规和条例。最好在早期就建立能耗预算方案，以免日后为了适应相应的限制而进行重新设计。

9. 维护和运营

照明系统的长期维护和运营是设计过程中不可忽视的部分。照明设计专家必须评估照明系统在项目周期内的可持续性，并且和用户进行沟通，获悉使照明系统保持高效运行的方法。在设计和维护之间进行取舍以平衡用户对于项目短期及长期的期望是很必要的。设计师应该在项目前期就邀请用户参与并在可接受的维护及运行方式上达成一致。

10. 照明系统的选择

选择合适的照明系统来完整实现设计理念也许是最值得考虑的事。照明系统及其相应的灯具类型的选择需针对具体项目的视觉需求。哪种或者哪些系统能最好地实现项目每个空间所要求的视觉表现？哪种系统能够适当地加强建筑的主要特色？哪个系统提供的光线分布和强度可以强化每个房间的预期印象？哪个系统提供合适的空间建模？

虽然某种照明系统可能成为大多数地区的主流选择，但是对于项目的特殊需求及特定条件的满足也许需要一系列灯具的组合。投影简报的墙面泛光照明、强调艺术品及标志的强调照明、表演礼堂内的舞台照明、室内植物的高强聚光照明等都是经常出现的且无法通过基本整体照明系统来满足的情况。

建筑师、室内设计师以及最终用户（可能的话）应共同选出项目中建筑整体照明和装饰性灯具的方案。尽管这些系统可能会增加房间内的功能性照明，它们的主要作用仍是创造及强化空间环境。

习 题

1. 利用光学原理控制照明的途径有哪些?
2. 选择灯具时需要考虑哪些因素?
3. 光环境设计中为什么要综合考虑自然光与人工光的搭配运用?
4. 简述照明设计过程。
5. 室内光环境设计需要考虑哪些因素?
6. 使照明系统更节能有哪些途径?

Chapter 8
Building Lighting

Abstract: This chapter introduces the basic knowledge of optical physics, the main parameters of lighting equipment, the composition of lighting systems, as well as the design method of building light environments.

Key points: brightness, luminous flux, luminous intensity, lighting control method, the basic factors of luminaires, the process of lighting design, architectural lighting requirements, lighting system selection.

Lighting is the utilization of either natural or artificially generated light to provide a desired visual environment for work and living. This chapter covers the properties of light, human vision, and the fundamentals of lighting applicable to the building's environment.

8.1 Light and Lighting

8.1.1 Light and Vision

The human eyes are so constructed that when light enters the cornea and lens, light energy is focused on the retina and transferred to the brain by optic nerve cells. The brain then translates the information back to the eyes, forming the optical image. The impressions from both eyes integrate the information into three-dimensional images.

Human beings see in two ways: by differences in color and by contrasts in luminance (brightness). We can see red projects on a blue background, but not easily on a background of the same red color. There must be a color difference for our eyes to see. Similarly, we can read black print on white paper, but not easily on dark gray paper and not at all on black paper. Thus, there must be a luminance contrast in order for our eyes to see.

1. Luminance and Luminance Contrast

Simple stated, luminance is the amount of light sensed by our eyes from an object. Light may be generated from an object, such as the sun or a light source, and maybe reflected from an object, such as the tabletop or the paper in a book, or may be transmitted from an object, such as a stained-glass window or a lamp shade. Luminance contract can be defined in a number of ways. For a reading task, we generally use the formula

$$C = |L_t - L_b|/L_b \qquad (8\text{-}1)$$

Where C—contrast;

L_t—luminance of the task, candela per unit area;

L_b—luminance of the background, candela per unit area.

The absolute value $|L_t - L_b|$ is used when L_t is darker than L_b, and C is always less than unity.

2. Visual Comfort

While high luminance contrast improves visual acuity, too high a contrast may cause eyestrain after prolonged viewing. It is often more desirable to print black text on slightly colored paper, such as tan, ivory, or light blue. Obviously, visual acuity is diminished when black text is printed on dark-colored paper, such as saturated red or blue, or other colors of low value.

3. Glare

When the luminance of a light source or an object is so high (so bright) that it begins to interfere with vision, it is called glare. When glare is so strong that it causes physiological discomfort, it is called discomfort glare. When glare actually affects the ability to see, it is called disability glare. Glare that originates from a light source is called direct glare, and glare reflected from a surface is called reflected or indirect glare. Direct glare can be avoided by relocating the light source away from the line of sight. If practical, indirect glare can be minimized by replacing the reflecting surface with non-glare (matte) or low-reflectance (dark) surfaces.

8.1.2 Physics of Light

1. Photometric Units

The basic photometric quantities are given in Table 8-1.

Table 8-1 Basic photometric quantities

Quantity	Symbol	Units and Abbreviations
Energy (luminous energy)	Q	Lumen-hours (lm-h)
Power (luminous flux)	F	Lumen (lm)
Intensity (candlepower)	I	Candela (cd)
Illumination (illuminance)	E	Lux (lx)
Brightness (Luminance)	L	Candela/m^2 (cd/m^2)

2. Energy of Light

Light energy can be converted from other forms of energy, such as heat, electrical energy, and chemical energy, although it is normally converted from electrical energy because that conversion process is most efficient. Light energy is not normally calculated in lighting design, since light energy quickly degrades to hear energy and thus can not be stored.

3. Power and Intensity of Light

Power is the rate of consuming energy. Inlighting, power is the luminous flux emitted by a light source in a unit of time. The unit of lighting power is the lumen (lm). If the conversion of electrical energy to light energy involves no loss, then one electrical watt converts to 683lm of a single wavelength of green light. If the conversion is into white light, the conversion is only about 200 lm per watt.

A lumen is defined as the lighting power emitted within a unit solid angle (one steradian) by a point source having a uniform luminous intensity of 1 candela (cd). A candela is a unit of intensity of light. In layman's term, 1cd is as the light intensity produced by a candle. This is a useful analogy, but it is not a scientific definition, since a candle can be of any size and material. By definition, 1cd is 1lm per steradian. A sphere consists of 4pai (12.57) steradian. Thus, a candle (1 candlepower) is equivalent to 12.57lm.

4. Illumination

Illumination is luminous power per unit area. The quantity is analogous to Btu/h/area (1 Btu = 1055.06J) in thermodynamics and watts/area in electrical power. Although illumination is replaced by illuminance in engineering terminology, illumination is still used widely in practice. In SI unites, illuminance is in lux (lx). By definition, illuminance is expressed as

$$E = \frac{\text{luminous flux}}{\text{area}} = \frac{F}{A} \tag{8-2}$$

Where E—illuminance (lux);

F—light flux (power, lumen);

A—area (square meters).

The relationship between lighting power and illuminance is best illustrated in Fig. 8-1a, which depicts the light flux radiated from a point source; and in Fig. 8-1b, which illustrates the relationship between intensity (candela), power (lumen), and illuminance (lux).

Fig. 8-1a shows one candela-source at the center of a clear sphere. Fig. 8-1b shows that the illuminance at any point on the sphere is lx (one lumen per square meter) when the radius is 1 m. The solid angle subtended by area $ABCD$ is one steradian. The flux density is therefore one lumen per steradian, which corresponds to a luminous intensity of one candela, as originally assumed. The sphere has a total area of 12.57 sq m and there is a luminous flux of 1lm falling on each square meter. Thus, the source provides a total of 12.57lm.

Illumination levels commonly encountered in natural and in buildings are given in Table 8-2.

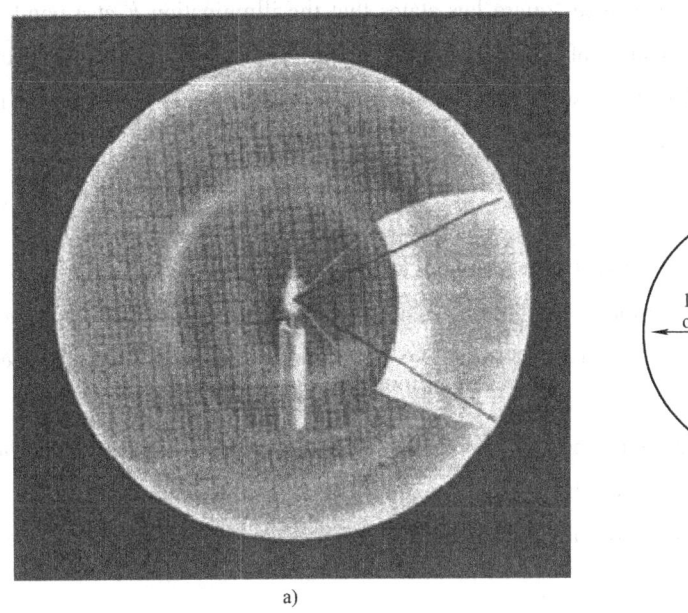 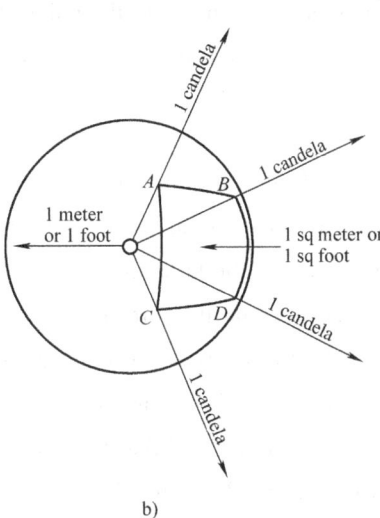

Fig. 8-1 The relationship between illuminance and power
a) One candela-source at the center of a clear sphere b) Light source and illuminance

Table 8-2 Illumination encountered in nature and in buildings

Position		Nominal Level/fc
Starlight		0.0002
Moonlight		0.02
Streetlight		1.5 ~ 10.0
Daylight	In shade (outdoors)	100 ~ 1000
	In direct sunlight	5000 ~ 10000
Transient space (corridor, etc.)		5 ~ 10
Office lighting		50 ~ 70
Classrooms (kindergarten to college)		20 ~ 70
Drafting rooms		70 ~ 150
Sport facilities (schools to professional facilities)		30 ~ 300

Note: 1 fc = 10.764lx.

5. Luminous Intensity

The light power in a given direction is defined as the luminous flux per unit solid angle, or the luminous flux on a surface normal to that direction, divided by the solid angle in steradian ($I = d\Phi/d\omega$). This definition applies strictly to a point source. In practice, however, light emitted from a larger light source, such as an incandescent lighting fixture whose dimensions are negligible in comparison with the distance from which the illuminance is measured, may also apply.

(1) Inverse-square Law The inverse-square law states that the illumination E at a point on a surface varies directly with the intensity I of the source and inversely with the square of the distance d between the source and the point. If the surface at the point is normal to the direction of the incident light, the law may be expressed as

$$E = \frac{I}{d^2} \tag{8-3}$$

Where E is in lux when d is in meters; I is in candelas when d is in meters.

This equation can be directly applied in lighting design calculations if the distance from the light source to the task surface is at least five times the maximum dimension of the source as viewed from the point on the surface.

(2) Cosine Law The Lambert cosine law states that the illuminance on any surface varies with the cosine of the angle of incidence. The angle of incidence (θ) is the angle between the normal to the surface and the direction of the incident light. The inverse-square law and the cosine law can be combined into the form

$$E = \frac{I}{d^2}\cos\theta \tag{8-4}$$

The inverse-square law shows how the same quantity of light flux is distributed over a greater area as the distance from the source to the surface is increased. The Lamert cosine law shows that the light flux striking a surface at angles other than the normal to the surface is distributed over a greater area.

6. Luminance and Brightness

Luminance is the luminous flux reflected from or transmitted through a surface. It is equal to the illuminance on the surface multiplied by the reflectance or transmittance factors of the surface. Luminance is perceived by our eyes as a sensation of brightness that is affected in part by the measurable luminance and in part by the state of adaptation of the eye. For example, if the eyes have become adapted to an environment with very low illuminance, as in a movie theater, a very dim light will appear to be bright. On the other hand, in daylight, a bright automobile headlight will appear dim. Thus brightness is not synonymous with luminance, although the two terms have often been used interchangeably in common practice. An object or a surface will appear bright if it is in a bright environment and more bright if it is in a dim environment. To minimize the sensation of brightness, the designer should avoid locating the light source within the normal line of sight and provide less contrast surrounding the source.

Luminance is a directional quantity. Depending on the viewing angle and characteristics of the surface, luminance is expressed as lumens/steradian or candelas/area. Luminance is expressed in the following units:

$$1 \text{ luminan} = 1 \text{cd/m}^2 \tag{8-5}$$

Table 8-3 provides typical approximate luminance values for natural and artificial light source.

Table 8-3 Approximate luminance values for various light sources

Light Source	Typical Luminance/ (cd/m^2)
Sun (as observed from earth)	1540000000
Moon (as observed from earth)	8000
Snow in sunlight	31000
Overcast sky	2000
Candle flame	10000
Filament lamp (60W inside frosted)	30000
40W fluorescent (cool white) lamp	17000

8.1.3 Light Controls

The lighting in a space may be too bright or may come from the wrong direction, causing visual discomfort or inefficient utilization. Or the light may be the wrong color, causing poor color discrimination. For all of these reasons, light must be controlled.

Light travels in clean air without bending or notable loss until it is intercepted by another medium, which will either reflect, absorb, transmit, refract, diffuse, or polarize the light. These characteristics of varying materials are utilized as a method of controlling light to achieve better lighting.

(1) Reflection Light is reflected from the surface of a material. If the surface is shiny, or specular, such as the surface of a mirror, then reflected light will follow the law of reflection: the angle of reflection is equal to the angle of incidence. Even a transparent material reflects some light from its surface.

(2) Diffusion When the surface is matte—that is, not shiny—then the reflected light will be diffused. The diffused light may be directional or totally non-directional, as a "cosine distribution".

(3) Transmission When the material is transparent (clear glass), spread (etched glass), or totally diffused (white glass), light will pass through it in a controlled mode.

(4) Absorption Light is absorbed when it is directed to an opaque material or passes through a transparent or translucent material. There will be a loss of light in either case. The amount of light absorbed is the balance of the incident light that is reflected or transmitted.

(5) Refraction The direction of light changes at the interface between two different materials, such as air and glass. This property is called refraction. Refraction is the most effective means of controlling light and is commonly used by lighting designers. Snell's law of refraction is

$$n_1 \sin i = n_2 \sin r \tag{8-6}$$

Where n_1—index of refraction of the first medium;

i—angle the incident light ray forms with the normal to the surface;

n_2—index of refraction of the second medium;

r—angle the refracted light ray forms with the normal to the surface.

(6) Polarization Light travels at high speed with waves vibrating in all planes at right angels to the direction of travel. Polarization is the phenomenon wherein the waves vibrate only in one plane. A polarizing material (filter) is called a polarizer. When light passes through two polarizers in tandem, but with their optical axes oriented at 90 degree, the light will be totally polarized. One of the more popular uses of polarizers is in polarized sunglasses, which are recognized as the most effective means of reducing glare from the sun. If we position two polarized sun-glasses at right angles to each other, we find that the sunlight is nearly 100 percent filtered. Polarization is used in lighting controls in the form of multilayered polarizing lenses (diffusers).

Any combination of the six methods of light control can be incorporated into lighting design.

8.2　Lighting Equipment and Systems

Light may originate in many ways, from solar energy (daylight), from combustion and chemical reactions, and from the conversion of electrical energy. Of all light sources, daylight is the most plentiful. It is also free of charge. However, daylight is not available at night and fluctuates widely during the day, sometimes being too bright for visual comfort or too hot to stay under for very long. Still, when properly controlled, e. g., with sunglasses and air conditioning, it is the most economical of all sources of light.

In building, electrical lighting has become the sole source of light at night and a supplemental source during the day. Frequently, electrical lighting must be used even if there is plenty of daylight—for example, during a visual presentation in a classroom or conference room, and during many sporting events, when daylight from low angles may cause glare that blinds the players or the spectators. Combustion type light sources, such as gaslights, are limited to decorative use only.

The fundamental component of lighting equipment is the light source, commonly called a lamp. The assembly that holds a lamp or lamps together to provide lighting is the luminaire, commonly called a lighting fixture. Although discouraged in academic circles, the term lighting fixture is more accepted than luminaire by the general public and among professionals in the design and construction industries. Thus, the two terms are used interchangeably in this chapter, as are light sources and lamps.

Lighting fixtures must be designed for a particular type of lamp and are usually not suitable forother types. One reason for this is the difference in configuration of the lamp holder (socket). Another reason is the amount of heat generated, which affects the material of the fixture, the ventilation, and the physical clearance between the lamp and the surrounding surfaces. Thus, lighting fixtures and lamps must be compatible and within the power (wattage) limit of the fixture.

Lighting fixtures are important elements of interior design, since they are often prominently displayed in the space. In addition to lighting performance, other features such as size, texture, shape, and color must be considered when selecting a fixture. To create a successful lighting design, the architect, interior designer, and lighting engineer must be knowledgeable about both light sources and the performance of various fixtures. This section presents the fundamentals of lamps, fixtures and lighting systems.

Lighting design professionals have a responsibility to minimize energy consumption by using efficient light sources and equipment, while creating an environment that is aesthetically pleasing and conductive to higher productivity. For example, lighting accounts for about 25 percent of all electrical energy consumed in the United States. For each kW · h of electrical energy consumed, a corresponding amount of pollutant is being released into the atmosphere.

8.2.1 Electrical Light Sources

Electrical light sources are called lamps. Although thousands of lamps are made for diverse applications, they can be grouped into four major classes, based on their operating principles.

Incandescent lamps convert electrical energy into heat at a temperature that causes the filament of the lamp to become incandescent (red or white hot). The process closely resembles the heating of a blackbody.

Fluorescent lamps contain mercury vapor. When proper voltage is applied, an electrical arc is produced between the opposing electrodes, generating some visible, but mostly invisible, ultraviolet radiation. The ultraviolet radiation excites the phosphor coating on the inside of the bulb, which then emits visible light.

High-intensity discharge (HID) lamps produce high-intensity light within an inner arc tube contained in an outer bulb. The metallic gas within the arc tube may be mercury, sodium, or a combination of other metallic vapors. The outer bulb may be clear or coated with phosphor. HID lamps are classified as mercury vapor, metal halide, and high-pressure sodium.

Miscellaneous lamps include a wide variety of lamps operating on different principles. Although they have limited application in buildings, future breakthroughs in technology and production may provide a new dimension to the world of architecture and environmental design. Some promising new types are the following:

1) Short-arc lamps, or compact-arc lamps, such as the xenon family of lamps, produce light in small arc tubes and are the closest thing to a true point source of high luminance. They are usedprimarily as search lights, in projectors, and in optical instruments.

2) Low-pressure sodium lamps (LPSs) are monochromatic lamps in the yellow region of the spectrum (589 to 589.6nm). The efficacy of an LPS lamp is as high as 180 lumens per watt, but because of its color, this lamp has limited applications. Typical applications are along highways and in storage yards.

3) Electroluminescent lamps emit light by the direct excitation of phosphor from an alternating

current. Therefore, they can be made in any shape, size, and form. Electroluminescent lamps can produce different colors by mixing phosphors. Although these lamps areextremely efficient at about 200 lm per watt, their use is limited to signs and decorative applications.

4) Electrodeless lamps are gaseous lamps excited by means of electromagnetic or microwave energy without the use of electrodes. These lamps have a promising future in building lighting applications through the use of specially designed fixtures or the use of "light pipes".

8.2.2 Factors to Consider in Selecting Light Sources and Equipment

There are many factors to consider in selecting lamps of all varieties.

1. Light Output

Light output, expressed in lumens, is defined as follows:

1) Initial lumens: rated light output when the lamp is new, typically measured after 100 hours of operation.

2) Average lumens: average of the initial lumens output and the lumens output at the end of the rated life of lamp.

3) Mean lumens: lumens output at 40 percent of the rated life of the lamp.

4) Beam lumens: initial lumens output within the central beam of a floodlight, usually defined to exclude light intensity less than 10 percent of the maximum intensity of the light.

2. Intensity

Light intensity is expressed in candelas (cd) at various angles from the lamp or fixture. The data are usually provided by manufacturers in the form of candlepower distribution curves.

3. Luminous Efficacy

Luminous efficacy, or simply efficacy is defined as the light output per unit of electrical power (watts) input, or lumens/watt (lm/W). Theoretically, 1 watt (W) of electrical power can be converted to 683 lm of monochromic green light, or about 200 lm of white light of equal energy level among all visual spectrum wave-lengths. With this as reference, the $10 \sim 25$ lm/W efficacy of incandescent lamps is far short of ideal. The efficacy of a lamp should include the power consumed by its accessories, that is lamp efficacy, in lumens/watt, for lamps only; or net lamp efficacy, of the lamps and accessories (e.g., ballast), for electrical discharge (fluorescent and HID) lamps.

4. Luminaire Efficiency

Luminaire efficiency is the ration of the total light output of the lumps in lumens versus the total light input of all lamps in the luminaire. It is expressed in percentages. Luminaire efficiency is a good measure for comparing luminaires of similar candlepower distribution characteristics, but it is not necessary a measure of how well the light is being utilized. For example, if one must illuminate a painting on a wall, a bare bulb fixture, which is 100 percent efficient, suspended in front of the painting will not be as good as a directional luminarie that is only 60 percent efficient.

5. Rated Lamp Life

The rated life of a lamp is defined as the time elapsed when 50 percent of a group of lamps remain burning. Rated life closely follows the mortality curve of most statistics for a large number of subjects. Figure 8-2 shows the mortality curve of incandescent lamps.

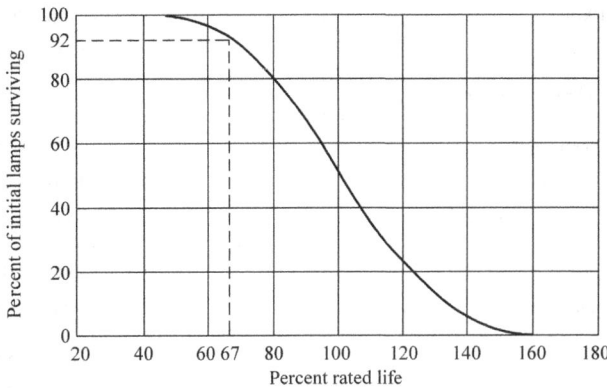

Fig. 8-2 Range of typical mortality or life expectancy curves for incandescent lamps

Example: If the rated life of an incandescent lamp is 750 hours, what would be the expected percentage of survival for a large number of lamps installed in a building after 500 hours of use?

Solution: The hours of use of the lamp are 2/3, or 67% of the rated life. As shown in Fig. 8-2, 92% of the lamps would probably survive.

6. Lumen Depreciation

Light output depreciates with time. The loss of light, known as lumen depreciation, may be as high as 20 to 30 percent of a lamp's initial light output. This characteristic must be taken into consideration in illumination design. Typical lumen depreciation characteristics for various lamps are listed in Table 8-4.

Table 8-4 Depreciation characteristics of lamps, percent of the initial light output

Type of Lamp		Approximate Light Output (%)	
		50% of Life	100% of Life
Incandescent	General-service type	90	82
	Tungsten halogen	97	92
Fluorescent	Light loading (low brightness)	92	90
	Mediumloading (standard)	85	82
	High loading (high output)	75	65
High-intensity discharge	Mercury (H)	77	60
	Metal halide (MH)	70	65
	High-pressure sodium (HPS)	90	70

7. Color Temperature

Color temperature is the color the lamp appears, expressed in kelvin (K). Table 8-5 lists the color temperature characteristics of some typical lamps.

Table8-5 Color temperature of typical light sources

Light Source		Color Temperature Range/K
Incandescent	60W	2500~2700
	100W	2700~2900
	500W	2900~3100
	Halogen, tungsten	3000~3200
Fluorescent	Warm white	2900~3000
	Cool white	4000~4500
	Daylight	6000~6500
Mercury	Clear	5500~5800
	Improved	4400~4500
Metal halide	Clear	3700~3800
	Improved	3200~4000
High-pressure sodium	Normal	2000~2100
	Color improved	3000~4000
Low-pressure sodium		1700~1800
Photoflood lamps		3200
Photoflash lamps		5500

8. Color-Rendering Index

The concept of the color-rendering index (CRI) is useful for measuring how well a lamp renders color, compared with a reference light source of the same color temperature range. An incandescent lamp with color temperature at 3000K has been selected by the CIE as the reference source ($CRI = 100$) for comparison with all other lamps having color temperature below 5000K. This selection of $CRI = 100$ does not mean that this particular incandescent lamp can render the true color of every object or material. Such a lamp is selected only because it has a smooth profile of spectral power distribution (SPD) without extremely narrow energy bands.

9. Color Preference Index

The color preference index (CPI) is useful in expressing the color quality of a light source on a preferential basis, such as red meat, green vegetables, blue sky, and pink complexions.

10. Flicker and Stroboscopic Effect

Theoretically, the cyclic flow of a 60Hz current through a lamp can have light fluctuations 120 times per second. This is called flicker. Because of the light retention characteristic of incandescent filaments and the phosphor coating of discharge lamps, flicker is not normally perceivable except in non-coated HID lamps. When a rapidly moving object is observed under a clear HID lamp, the object may appear to be at a standstill or moving at lower harmonic frequencies. This is called the stroboscopic effect. It can be eliminated or minimized by the use of lead-lag ballasts for multiple lamps and the wiring of fixtures on alternate three-phase circuits.

When the frequency of the electrical power system is lower than 60Hz, flicker and the stroboscopic effect will be exaggerated. Conversely, at higher frequencies, flicker will not be perceived.

11. Brightness

Physically, small light sources of high intensity, such as incandescent lamps, are excellent for light control, but they can be too bright for visual comfort. The location and aiming of the fixtures must therefore be carefully selected. Uncomfortable glare can be minimized by methods discussed in last section.

12. Intensity Control

Light intensity can be controlled by multilevel switching or by dimming. Incandescent lamps can be dimmed easily by the use of autotransformers or solid-state dimmers. Florescent and HID lamps can be dimmed by special ballasts and circuitry, but at a considerably higher cost.

13. Accessories

Among the many accessories that should be considered before selecting light sources are ballasts, starters, and dimmers.

8.2.3 General Comparison of Light Sources

Following is a summary of the factors that enter into these decisions:

(1) Efficacy   Incandescent lamps, including the tungsten and halogen types, are the lease energy-efficient light sources compared with fluorescent or HID lamps, which are three to five times as efficient.

(2) Spectrum power distribution   No light source can produce equal power across the entire visible spectrum. Even daylight at 7500K is richer in blue and poorer in red. Incandescent lamps are rich in the orange and red portion of the spectrum while fluorescent lamps are rich in blue and green. Low-pressure sodium lamps generate only a very narrow band of yellow spectrum light and lack all other colors.

(3) Color rendering   This is a very important aspect of lighting design. Many new light sources have excellent color rendering qualities as well as high luminous efficacy. The HPS lamp used in the illustration has a *CRI* of 80. The color rendition compares favorably with that of an incandescent lamp with a *CRI* of 100. Similar results can be achieved using metal halide lamps.

(4) Color temperature   The apparent color of white light sources, whether they are warm (yellowish reddish) or cool (bluish, greenish), can be expressed by the black body temperature along the Planckian locus in the CIE chromaticity diagram.

(5) Rated life   The lives of different light sources vary widely. In general, fluorescent and HID lamps last 10 to 20 times as long as incandescent lamps. The means that during the average life of a fluorescent or HID lamp, an incandescent lamp may have to be replaced 20 times.

(6) Cost of operation   The energy savings and cost of maintenance are considerably lower for

fluorescent and HID lamps than for incandescent lamps. The use of incandescent light sources should be limited to special-task illumination rather than general space illumination in most interior spaces, including highly decorative commercial spaces.

8.2.4 Luminaires

A luminaire, commonly called a lighting fixture, is a complete lighting unit that contains one or more lamps, structural supports, accessories, auxiliaries, wiring, and controls. Luminaires can be classified according to a number of constructional, physical, and photometric criteria, the most important of which are the following:

(1) Light source Whether the lamps within the lumiaire are incandescent, halogen, fluorescent, metal halide, high-pressure sodium, low-pressure sodium, etc.

(2) Wattage Whether the luminaire is designed for a single or multiple number of lamps, and what is the maximum size of the luminaire (s), etc.

(3) Power supply Whether the luminaire is wired for 110V, 220V, 380V and whether it is for AC or DC, etc.

(4) Application Whether the luminaire is for outdoor, indoor, underwater, underground, aviation, theater, roadway sign, etc.

(5) Construction Whether the luminaire is water-proof, weather-tight, dust-tight, explosion-proof, bug-tight, corrosion-resistant, etc.

(6) Method of mounting Whether the luminaire is to be ceiling surface, laid in, suspension, bracket, wall, floor, pole-mounted, etc.

(7) The control medium Prismatic lens, diffusing panel, or louver, and the specific cutoff angles, bafflers, reflecting characteristics, etc.

(8) Ballast Type and number of ballasts, and the ballast factor (BF), ballast efficiency factor (BEF), etc.

(9) Special features Whether there is EMI shielding, a built-in emergency lamp, a built-in battery, etc.

(10) Light distribution Interior luminaires are classified by the IES into six categories and by the CIE into five categories. The categories are based on the percentages and characteristics of the light flux distribution above and below the horizontal plane. The six categories are:

1) Direct, where 90 percent to 100 percent of the flux is directed downward.

2) Semi-direct, where between 60 percent to 90 percent of the flux is directed downward and the balance upward.

3) General diffuse, where between 40 percent and 60 percent of the flux is directed either upward or downward and the distribution is more or less uniform in all directions.

4) Direct-indirect, where between 40 percent and 60 percent of the flux is directed either upward or downward and there is very little flux in the horizontal direction. The CIE considers the di-

rect-indirect category as a part of the general diffuse type of luminaire distribution. From a designer's point of view, these two types should be classified separately, as they produce distinct spatial relations, in terms of such properties as wall luminance, glare, and coefficient of utilization.

5) Semi-indirect, where 60 percent to 90 percent of the flux is upward.

6) Indirect, where 90 percent to 100 percent of the flux is upward.

8.2.5　General Comparison of Lighting Systems

For each lighting system, thousands of luminaires are commercially available, and for each luminaire, there are many variations of lamp type, size, and control medium, such as lens, louvers, baffles, etc. Therefore, it would be meaningless to illustrate just a few of these combinations. However, an overview of lighting systems can be given as follows.

1) A direct system is a lighting system that is based on the use of direct-distribution luminaires. It is the most effective system for horizontal illumination. However, there is the potential for both direct and reflected glare. There are many ways to overcome the glare—for example, by using large low-brightness ceilings or sharp angle cutoffs.

2) A semi-direct system has small upward components. These will soften the high contrast between the ceiling and the luminaires and will improve the spatial brightness relations.

3) A general diffuse system uses luminaires with light flux more or less uniformly distributed in all directions. This system is likely to achieve more of a modeling effect, with soft shadows, but may have more direct glare. The fixtures are pendant-mounted. If they are too close to the ceiling, the system will behave like a semi-direct system.

4) A direct-indirect system is similar to a general diffuse system, except that the light flux within 10 to 30 degrees below the horizontal plane is reduced or shielded. This feature will greatly reduce direct glare, particularly on video display screens.

5) In an indirect system, as more light flux is directed above the horizontal plane, direct glare is reduced. In turn, however, the ceiling brightness may become too great for comfort. These systems should not be installed unless there is an adequate ceiling height and the fixtures are suspended within the recommendations of the fixture manufacturers. An indirect system is ideal for a video display space. If the overall illuminance level is not adequate for tasks such as close reading, the system may have to be supplemented with localized downlights.

With any of the preceding systems, the color and reflectance of wall surfaces is of great importance. The effects of color and reflectance of surfaces are quite different for different lighting systems.

8.3　Building Lighting Design

Human have physical instinct of needs and psychological dependence with the light. In terms of very rich material, products emerging, people are qualified to pursue a better quality of light, not only lighting, but also hope for precise light control on different occasions. At the same time, there is an increasingly high demand for decorative and artistic sense.

8.3.1　Natural Light and Artificial Light

Now, there are 3 kinds of the main natural light sources in the artificial environment, day light coming from diffuse reflectance through cloudy or partially cloudy sky, sunlight coming from direct reflectance through fine or partially cloudy sky, and reflected light that emitted by natural or artificial surface. It is very important to take corresponding measures to get reasonable natural light in buildings according to different light sources, so it's quite crucial in the course of building natural light design to take proper form of natural light lighting (side lighting, top lighting and atrium lighting). We should adopt the form of side lighting in the office, sitting room and other small civilian, public rooms. Side lighting not only can enable interior staff to see the external nature and people directly through lighting glass, but also isn't subject to height restrictions. But it will make interior staff feel a sense of vertigo in some certain positions, and to deal with the possibility of glare production, we can use partial separated block to control. As to warehouses, workshops and other buildings with less mobility, top lighting with low (especially when the solar elevation angle is low) glare rate, that is roof skylight, can be used. As to shopping center, office building and other large-scale buildings, atrium lighting should be adopted because it not only can meet people's requirements of visual appreciation of the outside world with low probability of glare, but also isn't subject to height restrictions with the access to get perfect light penetration depth. But not all of the architectures can meet the need of atrium design, and there will be larger temperature difference between the top and bottom under sunlight in sunny day if atrium is set, which will demand improvement design of load in the design of air-conditioner. So atrium lighting is confined to some building groups. Though natural light has many advantages, its application is limited by time, location, exterior climate condition and so on. So it can't meet one's need of building luminous environment sometime somewhere, but artificial light, that is artificial lighting, can substantially remedy the disadvantage. Not only does the building need artificial light in weaker natural light at night, but also it needs 24 hours' supply of artificial light in a particular environment. Artificial light can be separated into two parts according to its use: working lighting (functional lighting) and decoration lighting (artistic lighting), respectively focusing on meeting people's actual needs in physiology and their viewing needs in psychology. During the design of artificial lighting, light sources, lamps, installed power, lighting quality and the corresponding power supply line and equipment should be considered together. Because of the innovation of light sources and the development of decorative materials, artificial lighting isn't just used for the general interior lighting, but is further developing to ambient lighting and artistic lighting. It has become an indispensable element of interior design in the indoor environment of commercial, residential, and large public buildings.

Natural light and artificial light should be considered together during the design of the architecture luminous environment. The coordination of light sources and lamps should be taken into consideration during the design of artificial light. At the same time, the interior building staff's mood should also be in the consideration. In the design of luminous environment, psychological effects brought by luminous environment should be fully taken into account. Bright environment makes one feel open, with a uniform high-intensity white light makes one feel transparent. When a high-illumination region is in big space, lighting with uneven changes in brightness, including extreme flashing, moving or flashing lights, and the surrounding environment formed by stimulus colors, will give one a sense of excitement and make him or her happy to chat. Environment with non-irritating factors make one feel monotonous; one will feel unsafe and horrible when it is dark.

8.3.2 The Roles of Indoor Luminous Environment on the Interior Space Design

1) The proper use of indoor luminous environment can enhance the interface relationship and change the limit of the extent and scope in the indoor space.

2) Indoor luminous environment can enhance the overall atmosphere of the room, reflecting the indoor environment as the style and the mood effectively. In the different space occasions, the light can reflect the different spatial taste and style.

3) Indoor luminous environment can strengthen the interior space of the sequence and levels to enhance the directionality of the space environment and highlight the visual center of the indoor environment.

4) Indoor luminous environment can enrich the content space, improve the ratio of the room and limit the field of space.

5) Indoor lighting form itself has a certain space for art.

8.3.3 Effective Ways to Create Luminous Environment Meeting the Requirements of Interior Decoration

① The introduction and application of natural luminous environment should be focused on. Norman. Foster said, "Natural light is always changing. It can make building rich features. In space and the interaction of light and shadow, we can create dramatic." Although artificial lighting occupies an increasingly important role, the natural light is still one of the most expressive elements in environmental lighting design. As a compositing factor in contrast to environmental atmosphere, it expresses the mood of space. The people's thirst for the sun and the nature is gradually enhanced. Making good use of natural light indoor is an effective means to integrate indoor and outdoor space environment.

② Choose the proper lamps and light sources meeting the effects of overall space environment. The choice of lamps and light sources should start from the formation of the constiuent elements of the whole space environment. They should not only have personality traits, but also become decorative elements in the room.

③ The introduction of new equipment and intelligent control. In current society of which the lighting technology develops rapidly, intellectualization is the trend of development. The adoption of new ways and means helps to reach the required effect of luminous environment conveniently and efficiently, and contributes to energy saving and management control.

8.3.4 Lighting Design Process

The lighting design process may be divided into five phases, the last of which is actually an extension of the design phases covering pre-construction and post-construction activities.

1) Programming and conceptual formulation (PC).
2) Schematic design or preliminary design (SD).
3) Design development (DD).
4) Construction documents (CD).
5) Construction period services—bid negotiation (BN), construction administration (CA), and post-occupation evaluation (PE).

There is always an overlap between these phases. In simple projects, several phases may be consolidated. *The Lighting Handbook* contains a complete description of the design issues to be considered.

It is vitally important to consider lighting design as an element integrated into a project's overall design process. Lighting decisions made during each phase are, to varying degrees, influenced by the designs being developed by other disciplines. In fact, some lighting solutions may evolve through direct collaboration with one or more members of the project's other design teams. Ongoing communication with the project's various design professionals is critical to successful coordination and an integrated design.

In virtually, the lighting design process must be applied within a defined schedule in every project. Before work begins, the design professionals must insightfully budget time to each of the phases to permit attention to the project's specific needs. Failure to do so may result in missed deadlines, poor coordination, and cost overruns.

8.3.5 Design Considerations

1. Visual Performance

A lighting design is a plan to achieve the visual performance desired for the visual task or tasks for which the associated lighting system is to be used. Determining clearly the types of visual tasks to be performed in a space is fundamental to good design. The designer should seek this information from the user or key decision makers on the project. Also, it is often useful to survey a user's existing facility. Once these tasks are identified, levels of visual performance can be established that are in keeping with user's needs and expectations.

2. Selection of Illuminance

Specific luminance ratios for various applications such as offices, educational facilities, institutions, industrial areas, and residences can be found in the IES Lighting Handbook. In general, a higher luminance ratio (contrast) is desired between the task and its immediate background for better visibility and visual acuity. However, a low luminance ratio is actually more desirable for visual comfort. Good lighting design tries to balance these conflicting criteria and arrive at appropriate solutions.

3. Visual Comfort

Visual comfort is achieved when there is no prolonged visual sensation due to excessively high luminance within the visual field. One measure of visual comfort is the visual comfort probability (*VCP*) of a lighted space due to either daylight or an interior lighting system. A *VCP* of 70 or higher is considered acceptable for visual comfort. Reflected glare can cause a loss of visibility. A lighting system with low reflected glare can be designed with the equivalent spherical illumination (ESI) method, which requires specialized computer software. In general, reflected glare can be minimized by providing a proper surface texture for the task and by controlling the orientation of the luminous flux.

4. Architectural Lighting Needs

Lighting is called on in many situations to enhance architectural form or detail. Early in the design phase of a project, the lighting specifier should try to determine what architectural attributes may require lighting reinforcement. As the overall lighting design evolves, consideration of these architectural lighting needs should take place concurrently, fostering a more integrated solution. Indirect light coves for ceiling illumination, recessed wall slots to accent vertical surfaces, and concealment of a highlighting source within a column capital are a few common examples.

In many cases, an actual luminaire may become the architectural lighting embellishment. Themed or decorative luminaire in the form of chandeliers and sconces are often featured as focal points of architectural lighting in interior spaces.

5. Light Reinforcing Spatial Impressions

It has been clearly demonstrated through both research and practice that light plays an identifiable role in shaping human impressions. Although lighting's support of the performance of visual tasks is of prime importance, its ability to either enhance or detract from the users' experience cannot be overlooked.

Examples of how the distribution, intensity, and color of the light can reinforce users' impression of a space include these:

1) To create an impression of spaciousness, provide uniform wall lighting.

2) To create an impression of relaxation, create non-uniform light distributions, provide relatively low intensity, and emphasize peripheral light placement.

3) To create an impression of visual clarity, provide bright, uniform light.

A conscious awareness of these factors will help the lighting designer determine how and where to distribute light in order to reinforce the desired impressions. This use of light as a subjective influence can significantly enhance the user's experience of space.

6. Color

For a better understanding of color, chromaticity, color rendering, and the use of color, the lighting designer should refer to Section 5 of the reference volume of the IES Lighting Handbook. The terms chromaticity and color rendering are often misused. To put it simply, chromaticity refers to the color appearance of a light source, such as its color temperature, and color rendering refers to the ability of the light source to render colors of surfaces and objects as one would expect them to appear at the same color temperature. Both factors are important in finding the proper light source for a lighting design.

7. Systems Integration

Lighting is but one of the many systems incorporated into a building's design. Structural, HVAC, fire protection, plumbing, and power distribution are equally important to the success of a built environment. The designer must closely consider the impact that the lighting may have on these other systems, and vice versa. Ceiling cavity conflicts between luminaires and other systems are a frequent occurrence. Code-dictated sprinkler spacing can radically alter the intended placement of lighting equipment. High energy consumption for a lighting solution may force the selection of a larger than normal air conditioning unit, significantly increasing first cost. These are just a few examples of situations that frequently occur on multidisciplinary projects.

Although some conflicts in building systems are unavoidable, a close working relationship with members of the entire design team will result in a more integrated approach. Periodic design sessions and coordination meetings may be needed to ensure that important information is shared in a timely manner. Insightful consideration and understanding of the other systems' requirements is key to a well coordinated job.

8. Energy

Energy consumption in a lighting system should always be a prime design consideration. Since most electricity is generated from the consumption of fossil fuels, the more fuel is required to power a lighting system, the more pollution is produced. As lighting energy consumption goes up, the building owner or user must pay more to operate the system. The higher power requirements may also affect both first and long-term air conditioning costs.

National, regional, and local legislationrelated to energy has increased dramatically over the past decade and will continue to grow for the foreseeable future. The lighting designer must become familiar with the codes and ordinances that will affect a building's design. It is best to establish an energy budget early in the process rather than face the prospect of redesigning later in order to fit within imposed constraints.

9. Maintenance and Operation

The long-term maintenance and operation of a lighting system should not be neglected during the design process. The lighting design professional must assess the sustainability of the lighting system over the project's life and communicate to the user what measures will be necessary to ensure continued high performance. Trade-offs between design and maintenance are often necessary in order to balance the user's short-and long-term expectations for the project. The designer should engage the user in the process early and arrive at an understanding as to acceptable maintenance and operational characteristics.

10. Selection of Lighting Systems

Selecting the appropriate lighting systems to fully realize the design is, perhaps, the most pivotal consideration. Selecting the system and associated luminaire types that are appropriate for a specific project will be based on the various visual needs of the project. Which system or systems best fulfill the visual performance requirements of the tasks occurring in each space? Which will appropriately enhance the important architectural features? Which will provide light distribution and intensity that will reinforce the desired impressions for each room? Which will provide the appropriate spatial modeling?

Although one lighting system might serve as the predominant choice in most areas, it is likely that a range of luminaires will be required to address specific needs or special conditions. Wall washing for presentation surfaces, accent lights for artwork and signage, theatrical lighting for auditorium stages, and high-intensity spotlighting for indoor plants are just a few frequently encountered conditions in which the basic overall lighting system may not be sufficient.

Architecturally integrated lighting and decorative luminaires for a project should be selected collaboratively with the architect, the interior designer, and, if appropriate, the end user. Although these systems may add some functional light to a room, their primary role is to create spatial atmosphere and reinforcement.

Questions

1. What are the approaches to control lighting according to optical principles?
2. What factors need considering in the choice of lamps?
3. Why should the natural light and artificial light be integrated in the light environment design?
4. Introduce briefly the lighting design process.
5. What factors need considering in the indoor light environment design?
6. What approaches can cause the lighting system more energy efficient?

参考文献

[1] Alan Fry. Noise Control in Building Services 1~2 [M]. London：Pergamon Press，1988.

[2] 英国皇家屋宇装备工程师学会. 供热、通风、空调和制冷工程 [M]. 李百战，罗庆，译. 重庆：重庆大学出版社，2008：518.

[3] 侯梦超，武兰勤. 空调系统噪声控制 [J]. 河北企业，2009 (6)：68-69.

[4] Randall McMullan. 建筑环境学 [M]. 5版. 北京：机械工业出版社，2003.

[5] 钟宇. 浅析光环境在室内设计中的重要作用 [J]. 辽宁经济管理干部学院学报，2009 (5)：113-114.

[6] 冯愉. 室内设计中的灯光环境 [J]. 科技资讯，2009 (14)：227.

[7] 刘炜，王晓静，曾礼强. 办公室光环境设计要素 [J]. 照明工程学报，2007 (9)：36-40.

[8] Gregg D Ande. Daylighting Performance and Design [M]. 2nd ed. New York：John Wiley & Sons Inc，2003.

[9] 薛殿华. 空气调节 [M]. 北京：清华大学出版社，1995.

[10] 柴慧娟，等. 高层建筑空调设计 [M]. 北京：中国建筑工业出版社，1995.

[11] 陆亚俊，等. 暖通空调 [M]. 北京：中国建筑工业出版社，2002.

[12] 李德英. 供热工程 [M]. 北京：中国建筑工业出版社，2003.

[13] ASHRAE. 1991 ASHRAE Handbook：HVAC Applications [M]. Atlanta：ASHRAE Inc，1991.

[14] Wang Shan K. Handbook of Air Conditioning and Refrigeration [M]. 2nd ed. New York：McGraw Hill，2002.

[15] 陆耀庆. 实用供热空调设计手册 [M]. 北京：中国建筑工业出版社，1993.

[16] 电子工业部第十设计研究院. 空气调节设计手册 [M]. 2版. 北京：中国建筑工业出版社，1995.

[17] ASHRAE. 1996 ASHRAE Handbook：HVAC Systems and Equipment [M]. Atlanta：ASHRAE Inc，1996.

[18] William K Y Tao，Richard R Janis. Mechanical and Electrical Systems in Buildings [M]. 2nd ed. Englewood Cliffs：Prentice Hall，2001.

[19] Illuminating Engineering Society of North America (IESNA). Lighting Handbook：Reference and Application [M]. 8th ed. New York：Illuminating Engineering Society of North America 1994.

[20] General Electric Lighting Company. Fundamentals of Light and Lighting [M]. Cleveland：General Electric Lighting Company，1960.

[21] General Electric Lighting Business Group. Light and Color [M]. Cleveland：General Electric Lighting Business Group，1995.

[22] General Electric Lighting Company. Specifying Light and Color [M]. Cleveland：General Electric Lighting Company，1995.

[23] Minolta Corporation. Precise Color Communication [M]. Ramsey：Minolta Corporation，1995.

[24] IESNA. IES Education Series (Introductory) [M]. New York：Illuminating Engineering Society of North America，1995.

[25] Joseph B Murdoch. Illumination Engineering [M]. New York：Macmillan，1985.

[26] Ronald H Helms，M Clay Belcher. Lighting for Energy-Efficient Luminous Environments [M]. Englewood Cliffs：Prentice Hall，1991.

[27] M David Egan. Concepts in Architectural Lighting [M]. New York：McGraw Hill，1983.

[28] 钟宇. 浅析光环境在室内设计中的重要作用 [J]. 辽宁经济管理干部学院学报，2009 (5)：113-114.

信息反馈表

尊敬的老师：

　　您好！感谢您多年来对机械工业出版社的支持和厚爱！为了进一步提高我社教材的出版质量，更好地为我国高等教育发展服务，欢迎您对我社的教材多提宝贵意见和建议。另外，如果您在教学中选用了《建筑环境与能源应用工程概论（中英文对照）》（刘立　范慧方主编），欢迎您提出修改建议和意见。索取课件的授课教师，请填写下面的信息，发送邮件即可。

一、基本信息

　　姓名：_____　性别：_____　职称：_____　职务：_____
　　邮编：_____　地址：_____
　　学校：_____　院系：_____　专业：_____
　　任教课程：_____　　电话：_____（H）　_____（O）
　　电子邮件：_____　　手机：_____　　QQ：_____

二、您对本书的意见及建议

（欢迎您指出本书的疏误之处）

请与我们联系：

100037　机械工业出版社·高等教育分社
Tel：010 - 88379542（O）
E - mail：ltao929@163.com
http://www.cmpedu.com（机械工业出版社·教材服务网）
http://www.cmpbook.com（机械工业出版社·门户网）